GANGSTER TOUR OF TEXAS

T. LINDSAY BAKER

GANGSTER TOUR OF TEXAS

TEXAS A&M UNIVERSITY PRESS College Station

Library of Congress Cataloging-in-Publication Data

Baker, T. Lindsay.
Gangster tour of Texas / T. Lindsay Baker. — 1st ed.
        p. cm.
    Includes bibliographical references and index.
    ISBN-13: 978-1-60344-258-9 (flexbound : alk. paper)
    ISBN-10: 1-60344-258-8 (flexbound : alk. paper)
    ISBN-13: 978-1-60344-407-1 (e-book)
    ISBN-10: 1-60344-407-6 (e-book)
    1. Organized crime—Texas—History—20th century.
2. Gangsters—Texas—History—20th century.   3. Gangsters—
Homes and haunts—Texas.   4. Texas—History, Local.
5. Texas—Description and travel.   6. Heritage tourism—Texas.
I. Title.
HV6793.T4B35   2011
364.106'609764—dc22
2010054349

To state troopers

E. B. WHEELER *and* H. D. MURPHY,

who gave their lives while attempting to

serve others

CONTENTS

ACKNOWLEDGMENTS

Writing a guide to historic sites requires research similar to yet different from writing straightforward narrative history. Not only does the author frequent such document repositories as libraries, churches, and courthouses, but he or she also haunts lonely road intersections, otherwise nondescript urban neighborhoods, cemeteries, and the alleys where the backs of buildings sometimes are less changed than their fronts. It is not enough to learn merely what happened in a past event. Writers of guides have to discover specifically where the events took place. This means that considerable travel and lots of time in the field are required. Sometimes it means that the writer has to return to the scene of an event time and again as newly uncovered sources make possible fresh insights into what happened at a particular place and time.

A statewide study like this one entailed scores of people sharing what they knew about the history of notorious crimes in Texas. As I started conducting this research, I sent questionnaires to every one of the county historical commission chairs in the state, and their responses helped me to start assembling a list of potential sites and stories. Then, at the Texas Collection at Baylor University and the Dolph Briscoe Center for American History at the University of Texas at Austin, I paged through the issues of all the regional historical journals published in the state. That process turned up articles on even more potentially interesting crimes from the past. During this phase of research, two colleagues alerted me to criminal enterprises that eventually became chapters in the book. Carol Roark of the Dallas Public Library told me about O. D. Stevens and the Texas and Pacific Mail Robbery, while Rosalie Gregg of the Wise County Historical Commission opened my eyes to the importance of the Urschel Kidnapping. As I started making preliminary visits to crime sites that had potential for inclusion in the book, I started meeting the local people who knew about these places, and they greatly assisted by sharing their grass-roots knowledge of the events—information often unavailable in written sources. Along the way I occasionally came across individuals who are the acknowledged experts on particular events. Librarians and archivists across the state made their documentary sources available. As the project reached its close, many generous people read through chapters of the text dealing with events about which they had special knowledge. I gratefully thank everyone who so generously assisted, though I retain responsibility for any errors of fact and interpretation.

Many librarians, archivists, and custodians of public records facilitated this effort. Among those who went out of their way to be helpful were the following, in alphabetical order of location: Ann E. Hodges, Brenda S. McClurkin, Katherine R. Goodwin, Ben Huseman, Gary Spurr, and Catherine Spitzenberger, all in Special Collections at the University of Texas at Arlington Library, Arlington; Kevin Klaus, Archives and Records Division, Texas General Land Office, Austin; Brian Schenk, Texas Military Forces Museum, Austin; Don E. Carleton, Lynn Bell, and Margaret Schlankey, Dolph Briscoe Center for American History, the University of Texas at Austin; Robert L. Spence, Carnegie Library, Ballinger; Warren Stricker, Research Center, Panhandle-Plains Historical Museum, Canyon; Michael Cunningham, Library, Cisco College, Cisco; Senior Corporal Jesus Lucio Jr., Dallas Police Department, Dallas; Carol Roark and Rachel Howell, Texas/Dallas History and Archives Division, Dallas Public Library, Dallas; Willie Braudaway, Val Verde County Library, Del Rio; Lee Lincoln, Whitehead Memorial Museum, Del Rio; Ed Alcorn, Eastland County Museum, Eastland; Terry Holbert, Electra Public Library, Electra; Claudia Rivers and Anne Allis, C. L. Sonnichsen Special Collections Department, University Library, University of Texas at El Paso; Patricia H. Worthington, El Paso County Historical Society, El Paso; Laura Juarez and Sergeant Robert Vasquez, El Paso County Sheriff's Office, El Paso; Carmen P. Sifuentes, Texas Department of Transportation, El Paso; Dede Humphries, *Floresville Chronicle-Journal,* Floresville; Casey E. Greene and Carol Wood, Galveston and Texas History Center, Rosenberg Library, Galveston; Lily Foltz, Rusk County Library, Henderson; Roy Bermudez, Hondo Public Library, Hondo; Joel Draut, Mary McMillen, Ingrid Grant, Ron Drees, Fred Parris, and Kemo Curry, all at the Houston Metropolitan Research Center, Houston Public Library, Houston; Melissa Day, Kaufman County Library, Kaufman; Tai Kreidler, Monte Monroe, and Janet Neugebauer, Southwest Collection, Texas Tech University Library, Lubbock; J. P. "Pat" McDaniel and Jim Bradshaw, Haley Memorial Library and History Center, Midland; Keva Boardman, Sophienburg Museum and Archives, New Braunfels; Bill Welge, Research Center, Oklahoma Historical Society, Oklahoma City; Diana Guthrie, Pleasanton Public Library, Pleasanton; Terri Laurence, Office of County Clerk, Garza County Courthouse, Post; Linda Pucket, Garza County Historical Museum, Post; Suzanne Campbell and Shannon Sturm, West Texas Collection, Angelo State University, San Angelo; Tom Shelton, Library, Institute of Texan Cultures, San Antonio; Andy Crews, San Antonio Public Library, San Antonio; Stephanie Langenkamp, San Marcos Public Library, San Marcos; Susie Hull and Helen Castro, Office of District and County Clerk, Martin County Courthouse, Stanton; Joann Carrillo,

St. Joseph Catholic Church, Stanton; LeAnna S. Schooley and Bethany Kolter Dodson, W. K. Gordon Center for Industrial History of Texas, Tarleton State University, Thurber; Susan Anderson and Virginia Wood Davis, El Progreso Memorial Library, Uvalde; Janet Kent, Victoria Public Library, Victoria; Thomas L. Charlton and Michael Toon, Texas Collection, Baylor University, Waco; Jerry C. Hoke, Library, Wharton County Junior College, Wharton; and Brett A. Glenn, Wharton County Historical Museum, Wharton.

Whenever I learned something about any of the events recounted in this book, local people played an indispensable role in helping me find the specific locations where the events took place. These key individuals were, in alphabetical order by location, John Klingemann, Alpine; Jim Beck, Austin; Linda Raby, Buda; Joyce Glasgow, Donald Frazier, and Jason Terbush, Buffalo Gap; Ben Choate, Jane Willard, Carolyn Harvey, Corbett Howard, and Penny Rathbun, all in Celina; Glenn Rea, Cuero; Robin Gilliam and Sylvia Rushing, Denison; Janis Hayers, Ted Bishop, and Jeannette Miller, Electra; Tina Cotelleso and Ann Arnold, Fort Worth; Cecil Stubblefield, Hillsboro; Jim Willett and Weldon Svoboda, Huntsville; Diana Clemmo and Mickie Hooten, Kemp; James I. Fenton and George Ann Hobbs, Lubbock; Leslie Dare and Cozell McAfee, Mabank; Marie T. Neff, Post; Kelly Franks and Frank Thomas, San Marcos; Horace P. Flatt, Terrell; Kenneth Kelley, Uvalde; and Alton O'Neal Jr. and Jean Boles, Winters. Some of the people I met over the years of research are the acknowledged experts on several of these incidents, and they all generously shared their expertise. Among them are John Neal Phillips on the Barrow Gang; Sergeant Jonathan Hutson on the 1933 Texas and Pacific Mail Robbery; Bob Brinkman on "flapper bandit" Becky Rogers; Ken Towery on the Texas Veterans' Land Board Scandal; Doug Braudaway on Dr. John R. Brinkley's activities in Del Rio; and Vickie Bryant on Top O'Hill Terrace. Finally, a number of the most knowledgeable people generously reviewed chapters of the book. Among these kind friends and colleagues I would like to thank in particular Jesús F. de la Teja, Bob Brinkman, Bill O'Neal, Sergeant Jonathan Hutson, Doug Braudaway, Mildred Sentell, John Neal Phillips, Paul R. Scott, Sarah Jackson, Louis Aulbach, Vickie Bryant, and Casey E. Greene. I thank everyone for this generous help.

Members of the administration at Tarleton State University have encouraged my efforts throughout research for this work. These individuals include presidents F. Dominic Dottavio and Dennis P. McCabe; Dean Minix and Donald R. Zellman, deans of the College of Liberal and Fine Arts; and Malcolm Cross and Michael Pierce, chairs of the Department of Social Sciences.

For a decade my family members patiently put up with seemingly endless sordid tales about historic Texas punks and thugs, but they finally got tired. Whenever we took road trips and I queried, "Do you see that bridge over there?" my dear wife, Julie, in self-defense, finally started responding, "I don't want to know what happened over there." She, my parents, and other family members must be breathing a collective sigh of relief now that this particular research project has drawn to its close. They all, however, truly have been supportive. Julie even read and critiqued each chapter as it reached its intermediate stage, for which I am immeasurably grateful. Thanks, everyone, for the help.

INTRODUCTION

Growing up in Cleburne, Texas, in the 1950s, I remember my father telling me of his Uncle Lacey Robertson's encounter with a man he believed was bank robber and kidnapper Machine Gun Kelly. Uncle Lacey was a barber in Newcastle, Texas, and he related that in about 1933 an unidentified man came into his shop for a shave. Uncle Lacey proceeded to oblige the stranger, who after paying for the service stepped outside and reportedly "drove away in his fast little automobile." Only then did Uncle Lacey realize who had been sitting in his barber's chair: "Oh, my gosh, I've just shaved Machine Gun Kelly! I had my razor right at his throat." It's probably just as well that Uncle Lacey showed restraint, for the famous gunman time and again had demonstrated that he was wound as tightly as a spring.

Stories like this are told in many families and surprisingly often include tales of nationally known punks and thugs. While going to school, for example, I heard from my classmates multiple accounts of Bonnie and Clyde "sightings" by family members twenty years before, though I'll never know how many of them were legitimate. Maybe these associations from childhood and adolescence were what prompted me to join a tour of local historic crime scenes during the Western History Association annual conference in St. Paul, Minnesota, in 1997. There I had the chance to ride on a bus through the street where the Barker-Karpis Gang abducted William Hamm Jr., president of the Hamm Brewing Company, for ransom; to see the apartment building where John Dillinger, known as "Public Enemy Number One," resided for a time; and to walk in front of the South St. Paul Post Office, where Alvin Karpis and Fred Barker strode in and made off with a meatpacking house payroll. I couldn't resist buying a copy of *John Dillinger Slept Here*, Paul Maccabee's guide to organized crime sites in the Twin Cities.

The just completed tour had been so stimulating that I carried my new acquisition into the book exhibits at the meeting and walked straight to editor Mary Lenn Dixon at her table of wares from Texas A&M University Press. After showing her my prize and describing what a good time I'd had on the tour, I asked, "Wouldn't it be fun to do a book like this for Texas?" She nodded in assent, and on returning home I sent her a prospectus for such a volume. Time passed, other projects reached completion, and finally in the early 2000s I started work on the project that resulted in these pages.

I adopted the same strategy that Maccabee had found successful in assembling the Minnesota study—create a heritage tourist's guide for visiting actual places where offenses took place. Being less interested in the violence of psychopaths or sins of passion, I decided to pursue organized crime. My working definition was very close to that in the Texas criminal statutes, which characterize organized crime as any activity in which two or more people conspire to break the law for personal gain. I sought specific locations where transgressions based on greed had been perpetrated. For the next several years I prowled alleys, buildings, streets, sidewalks, and offices that had been the scenes of robberies, embezzlements, frame-ups, burglaries, moonshining, bribery, narcotics deals, and related murders and assaults. It has been a fascinating study, to say the least.

It made good sense to begin this book with the year 1918. That was when the Texas Legislature voted to prohibit the manufacture and sale of alcoholic beverages within the bounds of the Lone Star State, more than a year ahead of national prohibition. This act suddenly turned law-abiding Texans who had brewed beer or even tended bar into criminals if they continued their trade on the sly. At about the same time the United States entered two decades of what might best be described as an epidemic of bank robbery. The crime wave grew so great that the Texas Bankers Association in 1927 offered a five-thousand-dollar reward for dead bank robbers. (If someone caught a robber alive, he or she received no reward whatsoever.) Even though federal prohibition of the manufacture and sale of alcohol ended in 1933, crime did not. Texas abounded with illegal casinos, while crime bosses, gangsters, and their helpers roamed cities and countryside committing robberies and kidnapping the wealthy for ransom. Embezzlers secretly withdrew money from financial institutions, while elected officials freely took bribes. Drug lords dealt first in morphine and then in heroin. The following pages encompass events through the year 1957, when Texas Rangers closed the most famous of all the illegal Texas gambling casinos, those in Galveston. This event concluded what people popularly view as the "gangster era" in Texas. What a field this has been for the historian to till!

This guidebook begins with perhaps the best known of all the Texas lawbreakers: Clyde Barrow, Bonnie Parker, and the criminal partners who shared their company. Their trail of crime traversed much of the Lone Star State, extending as far as the midwestern states. Following the Barrow Gang are fifteen other unlawful enterprises in roughly chronological order, from the bank robbing Newton Boys of Uvalde in the 1910s and 1920s to the Maceo Brothers and their illicit gaming empire, shut down by law officers in 1957. The volume could have included many other crooks and could have told much more about illegal activities, but its purpose has been to lead visitors to the most interesting and best preserved of the historic crime scenes that I could find. The goal has never been to chronicle all organized crime in Texas.

Cast yourselves back in time. Imagine a Texas where air conditioning is unknown, where tiny banks operate in almost every little town, where liquor and beer come from bootleggers, and where the likes of Clyde Barrow, Joe Newton, and Machine Gun Kelly career in old-time cars down unpaved roads at breakneck speed. Welcome to a *Gangster Tour of Texas.*

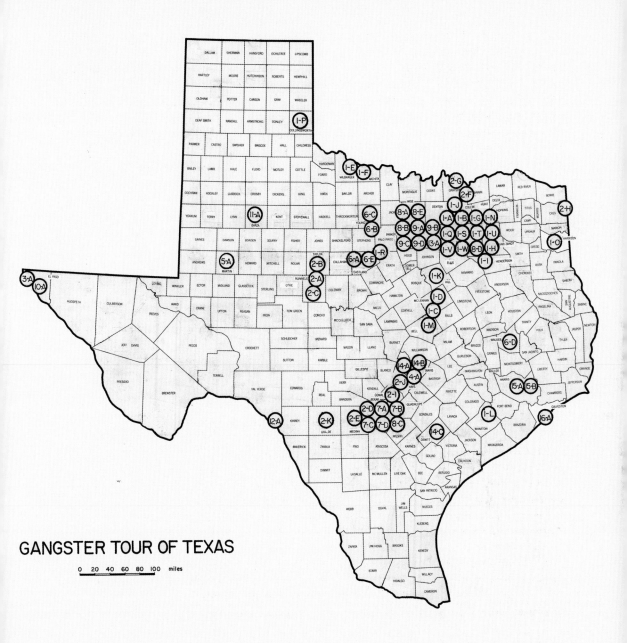

GANGSTER TOUR OF TEXAS

0 20 40 60 80 100 miles

GANGSTER TOUR OF TEXAS

1 BONNIE AND CLYDE SLEPT HERE ON THE TRAIL OF THE BARROW GANG

Among the best known of the criminal enterprises in Texas was the group of people known as the Barrow Gang. The only two individuals continuously associated with the group were Bonnie Parker and Clyde Chestnut Barrow, who have entered history and folklore as Bonnie and Clyde. Their trail of crime covered much of Texas as well as places as distant as Minnesota and Indiana.

Bonnie Parker came into the world in 1910 at Rowena, a small farming community in West Texas about twenty-seven miles northeast of San Angelo. When she was four years old, her bricklayer father died, leaving her mother to fall back on her family for support. In 1914 Bonnie's mother and three children moved in with her paternal grandparents, who lived on Eagle Ford Road in West Dallas. Outside the incorporated bounds of Dallas, this squalid neighborhood on the edge of the Trinity River floodplain west of downtown, surrounded by oil facilities and cement kilns, was one of the poorest and most crime-ridden white ethnic neighborhoods in the city. In this area that residents called "the Bog," Bonnie studied in the Cement City Independent School District. Bonnie demonstrated her scholastic ability in 1922 by winning first prize in spelling for her age category in a county-wide competition. Opportunities were limited even for a smart and pretty poor girl from a rough neighborhood. In 1926 she entered an abusive marriage with a West Dallas hoodlum named Roy Thornton, who ended up in the state prison for his crimes. On her own in January 1928, personable Bonnie started working in a series of waitress jobs in Dallas eating places, among them the Hargraves Cafe. She made the acquaintance of young Ted Hinton about this time, and he remembered her as freckle-faced and "perky, with good looks and taffy-colored hair that showed a trace of red." He added, "Several of the men my age flirted with her, and Bonnie could turn off the advances or lead a customer on with her easy conversation." Then in January 1930 she chanced to meet the person who changed her short life, Clyde Barrow.

Bonnie Parker as a young woman in 1926. Courtesy of Texas/Dallas History and Archives Division, Dallas Public Library, image PA 76-1/33005.

Like Bonnie, Clyde was born in the country, on a farm near Telico, Ellis County, Texas, in 1909. Unable to make a living by working on other people's land for a share of the crops, Clyde's father, Henry, moved his wife and their three youngest children to Dallas in 1922. Clyde's earliest days in the city were spent camped beneath his family's wagon under the Houston Street Viaduct in the Trinity River bottoms. The Barrows relocated to the impoverished "Bog" in West Dallas, where Henry used his horse and wagon to get around as he bought and sold scrap metal. After a car struck his wagon and Henry received a settlement for the damages, he used the money to purchase a cheap wooden filling station on the north side of Eagle Ford Road at Borger Street. The place of business doubled as a home for his family.

Clyde went to school for a time but then dropped out. The slight young man with boyish looks went to work for a series of businesses, among them United Glass and Mirror on Swiss Avenue, and then began stealing cars and burglarizing houses to get extra money. On October 29, 1929, Clyde, his brother Buck, and a friend named Sidney broke into a service station in Denton. Instead of cracking the safe inside, they hoisted it into their car to open in a more secluded location. When law officers began tailing the three young men, Clyde took a corner too fast, slammed into a light pole, and his two companions were arrested. He successfully hid out beneath a vacant house.

In January 1930, not long after brother Buck went to prison for the Denton burglary, Clyde chanced to call at the West Dallas home of Clarence Clay. Dropping in to see the man's daughter, who had been in an accident, he also met Bonnie Parker, who had come to see the friend as well. Clyde fell for the petite café waitress with blue eyes and reddish-blond hair. Soon they began spending all their free time together.

Henry T. Barrow's Star Filling Station in West Dallas, the home of the Barrow family, as it appeared in 1934. Courtesy of Texas/Dallas History and Archives Division, Dallas Public Library, image PA 76-1/33018A.

Then, in the second week of February 1930, police awakened Clyde at Bonnie's house and arrested him for the Denton burglary for which his brother had already been convicted. There was insufficient evidence to convict Clyde, but authorities transferred him to Waco, where he had been charged with burglary and auto theft. In early March Bonnie went to Waco for her sweetheart's sentencing—seven two-year terms for each of the seven counts—but to be served concurrently.

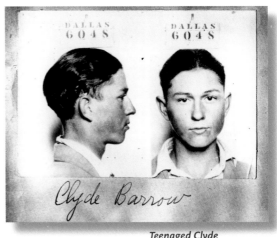

Teenaged Clyde Chestnut Barrow as he appeared in a Dallas mug shot after his arrest for auto theft in December 1926. Courtesy of Texas/ Dallas History and Archives Division, Dallas Public Library, image MA 83.7/MB.B-33.

Hoping to dodge the prison term, Clyde persuaded Bonnie to smuggle a pistol to him in jail. Concealing it between her breasts, she got the weapon into her lover's hands on March 11, 1930. A few hours later, as a jailer was delivering the evening meal to prisoners, Clyde shoved the pistol in his face, took the keys, and locked the officer in a cell. Getting the drop on another jailer, Barrow and two other prisoners exited the front door of the jail. Walking north from downtown, they stole a car at a boardinghouse at 724 North Fifth but then exchanged it for another taken from in front of Dr. William L. Souther's home at 2005 North Seventh and escaped out of town, heading for the Midwest. Freedom was brief for Clyde, who with the others surrendered to police in Middletown, Ohio, only a week later. When the local sheriff returned Barrow to Waco, the formerly lenient judge revised his sentence to seven consecutive two-year terms, a total of fourteen years.

Authorities transferred Clyde to the Walls Unit, the main section of the state prison at Huntsville, in April 1930. They held him there several months before transferring the young man to the Eastham Prison Farm, about thirty miles away. Texas governor Dan Moody had declared that the central unit at Huntsville was "not fit for a dog," but Eastham was far worse. Guards and trusty prisoners at the farm made it a hell on earth, beating and abusing many prisoners and causing others simply to "disappear." It was at Eastham that a building tender trusty known as "Big Ed" beat and repeatedly sodomized Clyde. In collusion with another building tender, Clyde lured his tormenter into a toilet at one end of the prisoner dormitory at Eastham Camp 1, where he brained the man with a short piece of pipe. The abuse by "Big Ed" and others at Eastham changed Clyde. In the words of his friend Ralph Fults, he went "from a schoolboy to rattlesnake," and this was no exaggeration. Before imprisonment Barrow had rejected authority, but at Eastham he began to equate official power with the abuse and injustice he saw all around him. From this time on, Clyde became focused on opposing governmental authority and seeking revenge for the suffering he experienced in prison. Some believed he became a psychopath. While still imprisoned at Eastham he developed a plan to revenge himself by staging a raid to free prisoners and kill hated guards. This effort became his goal in life and shaped much of what he did from this time onward.

While Bonnie wrote imprisoned Clyde a steady stream of letters, his mother worked for his early release. The efforts succeeded, and on February 2, 1932, Governor Miriam Ferguson granted him a conditional parole. Clyde returned to his family and Bonnie in Dallas, but his mother realized that he came back a different person, hardened and bitter. He returned to work at United Glass and Mirror, but his boss laid him off. "It's just because I'm a con and my name's Barrow," he declared to his mother, adding that manager P. H. "McCray says, 'I know you ain't doing nothing wrong, but all them cops hanging around is making my business even worse than it already is.'" With time on his hands and no steady source of income, Clyde went back to what he knew well—burglary. Joining with friend Ralph Fults, whom he had met in prison, and neighborhood thug Raymond Hamilton, Barrow and his accomplices attempted to stick up the Simms Oil Refinery at 2435 Eagle Ford Road, not far from Henry Barrow's filling station. They bound and gagged four employees and broke open the office safe only to find it empty, making good their empty-handed escape.

After pulling off several other penny-ante burglaries, the threesome headed out of state—where no one would recognize them and where they had no criminal records—to rob a bank. Driving hundreds of miles north into the Midwest in April 1932, they scouted out a bank at Okabena, Minnesota, but then settled on another said to have been in Lawrence, Kansas, that they had seen on the outbound trip. The armed robbery reputedly netted them several thousand dollars. Once they returned home the hoodlums lived on the proceeds. Then Clyde, Ralph, and a young man named Red took a trip to Amarillo in hopes of linking up with two brothers they had met at Eastham. On the way they stole a Ford coupe in Memphis, Texas.

About halfway home to Dallas, their stolen vehicle broke down on April 14 in the oil town of Electra, near Wichita Falls. As the three young men walked eastward from the car, Chief of Police James T. Taylor and water department employee J. C. Harris approached them to investigate. One of the young strangers pulled a gun on the two men just as the local Magnolia Petroleum agent, A. F. McCormick, drove up from behind. The outsiders ordered everyone into McCormick's Chevrolet sedan at gunpoint, just as frightened teenager Red ran away on foot. Undaunted, the remaining two hoods drove their three captives

eight to ten miles south from Electra, forcing them out at the side of a
dirt road on the Lazy J Ranch.

Barrow and Fults proceeded northward by a ranch road toward the
Fort Worth–Amarillo highway, where they spied a U.S. Mail delivery vehicle. Driving alongside postman William N. Owens, one of the strangers called out, "If you value your life, stop." Threatening the rural mail
carrier with firearms, they abandoned McCormick's Chevrolet, Clyde
taking the wheel of the postal vehicle. He headed northward across
the Fort Worth–Amarillo highway toward the Red River, crossing at
the Randlett toll bridge. They proceeded into the Wichita Mountains,
hiding out for the afternoon but emerging in the evening to mooch a
meal from the manager of a small roadside eating place. Barrow and
Fults then drove on a few more miles, leaving Owens at the side of the
road near Fletcher, Oklahoma. During the kidnapping, Owens told his
kidnappers that if they burned the truck when they finished with it, he
would likely receive a new replacement. That they did, and Owens, on
return home, did eventually get a new vehicle.

No sooner was Clyde back in Dallas when he had the opportunity,
on April 17, 1932, to demonstrate to Fults the ability as an automobile

A typical rural gasoline station during the days when the Barrow Gang stalked Texas roads. Courtesy of Texas/ Dallas History and Archives Division, Dallas Public Library, image PA 76-1/33012.

driver that later made him famous. The two were motoring westward on West Davis Street, west of Dallas, when they noticed a law enforcement patrol car on their tail. Already driving fast, Clyde accelerated several car lengths ahead of the officers, aiming for the top of Chalk Hill, where he knew the unpaved road would begin descending toward Arcadia Park. Just past the crest, Clyde shut off the headlights, tramped on the brakes, and cut the steering wheel to the left. The fast-moving vehicle swung around completely, headed back toward Dallas, whereupon Barrow turned on his lights and proceeded back to the top of the hill just as the lawmen with lights flashing and siren wailing sped past going the opposite direction.

Hoping to proceed with plans for raiding Eastham Prison Farm, Clyde knew that he needed one or two large cars and more firearms. He, Bonnie, and Ralph Fults on April 18, 1932, drove to Tyler, where they stole a new Buick and a late model Chrysler. Late that night, on the way back to Dallas, the thieves stopped off in Mabank, where Fults had purchased two boxes of firearms shells earlier in the day. He had observed that Hyman Bock's store at 112 Market Street had a good stock of guns, so the three decided to help themselves after hours. About one o'clock on the morning of Tuesday, April 19, 1932, they quietly rolled into town, headlamps extinguished, and stopped in the alley behind the Bock store. While they were attempting to force the lock on the back door, City Marshal Dave Drennan disturbed their efforts.

Gunshots were exchanged in the dark, and the two cars roared out of town as the fire bell started clanging.

The night had turned rainy, and the erstwhile burglars discovered that the local roads had been converted into muddy gumbo. Not far from town, both bogged down to the hubs of their wheels. The three criminals made their way cross-country to a farm where there were no cars—only two mules. With Bonnie and Fults astride the recalcitrant animals, the threesome proceeded to the town of Kemp. There they took an automobile belonging to a local physician named Scarbrough, but it, too, became stuck in the mud. By now it was daylight, and the fugitives hid out in a wooded area near Kemp until lawmen discovered them about seven o'clock in the evening. In a gunfight that ensued, Clyde escaped into the brush, but posse members captured Fults after he was shot in the left arm and ankle and also Bonnie, who was unin-jured but whose clothes had been torn to pieces by the day's pursuit. Locals hauled both prisoners to Kemp, where Dr. Scarbrough refused to attend to Fults's wounds in anger over the theft of his car. Posse members locked the two muddy fugitives in the Kemp jail overnight before authorities the next day transferred them to the county jail in nearby Kaufman.

Even though Bonnie and Fults were locked up, Clyde proceeded with his efforts to gather more guns for the planned prison farm raid. Con-tacting two local hoods whom he had already recruited for the raid—Ted Rogers and another known as Johnny—the three young men headed for the little cotton-farming town of Celina, about forty miles north of Dallas. Their goal was new firearms, said to be in the Patrick & Seitz hardware store. In the early hours of April 21, 1932, two of the young strangers took a position sitting on a bench in front of the Nelson Hotel on the southeast corner of the town square. Night watchman Floyd C. Perkins approached them from the city hall, just across the street, and asked whether they needed any assistance. One of them replied that they were looking for the home of "the widow Taylor." About this time Celina mayor S. M. Francis emerged from the city hall, whereupon one of the outsiders drew a gun, took the watchman's visible firearm, and marched both men down the sidewalk to the west. A suspicious move by the watchman drew a pistol-butt blow to his head, followed by one of the intruders taking a second secreted pistol from him. Then the two young men marched their two prisoners in the opposite direction, east two blocks to the Frisco Railway tracks, where they forced them into an empty boxcar on a siding near the station.

With the mayor and watchman locked up, the three strangers headed to their actual destination, the hardware store on the northeast corner of the square. Encountering two more locals on the way, the outsiders likewise coerced them into the boxcar. Finally the thieves reached the alley on the north side of the store, whereupon they broke into the wrong building, the Choate drugstore. Discovering their mistake, the three burglars next forced the door at the back of the Patrick & Seitz hardware, taking two shotguns and ammunition. By this time others had observed the suspicious late-hour movements, and they switched on the streetlights and sounded the fire alarm. The intruders escaped into the darkness while locals responded to the cries and pounding of the four men inside the boxcar.

Clyde, Ted, and Johnny headed for a hideout near Lake Dallas, but their testing of newly stolen firearms the next day attracted lawmen's attention. As police cars approached the scene of the shooting, they successfully evaded apprehension by diving into a thicket. The officers, however, found the weapons taken in Celina, as well as a chrome-plated automatic pistol. About this time two more young hoodlums who had missed the car-stealing foray to Tyler drove up and were arrested. Then officers connected the fancy pistol with the Electra incident, in which Chief of Police James T. Taylor had lost this very gun. Lawmen realized that the seemingly unrelated Electra kidnappings, the attempted burglary in Mabank, and the Celina thefts were all connected to the same gang of criminals. Although East Texas authorities released Bonnie Parker, they transferred Ralph Fults to be prosecuted and eventually imprisoned for the Electra abductions. Unknowingly the officers had thrown a monkey wrench into Clyde Barrow's plans to raid the Eastham Prison Farm.

By the end of April 1932, Clyde had started running short of money. He had spent the proceeds from their midwestern bank robbery. He remembered that a boyhood friend had family members who operated a jewelry store on the extreme north side of Hillsboro, Texas, and decided that the safe in that secluded store probably was full of fenceable baubles. Having choreographed the heist, Clyde waited in the getaway car while Ted and Johnny approached the store sometime late in the night of April 30. They pounded on the door to the shop, saying they wanted to buy guitar strings, until sixty-one-year-old John N. Bucher came down from the family's apartment upstairs. After picking out the strings, everyone proceeded to the front of the store, where Ted proffered a ten-dollar bill in payment. He knew that late at night the jeweler would be unable to break the note. No sooner had Mrs. Bucher opened the safe to get change than her husband unexpectedly reached inside for a hidden pistol. Ted almost instantly fired his .45 right into Bucher's chest, and he fell to the floor gasping for air. Retrieving their victim's pistol, the bandits emptied the safe of forty dollars and about two thousand dollars worth of rings and other jewelry before exiting to the car and retreating in the darkness. The diminutive Ted Rogers bore a striking resemblance to a contemporaneous West Dallas criminal, Raymond Hamilton, which led to the latter being falsely convicted of John Bucher's murder.

The accusations of murder prompted Hamilton into more criminal activity, including one robbery with Clyde Barrow and a young man called Ross. With apparent inside information about the pay schedule at the Neuhoff Packing Plant just north of downtown Dallas, Clyde and Raymond walked into the office about four o'clock on Monday, August 1, 1932. Seeing clerk Elsie Wullschleger counting out payroll money, Raymond, with pistol drawn, scooped the cash into a grocery sack while Clyde examined the contents of a mostly empty safe. Almost as quickly as it can be told, the bandits exited the office, escaping in a sedan with Ross at the wheel. Because the day's packing house receipts already had been deposited in the bank, the thieves absconded with only about $440.

As all had expected, in mid-June Kaufman County authorities released Bonnie from jail. After returning home to Dallas, she eventually told her family that she had a new waitress job in Wichita Falls. Actually she went there with Clyde. They checked into a local tourist court and stayed there as a vacationing couple until about the end of July. Bonnie then returned to see her family in Dallas while Clyde, Raymond, and Ross made an excursion into Oklahoma, picking up a hitchhiker along the way. The group stopped at an outdoor dance in Stringtown, northeast of Atoka. While Ross and the hitchhiker tried to find some bootleg liquor, Raymond and Clyde started checking out nearby parked cars, thinking they might leave with a different vehicle. Two local law officers strolled over to investigate but were met with a volley of pistol fire. Clyde and Raymond made for their car, leaving Sheriff C. G. Maxwell dead in the parking lot.

A day later back in Dallas, Clyde picked up Bonnie. Telling her family that a ride had arrived to carry her back to Wichita Falls, she actually departed with her lover and Raymond Hamilton for a trip across West Texas to Carlsbad, New Mexico, where her aunt lived. Her male companions hoped that the trip would take them far enough away to evade Oklahoma and North Texas officers on the hunt for the Stringtown murderers. Little could they know that at the same time New Mexico officers had been cleaning up a series of auto theft rings and were on the lookout for unfamiliar cars with out-of-state license tags. On Sunday, August 14, 1932, Sheriff Joe Johns followed Clyde and Raymond to the rural home of Bonnie's aunt, rapping on the farmhouse door and asking, "Whose Ford is this?" Moments later Clyde burst out with a shotgun in his hand, ordering the officer to "stick 'em up." Forcing

Johns into their single-seated coupe at gunpoint, Clyde, Raymond, and Bonnie all piled inside and headed back into Texas with their captive. Twelve hours later they pulled into San Antonio, where they looked in vain for a second likely car to steal, and then after daybreak they proceeded another fifteen miles out of town. There they abandoned Sheriff Johns alongside the road.

Clyde, Raymond, and Bonnie proceeded about a hundred miles farther to the southeast, to Victoria, where about two o'clock in the afternoon they finally managed to steal another car. Now in two vehicles, the criminals turned eastward toward Houston. They had taken no rest for twenty-four hours. News of Sheriff Johns's abduction and a description of the auto taken in Victoria quickly spread among lawmen on the coastal plain. Among those notified were City Marshal W. W. Pitman and Deputy Sheriff Carl Siebrecht at Wharton, where U.S. Highway 59 crossed the Colorado River on a new overhead truss bridge. Pitman parked his car where he would be able to pull across the north end of the bridge, while Siebrecht positioned himself at a slight curve in the road just to the south, where he could see both oncoming traffic and Pitman. His plan was to signal the marshal to block the road as soon as the stolen car appeared. With Clyde at the wheel, the couple in the coupe first approached Siebrecht. As he passed the officer, Clyde slammed on his brakes and spun the car around as he reached for a pistol. Attempting to run down the deputy, Clyde started shooting at him directly through the windshield, spraying broken glass everywhere. In the meantime Raymond Hamilton, following in the sedan from Victoria, swung around and likewise headed for the deputy, awkwardly shooting from the window. Siebrecht fired at both cars, noting that Hamilton "leaned way down in the seat as he went past and I had to shoot through the door." In a matter of moments the two cars disappeared.

For six months, Bonnie and Clyde lay low, and we know little of their activities. Raymond Hamilton for his part spent several months hiding out in Michigan. The couple showed up in Dallas in late December, exchanging gifts with family members on Christmas Eve. During this visit they recruited a helper, William Daniel Jones, saying, "We been driving a long ways. We need someone to keep watch while we get some rest." Known as "Deacon" or W. D., the teenager had known Clyde since childhood and idolized him. That night the threesome headed south in a single-seated coupe, arriving at a tourist court near Temple, Texas, about two o'clock in the morning. Checking into a room, the couple took the bed while Jones made a pallet on the floor. After sleeping late, they got up about midday and drove into Temple to "get us some spending money." They found almost all places of business closed on the quiet Christmas Sunday afternoon.

The criminals cruised along Avenue G between the Santa Fe and the Scott & White hospitals, where they found a drugstore open to serve the patients. While Bonnie parked a block away on Avenue F, Clyde gave Jones a .41-caliber pistol and told him to follow him inside as a backup. The accomplice got cold feet and left the store before his partner could begin a heist, infuriating Barrow. Once outside he called W. D. a "yellow punk" and showered him with other verbal abuse. The frightened teenager stammered, "I want to go home." Just then they walked past Doyle Johnson's house at 606 South Thirteenth. Barrow gestured to a Ford Model A roadster with a key in the ignition and said, "Well, climb in that car and take yourself back to Dallas." Jones tried the starter, but cold weather prevented the engine from turning over. Clyde in exasperation then began pushing the lightweight vehicle so W. D. could start the engine. The movement attracted attention, and people who had gathered for a Christmas celebration began pouring out of a house. Twenty-seven-year-old grocery salesman Doyle Johnson clambered onto the driver-side running board of his car as Clyde yelled, "Get back, man, or I'll kill you." The car owner began choking Barrow, who now was at the wheel and was again warning, "Stop, man, or I'll kill you." Two shots rang out, one striking Johnson in the neck. As he fell into the street, Clyde and W. D. drove off in the now-running roadster, only to abandon it a short distance away when Bonnie picked them up on Avenue F. All three fled the town. When Johnson was laid to rest two days later, his family knew only that his slayers had been two unidentified men and a woman.

Bonnie, Clyde, and W. D. hid out in East Texas for just a few days. Early in January 1933 they delivered a radio containing hidden hacksaw blades to Lillian McBride in West Dallas, with the request that she deliver the set to her brother, Raymond Hamilton. He was in jail at Hillsboro, being tried for the murder of John Bucher, and Barrow hoped that he would be able to use the playing of the radio to drown out the sound of him sawing through the iron bars of his cell with the blades. About midnight on Friday, January 6, he, Bonnie, and W. D. drove to McBride's house to see whether she had been successful in making the delivery.

Unknown to the Barrow party, Dallas police officers already were at Lillian McBride's house, though not looking for Clyde. They had heard that another criminal, Odell Chambless, might be there. They arrived on the afternoon of Friday, January 6, but found only young McBride and a baby. Then six men returned around eleven o'clock in the evening,

Lillian McBride's home in West Dallas, where Clyde Barrow killed Deputy Sheriff Malcolm Davis on the night of January 6, 1933. In this staged photograph, Dallas County chief of detectives Bill Decker stands on the right, where Clyde Barrow fired the shots that took the life of Deputy Davis. Courtesy of Texas/Dallas History and Archives Division, Dallas Public Library, image PA76-1/33024.

this time finding another Hamilton sister, eighteen-year-old Maggie Farris, with a child and an infant. While four of them interviewed Farris inside a front room illuminated by a red night light said to be for the sleeping children, two more lawmen lounged on the back porch in the dark. All of them hoped that they might snag Chambless.

When Clyde, Bonnie, and W. D. drove up to the McBride home, they saw the red light, which actually was a warning signal that they should not stop. Then they circled the block and saw that the lamp had been extinguished, not knowing that a detective had instructed Farris to turn it off. Stopping in front, Clyde emerged from a coupe automobile wearing an overcoat that concealed a sawed-off 16-gauge shotgun. As he approached the porch, Maggie Farris cried out, "Don't shoot! Think of my babies." Instead Barrow emptied double-aught buckshot through the window, where in the faint red light of his first pass in the car he had seen the shape of a man. The two officers from the back porch came running around the house, whereupon Barrow blasted Deputy Malcolm Davis in the chest, the impact throwing him across the porch steps. In the chaos Clyde ran around the side of the house and then sprinted south a block and a half down the alley to Eagle Ford Road. There he linked up again with Bonnie and W. D. in the car and escaped to spend the next weeks in the area where the corners of Oklahoma, Arkansas, Kansas, and Missouri come together.

On March 22, 1933, Buck Barrow received a full pardon from Texas governor Miriam Ferguson, and the next day he was reunited with his wife, Blanche. They discussed many things, but looming in Buck's mind was guilt that he felt over having led his little brother into a life of crime. Fresh out of prison, he wanted to spend some time with Clyde and persuade him to give up, though friends advised him that his brother would never change. "Don't get in that car with Clyde," Ralph Fults warned him. "If you do, you're a goner." Even so, Buck, Clyde, Blanche, Bonnie, and W. D. Jones planned a vacation trip

Mug shots of Marvin Ivan "Buck" Barrow, brother of Clyde Barrow, who received a gubernatorial pardon and was released from the Texas State Prison in March 1933. Courtesy of Texas/ Dallas History and Archives Division, Dallas Public Library, image MA 83.7/ MB.B-28.

together. It was about this time that Clyde stole yet another Ford V-8 sedan, this time in Marshall, Texas. Teenaged Robert F. "Bobbie" Rosborough had just returned home to the red-brick bungalow where he lived with his parents and was preparing for a date when his mother asked him to bring in some milk bottles from the porch. "I went outside and my car was gone," he remembered. It was several weeks before the teenager got his car back—with thirty-five hundred additional miles on the odometer together with a gun tripod, holes shot through the floor, and soiled women's clothing.

Clyde, Bonnie, and W. D. drove the Rosborough Ford to an initial reunion meeting at a roadside, probably somewhere in northeastern Oklahoma, where they took a number of snapshot pictures. The party then proceeded in two cars to Joplin, Missouri, where they rented a garage apartment. Suspicious local law officers approached the residence on the afternoon of April 13, 1933, and were met with gunfire that downed two of them. Amid a hail of shots, the five criminals in one car exited the building and drove 450 miles nonstop to Amarillo, Texas, though they later hid out in other places, including Ruston, Louisiana. At the apartment officers found personal belongings, firearms, Blanche's purse with Buck's pardon, a guitar, several handwritten pages of poetry by Bonnie, and a camera with one or two rolls of undeveloped film. Within hours authorities had the film processed, and soon newspapers across the country began publishing the photographs from the roadside rendezvous showing all five individuals and the V-8 Ford from Marshall.

By June 9, 1933, Bonnie and Clyde were back in Dallas for a visit, but then they departed again with W. D. Jones. They took a circuitous route via the eastern Texas Panhandle, planning to meet up with Buck and Blanche Barrow in western Oklahoma. The next evening around ten o'clock Clyde was heading northward from Wellington toward

Bonnie and Clyde posed for a snapshot behind Robert F. Rosborough's 1932 Ford V-8 as the pair motored toward Joplin, Missouri, in late March or April 1933 for a reunion with Clyde's brother and sister-in-law, Buck and Blanche Barrow. After police confiscated the camera and film in Joplin, pictures like this one showing the license plate number conclusively connected the theft of this car with the Barrow Gang. Courtesy of Texas/Dallas History and Archives Division, Dallas Public Library, image MA 83.7/MB.B-32.

Shamrock, Texas, in an area where the old road paralleled new highway construction. As he approached the Salt Fork of the Red River, he saw a barricade across the road. Suspecting that it had been set up by lawmen, he crashed through. In reality the barricade was intended to keep motorists from driving off into the river. Soon the Ford V-8 was tumbling down a thirty-foot embankment, rolling twice, crashing into the sandy riverbed, and landing upside down. The impact of the accident threw Clyde out of the car, but it pinned Bonnie beneath. As W. D. Jones retrieved guns and ammunition, Clyde struggled to free his sweetheart. Then a spark ignited leaking gasoline that burned her right leg and arm. Just then two men from a nearby farm came to help, and together the four people lifted the wrecked car enough to pull the severely battered and burned Bonnie Parker free. They carried her to the nearby Steve Pritchard farm, where lantern light revealed the extent of her injuries. In the confu-

Bonnie Parker in a jaunty pose in front of Robert F. Rosborough's V-8 Ford during a roadside rest stop on the way to Joplin, Missouri, in late March or April 1933. Courtesy of Texas/ Dallas History and Archives Division, Dallas Public Library, image MA 83.7/MB.P-2.

sion Pritchard's son-in-law disappeared, pushing the family's car down a lane toward the highway and then driving into Wellington to report the accident and the suspicious wrecked car full of guns.

Clyde saw the shining headlamps when Collingsworth County sheriff George T. Corry and Wellington city marshal Paul Hardy turned off the highway toward the Pritchard farm about 11:30 PM. He and W. D. hid outside the farmhouse in the dark, surprised the officers, and seized their firearms. They then commandeered the officers' vehicle, placing Bonnie in the laps of Corry and Jones in the back seat, while Barrow and Hardy took the front as Clyde proceeded toward the planned Oklahoma meeting with Buck and Blanche. "You hold her easy," Clyde ordered the men in the back. Driving northward through Shamrock to Pampa, they proceeded eastward toward a bridge between Erick and Sayre, Oklahoma, where the rendezvous was made about 3:30 AM. W. D. asked, "What are we going to do with these men, kill them?" to which

Clyde replied, "No, I have been with them so long that I am beginning to kind of like them." Handcuffing two of their wrists together, Jones then spread the lawmen apart and fastened their free hands to trees with barbed wire.

Bonnie's injuries were not only painful but also life threatening. Blanche remembered, "Bonnie was a mass of burns and cuts on her face, right arm, and left. Her chin was cut to the bone. . . . All of us thought she would die before daybreak." The Barrow party in two cars headed to Fort Smith, Arkansas, and then after several weeks to Great Bend, Kansas, where Bonnie convalesced in tourist courts. Her sister, Billie Jean Mace, came up from Texas to help serve as Bonnie's nurse. In the meantime the men staged local heists to pay for their living expenses. Then on July 18, 1933, with Buck and Blanche Barrow, they moved to a tourist court adjacent to the Red Crown Tavern outside Platte City, Missouri, but there the out-of-town group attracted the attention of local authorities. The next night lawmen gathered to investigate and possibly arrest the strangers but were met with gunfire from Browning Automatic Rifles that were far more powerful than any guns the officers could muster. Again the Barrow Gang escaped, though all the members suffered injuries of one form or another. Buck received a dreadful bullet wound in his head. Clyde drove 180 miles to Dexter, Iowa, where the injured fugitives sought shelter at an abandoned rural amusement park called Dexfield. They camped for several days and nights, but Buck's condition grew worse. The strangers again attracted the attention of neighbors and eventually law of enforcement officers, about a dozen of whom raided the camp just after five o'clock on the morning of July 24, 1933. Lawmen captured Blanche and Buck, who died from his head wound five days later. After trial Blanche went to the Missouri State Penitentiary for five and a half years. Despite their injuries, Clyde, W. D., and Bonnie managed to get away. They all spent the next weeks as invalids on the lam, moving back and forth across Kansas, Missouri, Colorado, and some southern states as they recovered from their injuries. They did, however, burglarize National Guard armories in Illinois and Oklahoma to restock their supply of high-powered military weapons and ammunition. W. D. Jones departed their company in Mississippi, catching a bus home to Texas.

Bonnie and Clyde were physically

Prison mug shots of Blanche Barrow following her arrest in Iowa in July 1933. She was tried for offenses associated with the shoot-out in Joplin, Missouri, earlier that year, and the jury sentenced her to five and a half years of imprisonment. Courtesy of Texas/Dallas History and Archives Division, Dallas Public Library, image MA 83.7/MB.B-5.

able to return to West Dallas to see their family members in early September 1933. Having not slept indoors since midsummer and still recuperating from their injuries, they both looked haggard. Bonnie's mother commented that her daughter looked "miserably thin and much older. Her leg was drawn up under her. Her body was covered with scars." These family visits generally took place in rural settings, usually around dusk. From that fall onward, the couple tried to come back to visit more than before. After losing her ability to walk without a cane or assistance, Bonnie could no longer help Clyde as backup in robberies or serve as a getaway driver, so she ended up in hideouts with Barrow or Parker family members while Clyde recruited new male accomplices and used them to help stage robberies.

Dallas County sheriff Richard Allen "Smoot" Schmidt with a Thompson submachine gun about 1933. Courtesy of Texas/Dallas History and Archives Division, Dallas Public Library, image PA 76-17/33003.

Only once did the fugitive couple attempt to get together with their families twice in the same place, and the try almost ended their lives. Late on the afternoon of November 21, 1933, they joined their family members in a quiet spot near the crest of a hill about midway between Dallas and Fort Worth on unpaved State Highway 15 just east of its intersection with Esters Road. The occasion was the fifty-ninth birthday of Clyde's mother, Cumie. Everyone had a good time, but Clyde failed to bring a gift. The participants decided to gather again at the same location around dusk the next day for further gift exchanges. An informant shared this information with officers of the Dallas County sheriff's department, and they too made plans to be a part of the gathering.

Sheriff Richard Allen "Smoot" Schmidt, with deputies Ted Hinton, Bob Alcorn, and Ed Castor, arrived at the scene well before sunset, secreted their two cars, and then hiked some distance to a ditch about seventy-five feet away from the road. There they lay low, watching as a car carrying Barrow and Parker family members came north up Esters Road about 6:30 pm, turned onto Highway 15, and parked facing east. Then about 6:45 everyone heard the whining sound of a V-8 engine in a car being driven fast as Bonnie and Clyde came south on Esters Road and also turned east onto the highway. Clyde commented, "How do you feel about it, honey? It seems phony tonight." Then as Barrow began approaching the vehicle bearing family members, he saw something out of the corner of his eye, shifted down to second gear, and pressed the accelerator to the floor. At that very moment the lawmen stood up and opened fire with a Browning Automatic Rifle, two Thompson submachine guns, and an automatic rifle. Thirteen of their bullets pierced the black Ford coupe, shattering windows and puncturing three out of four tires. Bonnie and Clyde felt the impact as one of the shots passed through the fleshy parts of both their knees. They escaped because the lawmen had parked their cars too far away to make pursuit. In about four miles Clyde forcefully commandeered a four-cylinder 1932 Ford coupe from two motorists, and he and Bonnie headed north toward Oklahoma.

After the fugitive couple recovered from gunshot wounds, Clyde finally achieved his goal of raiding the hated Eastham Prison Farm. He sought to liberate a handful of inmates while killing as many guards as possible. As the plans were worked out, he decided to free convicts Joe Palmer, Henry Methvin, Hilton Bybee, and his old colleague in crime Raymond Hamilton. Early on the morning of Sunday, January 14, 1934, Bonnie and Clyde transported conspirators James Mullens and Raymond's brother, Floyd Hamilton, to the prison farm. In the dark the latter two walked to a simple wooden bridge, beneath which they secreted two .45-caliber automatic pistols inside a rubber cover and then returned to the car. Inmates Joe Palmer and Raymond Hamilton later retrieved the guns. Two days later on January 16 about six o'clock in the morning, while it was still dark, a black Ford V-8 carrying Bonnie, Clyde, and Mullens returned through fog to the prison farm and stopped. After about an hour inmates began arriving in nearby fields, and then gunfire rang out as Joe Palmer shot two of the mounted guards. Then Clyde and James Mullens, nearer the car, began firing bullets over the heads of prisoners as the four escapees made their way through the fog to the noise of a car horn that Bonnie was sounding. In the ensuing confusion, Clyde drove the crowded vehicle away and made good the breakout. He had followed through on his vow to strike back at the Eastham Prison Farm.

From Texas, the fugitive party proceeded north across Arkansas and Missouri. They paused at Rembrandt, Iowa, on January 23, 1934, to rob a bank of eight hundred dollars. They zigzagged across the center of the country, robbing additional banks at Poteau, Oklahoma, and Knierim, Iowa, with conspirator Mullens and escapees Bybee and Palmer finally separating from the party. By February 19, 1934, Barrow and Raymond

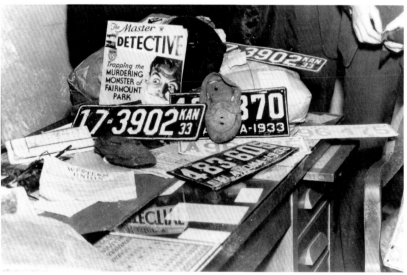

License plates from multiple states, clothing, and personal items that lawmen recovered from the Ford V-8 coupe that Bonnie and Clyde abandoned after escaping from an ambush near Esters Road on November 22, 1933. Courtesy of Texas/Dallas History and Archives Division, Dallas Public Library, image PA 76-1/35058.

The bullet-riddled Ford V-8 coupe that Clyde Barrow and Bonnie Parker abandoned following the ambush that Dallas sheriff "Smoot" Schmidt orchestrated on old Texas Highway 15 near Esters Road between Dallas and Fort Worth on the night of November 22, 1933. Courtesy of Texas/Dallas History and Archives Division, Dallas Public Library, image PA 76-1/33023.1.

Raymond Hamilton, one of the convicts that Bonnie Parker and Clyde Barrow liberated from the Eastham Prison Farm in January 1934. He spent much of the next several months operating in partnership with the couple. Courtesy of Texas/ Dallas History and Archives Division, Dallas Public Library, image PA 76-1/37215.

Hamilton had returned to the Lone Star State, for that night they broke into the National Guard armory next door to the Masonic lodge in Ranger, Texas, to restock their supply of military-type automatic weapons and ammunition. They chose an ideal night for a burglary, for a winter "norther" had just passed through, dropping temperatures across the state into the teens and twenties, so most law-abiding people were inside their homes trying to keep warm. From the armory the party went to the Dallas area to plan another heist.

They chose as their next target the R. P. Henry and Sons Bank in Lancaster, just south of Dallas. On Tuesday, February 27, Henry Methvin drove a green Chevrolet bearing Clyde Barrow and Raymond Hamilton to the side of the red-brick, tile-floored building. Just before lunchtime Clyde and Ray entered the front door and at gunpoint ordered employees and customers to the floor. Cashier L. L. Henry related, "They just walked in and quietly told us what to do. . . . One man covered us with the shotgun, while the other, without hurrying, gathered up all the money in sight." The haul was just over four thousand dollars. The bandits ordered the teller to open the side door to the bank, through which they escaped into the waiting car, making good their departure. After dividing the loot, Raymond separated from the group, leaving the Barrow Gang to consist just of Bonnie, Clyde, and Henry Methvin.

Weeks passed, with the threesome mostly lying low, but then they returned to public attention on Easter Sunday, April 1, 1934. About ten-thirty that morning they parked a black Ford V-8 with bright canary wheels at the side of Dove Road, about a hundred yards up the dirt lane just east of Texas Highway 114 about five and a half miles north of Grapevine. There they planned to rendezvous with family members and friends. On this beautiful, warm morning Bonnie played with a pet rabbit named Sonny Boy, which she planned to give to her mother, while Clyde dozed in the back seat and Henry lounged outside. Then three highway patrol officers riding motorcycles north on Highway 114 passed its intersection with Dove Road. Two

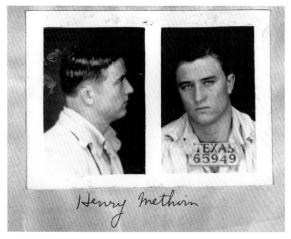

of them, E. B. Wheeler and H. D. Murphy, circled around and headed up Dove Road to see whether the west-facing Ford had broken down and if the motorists needed help. Bonnie awakened Clyde as soon as the officers turned up the byway, and he climbed into the front seat. He told Henry, "Let's take them," meaning he wanted to capture the unsuspecting

Henry Methvin, another of the prisoners that Bonnie and Clyde freed from the Eastham Prison Farm in January 1934 and an accomplice in some of their later crimes. In order to avoid his prosecution in Texas, he and family members played instrumental roles in the subsequent ambush and killing of the criminal couple near Arcadia, Louisiana, in May 1934. Courtesy of Texas/Dallas History and Archives Division, Dallas Public Library, image MA 83.7/MB.M-10.

By spring 1934, lawmen were stopping cars throughout Texas and adjoining states when their drivers and passengers were mistaken for members of the Barrow Gang. This was the fate of Jack Moates (left) and Ira Allison (right), whom San Antonio detectives stopped on April 30 because Clyde Barrow had been reported in an automobile with the same license number. San Antonio Light Collection, UTSA's Institute of Texan Cultures, San Antonio, Texas, image L-0381-C.

officers. Methvin misunderstood, and as the troopers racked their cycles, he began shooting. When one of the officers reached for a weapon, Clyde joined in as well. Within moments both patrolmen lay beside Dove Road, one dead and the other dying. Clyde, Bonnie, and Henry hastily departed the crime scene, heading northward into Oklahoma. There, six days later, they shot dead a constable and abducted the city marshal at the town of Commerce.

With the cold-blooded killings of the two highway patrolmen near Grapevine, public attitudes toward Bonnie and Clyde began to change. Even though it was fanciful, many people up to that time had viewed them as Robin Hood–like characters who stole from the rich and shared with the poor. After they murdered the two unsuspecting motorcycle officers, who still had their guns holstered, people realized that the members of the Barrow Gang were cold-blooded killers. The editor of the *Dallas Morning News* declared, "The fugitive Barrow and his companions are . . . like the mad dog[;] the only remedy for their ailment is extinction. They must be hunted up and disposed of." Unknown to the public, professional manhunters were already on their trail. Lee Simmons, manager of the Texas State Prison, embarrassed by the Eastham raid, on February 1, 1934, commissioned former Texas Ranger Frank Hamer to track down Clyde Barrow. Within a matter of days the ranger learned that Henry Methvin might be the key to ending Barrow's career in crime.

Intermittently since engineering the Eastham escapes, Bonnie and Clyde had stayed in an abandoned bungalow in the country about ten miles south of Gibsland, Louisiana. Henry Methvin's family lived in the same general neighborhood, and a number of them knew and had befriended the Texas desperadoes. Exercising the utmost secrecy, Frank Hamer offered a pardon for Henry Methvin's Texas crimes in exchange for a tip-off that would lead to the arrest or elimination of Barrow and Parker, and a deal was struck. Unknowingly, the couple and their accomplices continued on their trail of crime, stealing a tan-colored Ford V-8 sedan in Topeka, Kansas, on April 29, and then using it in the robbery of a bank in Iowa a few days later. They turned south toward Dallas and then headed east to the hideout in Louisiana.

Having gained the trust of certain Methvin family members, Frank Hamer assembled a modest group of lawmen to assist in either apprehending or killing Clyde Barrow. First he recruited Dallas police officer Bob Alcorn, a former friend of both Bonnie and Clyde. Then he added

Bonnie Parker and Clyde Barrow posed probably during the winter of 1933–1934 in one of the last photographs made of them together. Clyde supports Bonnie, whose injuries from the car crash on the Salt Fork of the Red River prevented her from standing without assistance. Courtesy of Texas/ Dallas History and Archives Division, Dallas Public Library, image PA 76-1/33006.

another former Texas Ranger, B. M. "Manny" Gault. Alcorn asked for backup in the form of another Dallas officer, and Ted Hinton joined the group. As part of the betrayal, Henry Methvin separated from Bonnie and Clyde on May 21, and then on the morning of May 23, his father, Iverson Methvin, stopped his logging truck in the middle of the road leading to the hideout south of Gibsland. Removing a tire, he gave the vehicle a disabled appearance. Hidden in the roadside brush were the four Texas lawmen together with two members of the Bienville Parish sheriff's department.

About 9:10 on the morning of May 23, old man Methvin and the six officers heard the distant high-pitched whine of a fast-running Ford V-8 engine. Then a tan-colored Ford V-8 sedan pulled into view. The young man and woman inside slowed down and then paused when they recognized old man Methvin's seemingly disabled truck. Then the first of more than a hundred gunshots began striking the car, which in moments became perforated with bullet holes. The shots killed Bonnie and Clyde almost instantly. Inside the car the lawmen found two bullet-mangled bodies, almost an arsenal of firearms, clothing, a pair of purple-tinted sunshades, Clyde's saxophone, and a partially eaten sandwich in Bonnie's lap. The Barrow Gang was no more.

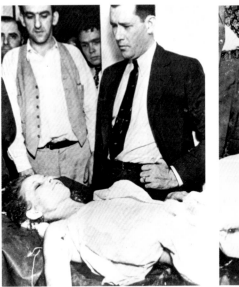 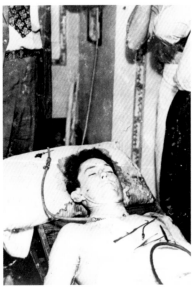

(left) *Bonnie Parker on the mortician's table in Arcadia, Louisiana, following her death by gunshots on May 23, 1934. Courtesy of Texas/Dallas History and Archives Division, Dallas Public Library, image PA 76-1/33020.*
(right) *The body of Clyde Barrow being embalmed in Arcadia, Louisiana, on May 23, 1934. The partially visible man standing on the left and wearing a suit with a distinctively patterned necktie is Dallas County sheriff Richard Allen "Smoot" Schmidt. Courtesy of Texas/Dallas History and Archives Division, Dallas Public Library, image PA 76-1/33010.*

Officers had the bullet-riddled Ford sedan with the bodies still inside towed through Gibsland to the seat of the parish in Arcadia. There a coroner examined the corpses, after which the local mortician embalmed them. Despite crowds of morbid sensation seekers that began thronging the little town, family members were able to arrange transfer of the bodies to mortuaries in Dallas. A memorial service was held for Clyde on May 25. It took place in a funeral home located in the former Belo family mansion in downtown Dallas, with his burial being beside his brother Buck in the family plot at the Western Heights Cemetery.

Some of the crowd gathered outside the Sparkman-Holtz-Brand Funeral Home in Dallas for the funeral of Clyde Barrow on May 25, 1934. Courtesy of Texas/Dallas History and Archives Division, Dallas Public Library, image PA 78-2/501c.

Mourners carrying the casket of Bonnie Parker from the McKamy-Campbell Funeral Home in Dallas following her memorial service on May 26, 1934. Courtesy of Texas/Dallas History and Archives Division, Dallas Public Library, image PA 78-2/513c.

Bonnie's service followed the next day, with her family placing her remains in the Fishtrap Cemetery in West Dallas. Though their families separated Bonnie and Clyde in death, Ted Hinton, who knew both of them, summarized their lives by avowing, "They stuck together, and they loved each other. That just about tells it."

VISIT THE CRIME SCENES

HENRY BARROW'S STAR FILLING STATION, 1221 SINGLETON BOULEVARD (FORMERLY 1620 EAGLE FORD ROAD), DALLAS

Henry and Cumie Barrow purchased a tiny combined residence and gasoline filling station with the settlement they received after a motorist crashed into Henry's horse-drawn scrap metal wagon. The youngest Barrow children lived at the station, while the older ones, including Clyde and Buck, came and went. It served members of Clyde's criminal circle as a rendezvous point and place for leaving messages. The family continued operating the station until 1940, when they sold it to others. Substantially modified over the years, it still stands beside the busy

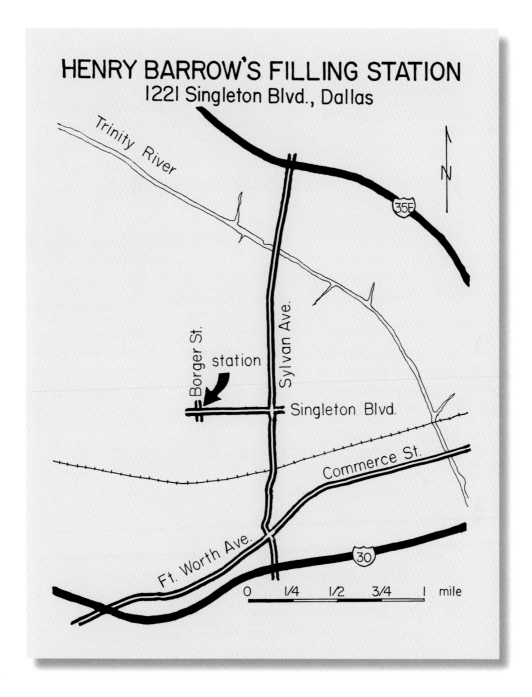

HENRY BARROW'S FILLING STATION
1221 Singleton Blvd., Dallas

Trinity River

35E

Borger St.

Sylvan Ave.

station

Singleton Blvd.

Commerce St.

Ft. Worth Ave.

30

0   1/4   1/2   3/4   1   mile

street. Even after the passage of decades, the rough West Dallas neighborhood is still known for its gang and criminal activity.

To reach the Barrow service station, leave Interstate 30 at exit 44A and drive north 0.8 mile on Sylvan Avenue (crossing Fort Worth Avenue and West Commerce Street) to Singleton Boulevard. Turn west (left) and proceed 0.3 mile on Singleton to the gray-painted building on the north side of the intersection with Borger Street. Alternatively,

Henry Barrow's filling station and Barrow family home as it stands today at the side of Singleton Boulevard, formerly Eagle Ford Road, in West Dallas. Photograph by the author, 2009.

leave Interstate 35E at exit 340B and drive south on Wycliff Avenue (which becomes Sylvan Avenue) 1.7 miles (crossing the Trinity River) to Singleton Boulevard. Turn west (right) on Singleton and continue 0.3 mile to the building.

WORKPLACES OF CLYDE BARROW AND BONNIE PARKER, UNITED GLASS AND MIRROR, 2614–16 SWISS AVENUE, DALLAS, AND HARGRAVES CAFE, 3308 SWISS CIRCLE, DALLAS

Clyde Barrow found employment at several places during the late 1920s and early 1930s, among them United Glass and Mirror. He worked at that business just east of downtown Dallas both before and after his imprisonment for auto theft and burglary. Clyde's sister, Nell, related that as a glazier he "built church windows for many Dallas churches" and "made lovely mirrors." Eventually the manager at United laid off Clyde in 1932 because local law officers repeatedly came to the workplace to ask the ex-con employee questions about suspected criminal activities.

Bonnie Parker found employment in several Dallas eating places, but the only one that remains standing today is the former Hargraves Cafe, about half a dozen streets northeast of United Glass and Mirror just off Swiss Avenue at 3308 Swiss Circle. The business occupied the storefront next to the west end of a crescent-shaped complex of five attached red-brick commercial buildings built on an irregularly shaped block where Swiss Avenue jogged half a block to one side near its intersection with Hall Street. Bonnie went to work here in January 1928,

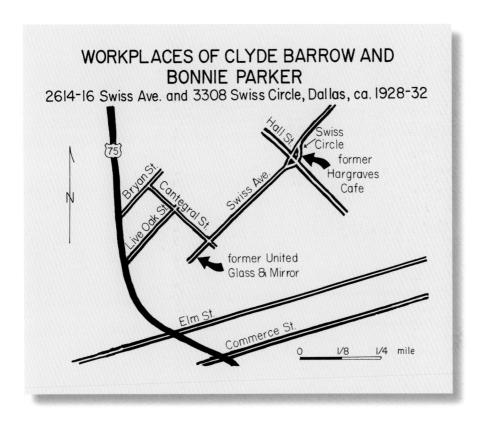

WORKPLACES OF CLYDE BARROW AND
BONNIE PARKER
2614-16 Swiss Ave. and 3308 Swiss Circle, Dallas, ca. 1928-32

taking orders and serving meals. She brought extra business to the
café from employees at the Yates Laundry Company, whose building
stood across Floyd Street from the rear of the row of stores. Unable to
leave their work stations, laundry employees whistled loud enough for
Bonnie to hear, whereupon she ran across to take orders and then delivered the prepared food wrapped in paper.

To reach these sites from the north, leave U.S. Highway 75 (North
Central Expressway) southbound at exit 284C on the left and drive 0.6
mile toward Downtown/Live Oak Street. Turn sharply to the northeast (left) onto Live Oak Street and drive 0.2 mile to Cantegral Street.
At Cantegral, turn southeast (right) and drive two blocks to Swiss Avenue. To view the buildings that housed United Glass and Mirror, turn
southwest (right) and drive half a block to "The Club," an athletic club,
at 2614–16 on the left. The portion of the present-day complex that
housed the historic glass and mirror shop consisted of the central two
buildings: the recessed structure with a parking lot in front and the east
half of the full-depth commercial building to the west (with 2616 on its
glass door). To view the former Hargraves Cafe location, turn northeast
on Swiss Avenue from the site of United Glass and Mirror and drive
five blocks to Swiss Circle and the curve of low red-brick commercial
buildings just after the intersection with Hall Street. To approach these

The commercial building that for years housed Clyde Barrow's employer, United Glass and Mirror, at 2614–16 Swiss Avenue on the immediate northeast side of downtown Dallas. Today an athletic club operates in the remodeled structure. Photograph by the author, 2009.

Hargraves Cafe, one of the several eating places where Bonnie Parker worked as a waitress, occupied the storefront at 3308 Swiss Circle, second from the west (right) end of this curved row of commercial buildings, a short distance northeast of downtown Dallas. Today the modern Baylor University Medical Center looms up behind it just to the southeast. Photograph by the author, 2009.

sites from the south, leave northbound U.S. Highway 75 (North Central Expressway) at exit 285 for Bryan Street East and take the access road 0.2 mile to its intersection with Bryan Street. Turn northeast (right) and drive one block on Bryan to its juncture with Cantegral Street. Turn southeast (right) on Cantegral and proceed four blocks to Swiss Avenue and follow the directions above to go from Swiss Avenue to the two sites.

WACO JAIL BREAK AND AUTO THEFTS, WACO, MARCH 11, 1930

On the afternoon of March 11, 1930, Bonnie Parker smuggled a .22-caliber pistol to her sweetheart, Clyde Barrow, inside the McLennan County Jail in Waco, Texas. That very evening he and two other prisoners used this weapon to force their way out of the calaboose, fleeing first on foot and then by stolen automobiles.

Although the historic jail building no longer stands adjacent to the courthouse in Waco, it is relatively easy to follow the route of the escapees as they fled on foot. Leaving the jail by an entrance on North Sixth Street, the three young men ran north on North Sixth across Columbus Avenue to Jefferson Avenue. There they cut diagonally across

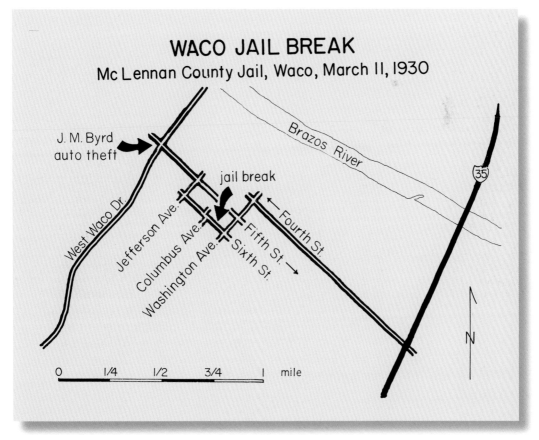

to North Fifth Street, which today has one-way traffic (southbound). They continued north on foot a block and a half to 724 North Fifth, where outside a boardinghouse they took a car belonging to J. M. Byrd. (Today this site is a vacant lot.) They proceeded north in the auto about fifteen blocks to the still-standing home of Dr. W. L. Souther at 2005 North Seventh Street, where they stole a vehicle parked in front and abandoned Byrd's car.

To reach the site of the former McLennan County Jail, today the location of the Courthouse Annex Building, leave Interstate 35 at exit 335A marked for Fourth/Fifth Streets/Downtown and drive 0.7 mile northwest on South Fourth Street to its intersection with Washington Avenue. Turn southwest (left) at Washington and drive two blocks to North Sixth Street. The present-day Courthouse Annex Building at the west corner of the courthouse block at Washington and North Sixth marks the place where the former jail stood.

To reach the former home of Dr. W. L. Souther, where the three young criminals stole their second automobile, drive north from the courthouse on North Sixth Street 1.2 miles (fourteen blocks) to its junction with Brook Avenue at a "T" intersection. Turn southwest (left) on Brook and proceed one and a half blocks to its juncture with North

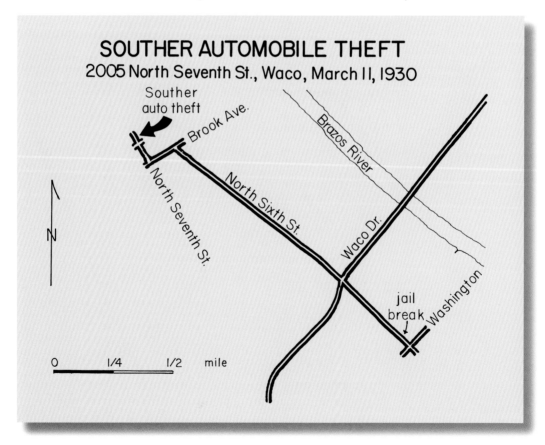

SOUTHER AUTOMOBILE THEFT
2005 North Seventh St., Waco, March 11, 1930

On the afternoon of March 11, 1930, Clyde Barrow and two fellow escapees from the McLennan County Jail stole an automobile belonging to Dr. W. L. Souther that he had parked in front of this house located at 2005 North Seventh Street in Waco, Texas. Photograph by the author, 2010.

Seventh Street. At North Seventh, turn northwest (right) and proceed one and a half blocks to the site of the auto theft, a light blue bungalow on the northeast side of the street at number 2005.

FIRST ELECTRA ABDUCTION AND AUTO THEFT, ELECTRA, APRIL 14, 1932

When the vehicle occupied by Clyde Barrow, Ralph Fults, and a teenager named Red broke down in Electra, Texas, on April 14, 1932, it came to a halt in the vicinity of an ice plant in the 400 block of West Railroad Avenue, the site today of a vehicle and trailer maintenance yard. The three young men started walking east on West Railroad Avenue, observed by A. F. McCormick, who was working on the second floor of the Magnolia Petroleum Company building on South Waggoner Street about two blocks away. After telephoning the chief of police, McCormick drove around on West Railroad Street behind the strangers just as they pulled pistols on the chief and another citizen near the street intersection with South Waggoner. There Red broke and ran, while Clyde and Ralph abducted all three locals at gunpoint.

To reach the crime scene, turn southwest from Business U.S. Highway 287 in Electra, Texas, onto Texas Highway 25. Drive one block, crossing the Union Pacific Railroad tracks, to West Railroad Avenue. Turn southeast (left) onto West Railroad Avenue and drive two blocks to the intersection with South Dunbar Street. The stolen car broke down opposite the ice plant that formerly stood at the west corner of the intersection. Proceed two blocks along West Railroad Avenue to the juncture with South Waggoner Street and the area of the armed

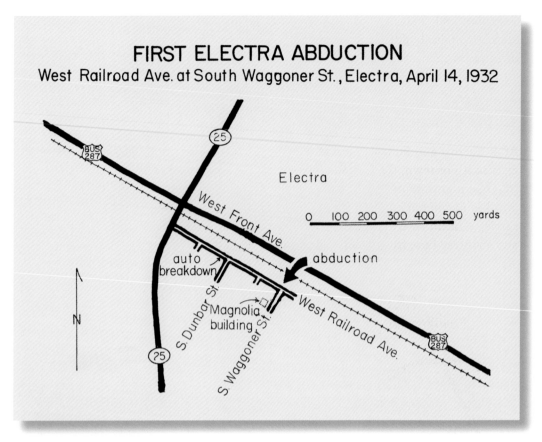

FIRST ELECTRA ABDUCTION
West Railroad Ave. at South Waggoner St., Electra, April 14, 1932

BUS 287

25

Electra

West Front Ave.

0   100   200   300   400   500   yards

auto
breakdown

abduction

S. Dunbar St.

Magnolia
building

S. Waggoner St.

West Railroad Ave.

BUS 287

N

?5

View south on West Railroad Avenue in Electra, Texas, from its juncture with South Waggoner Street (on the left), where Clyde Barrow, Ralph Fults, and a companion encountered local citizens and staged the first of two abductions and auto thefts on April 14, 1932. Photograph by the author, 2009.

abduction and theft of A. F. McCormick's automobile. The two-story brick Magnolia building, from which McCormick first observed the three young men, still stands nearby at 207 South Waggoner Street.

SECOND ELECTRA ABDUCTION AND AUTO THEFT, ELECTRA, APRIL 14, 1932

After Barrow and Fults dumped the first three abducted Electra citizens south of town, they turned north, back toward the Fort Worth–Amarillo highway, present-day Business U.S. 287. In the vicinity of the Fowlkes community, southeast of Electra, they drove alongside mail carrier William N. Owens and at gunpoint commandeered his vehicle and abducted him, freeing him in Oklahoma the next day.

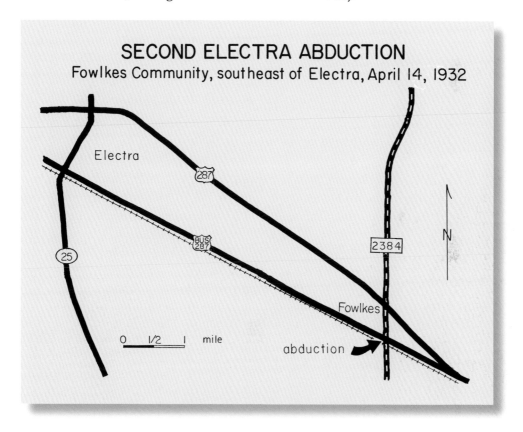

To reach the location of this second abduction, leave U.S. Highway 287 at its intersection with Farm to Market Road 2384 (Fowlkes Station Road) about five miles east of Electra. Drive south 0.4 mile on FM 2384 to its junction with Business U.S. Highway 287, the area of the former Fowlkes community. This crossroads is the general area where the Owens kidnapping took place.

CHALK HILL EVASION OF LAW OFFICERS, WEST DAVIS STREET, DALLAS, APRIL 17, 1932

On the night of April 17, 1932, Clyde Barrow demonstrated his soon-to-be-famous driving abilities to Ralph Fults when he skidded his vehicle around 180 degrees and eluded lawmen in pursuit.

To reach the site of this incident, leave Interstate 30 at exit 39 on the west side of Dallas, following either westbound or eastbound access roads to a juncture with North Cockrell Hill Road. Drive south on North Cockrell Hill 1.2 miles to its intersection with Texas Highway 180 (West Davis Street). Turn west (right) on Texas 180 and drive 0.6 mile toward the intersection with Chalk Hill Road. Once on Texas 180, you are driving where Barrow and Fults traveled. In approaching the juncture with Chalk Hill Road, notice the start of a substantial downhill grade. It was on this slope, as Barrow dropped out of sight of the pur-

West on West Davis Street (Texas Highway 180) on the west side of Dallas looking toward the drop-off of a substantial downhill slope near the intersection with Chalk Hill Road. It was on this road, at the time a gravel byway, that Clyde Barrow and Ralph Fults evaded law officers when Barrow used his considerable driving skills to pull a 180-degree turn on the night of April 17, 1932. Photograph by the author, 2009.

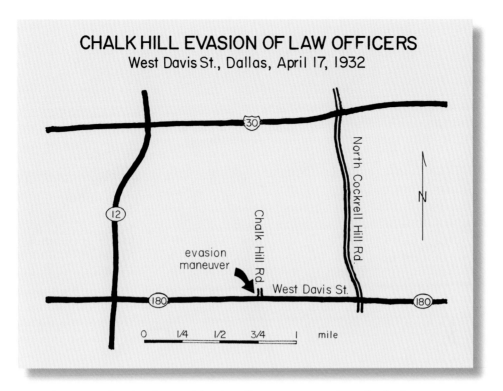

CHALK HILL EVASION OF LAW OFFICERS
West Davis St., Dallas, April 17, 1932

suing lawmen, that he dimmed his headlamps, tramped on the brakes, turned the steering wheel sharply, and swung the vehicle around on the gravel road to head back uphill toward the unsuspecting officers.

MABANK ATTEMPTED BURGLARY, 121 EAST MARKET STREET, MABANK, APRIL 19, 1932

In order to stage his hoped-for raid of the Eastham Prison Farm, Clyde Barrow needed more firearms. He and Ralph Fults attempted to break into the rear of Hyman Bock's general mercantile store in Mabank during a return auto-stealing trip from Tyler early on the morning of April 19, 1932. The store operated at 121 East Market Street, the main commercial thoroughfare in the little East Texas town. City Marshal Dave Drennan interrupted the burglary before the thieves could force the back door.

To reach the crime scene, exit U.S. Highway 175 on the north side of Mabank at its intersection with Texas Highway 198. Drive south on Texas 198 (Third Street) a distance of 0.5 mile to its intersection with East Market Street, then turn east (left) and drive one-half block. The single-story masonry commercial building at 121 East Market Street stands in the middle of the block on the north side of the street. At the time of research the structure housed a dance studio. To view the rear of the store, where the thieves attempted to force entry, just walk around to the alley behind the building.

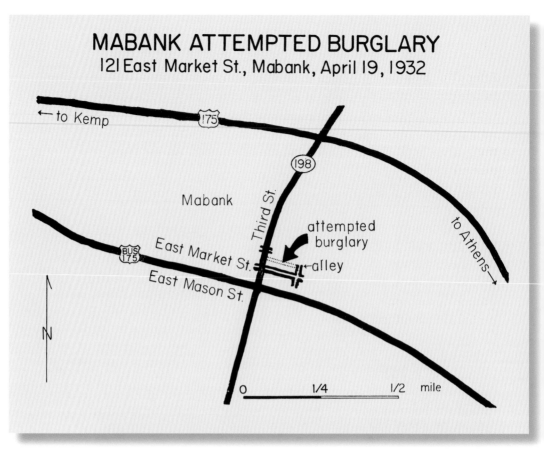

MABANK ATTEMPTED BURGLARY
121 East Market St., Mabank, April 19, 1932

← to Kemp

175

198

Mabank

Third St.

attempted burglary

to Athens →

BUS 175

East Market St.

←alley

East Mason St.

N

0   1/4   1/2   mile

The front of the commercial building at 121 East Market Street in Mabank, Texas, where Clyde Barrow and Ralph Fults unsuccessfully attempted a burglary to obtain firearms and ammunition in the early hours of April 19, 1932. Photograph by the author, 2009.

KEMP JAILING OF BONNIE PARKER AND RALPH FULTS, CITY JAIL, KEMP, APRIL 19, 1932

After Clyde Barrow, Bonnie Parker, and Ralph Fults left Mabank following the unsuccessful burglary of the Bock store, the car in which they were riding bogged down in mud. After spending the entire day evading a posse, Clyde escaped but Bonnie and Ralph fell into the hands of the local authorities on the evening of April 19, 1932. The fatigued lawmen secured the two fugitives for the night in the tiny one-room brick jail half a block off Main Street before transferring them to the county jail in Kaufman the next day.

To reach the now disused Kemp jail, exit U.S. Highway 175 at its intersection with Farm to Market Road 1895 on the northeast side of Kemp in Kaufman County. Drive southwest 0.5 mile into Kemp to the intersection with Business U.S. Highway 175/State Loop 346 (Elm Street). Turn southeast (left) onto Business U.S. Highway 175 and drive two blocks to an intersection with East Eleventh Street. There turn

The tiny one-room brick jail at Kemp, Texas, that housed Bonnie Parker and Ralph Fults on the night of April 19, 1932. Photograph by the author, 2009.

southwest (right) onto East Eleventh and proceed one and a half blocks to the historic Kemp jail, a small, red-brick cubicle with iron bars facing an unpaved alley behind a row of historic commercial buildings. This alley may be muddy after wet weather.

CELINA KIDNAPPINGS AND BURGLARY, CELINA, APRIL 21, 1932

Clyde Barrow, Ted Rogers, and a companion called Johnny made their way into sleepy Celina, Texas, in the dead of the night on April 20–21, 1932, intent on breaking into the Patrick & Seitz hardware store to steal guns and ammunition. In addition to burglarizing the store, they accidentally broke into another business and abducted four local men at gunpoint, locking them into a convenient railway boxcar.

To reach the town square in Celina, the focus of these crimes, drive north 7.7 miles on Texas Highway 289 from its intersection with U.S. Highway 380 between McKinney and Denton. At the juncture of Texas Highway 289 with Farm to Market Road 455 (East Pecan Street), turn west (left) and drive 0.6 mile to North Ohio Street in downtown Celina. Park in one of the several free spaces on the rectangular public square. Walk to the southeast corner of the square, where the two-story former Nelson Hotel building stands at 222 West Walnut Street, today the location of a real estate office. Directly across North Ohio Street to the west is the two-story historic city hall at 302 West Walnut. It still houses municipal offices. Two of the criminals got the drop on the mayor and watchman in the street between these two buildings.

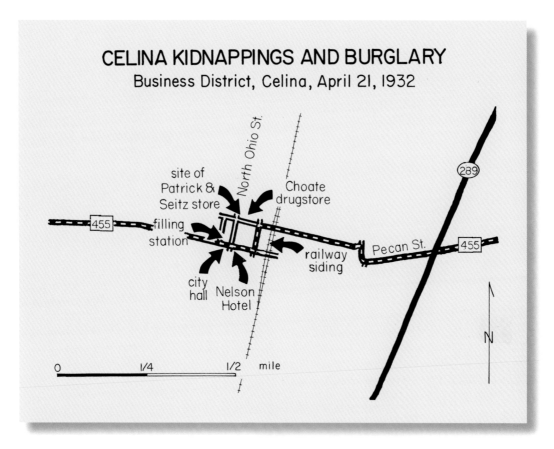

CELINA KIDNAPPINGS AND BURGLARY
Business District, Celina, April 21, 1932

North Ohio St.

site of
Patrick &
Seitz store

Choate
drugstore

289

455

filling
station

railway
siding

Pecan St.

455

city
hall

Nelson
Hotel

N

0   1/4   1/2   mile

View eastward across North Ohio Street past the city hall in Celina, Texas, toward the former Nelson Hotel. It was between these two buildings that Clyde Barrow and companions accosted the mayor and the night watchman sometime after midnight on April 21, 1932. Photograph by the author, 2009.

The main line with adjacent siding of the Frisco Railway just east of the town square in Celina, Texas, where Clyde Barrow and associates at gunpoint locked four community members into a boxcar on April 21, 1932, so that they could burglarize local businesses. Photograph by the author, 2009.

When Clyde Barrow, Ted Rogers, and an accomplice set about breaking into the Patrick & Seitz hardware for guns and ammunition in Celina, Texas, in the early hours of April 21, 1932, in the dark they mistakenly broke into the Choate drugstore, the brick commercial building shown on the right. On discovering their mistake, the criminals next forced the back door of the hardware store, which stood at the site of the present-day vacant lot just to the west. Photograph by the author, 2009.

To retrace the steps of the criminals with the two locals, first proceed west along the south side of the square to its southwest corner in front of 312 West Walnut. Just across the street to the north is a gray-painted former gasoline station where the outsiders washed blood from the face of night watchman Perkins after they had struck him in the head with a pistol butt. Next follow the route of the group back east on West Walnut Street, past the square, to the Frisco Railway tracks, just over two blocks. There the criminals locked the locals in a boxcar on a railway siding immediately east of the present-day Founders Station Park, where the tracks and the concrete foundations of the train station still may be seen. After adding two more Celina citizens to the boxcar, the thieves made their way on foot to the rear of the Choate drugstore and broke inside. This store operated at 241 West Pecan Street in a still-surviving single-story brick commercial building on the north side of the street just off the northeast corner of the square. Discovering their error, the burglars moved next door to force their way inside the hardware store at 243 West Pecan Street, the site of which today is a vacant lot.

ROBBERY AND MURDER OF JOHN N. BUCHER, COUNTY ROAD 4281, NEAR HILLSBORO, APRIL 30, 1932

On the night of April 30, 1932, Ted Rogers and a young man known as Johnny robbed the combination jewelry store and residence of John N. Bucher just outside Hillsboro, Texas. Clyde Barrow waited outside behind the wheel of a getaway car. As the businessman reached for a pistol secreted in his safe and his wife looked on, Ted fired a fatal gunshot into his torso. The thieves escaped into the darkness.

The modified remains of the Bucher store/residence still stand on the old Fort Worth highway, now a county road, on the northern outskirts of Hillsboro. From the Hill County Courthouse in town, drive north on Texas Highway 81 (North Waco Street) just over four blocks to an awkward intersection with Pecos Street to the left. The juncture is marked by a liquefied petroleum gas outlet on one side of North Waco Street and a monument works on the other and is located just where Texas Highway 81 begins bending toward the north-northeast. Veer north (left) onto Pecos Street and proceed north one block on Pecos to its intersection with Hill County Road 4281 (the old Fort Worth highway). Turn northwest (left) onto the paved county road, immediately pass beneath double railway tracks, and stay on the road 0.1 mile as it bears to the right. The south-facing white stucco Bucher house is on the right side of the road. The rural roadway is still paved with historic twenty-foot-wide concrete that dates from the days when it served as the main highway northward from Hillsboro toward Fort Worth and Dallas.

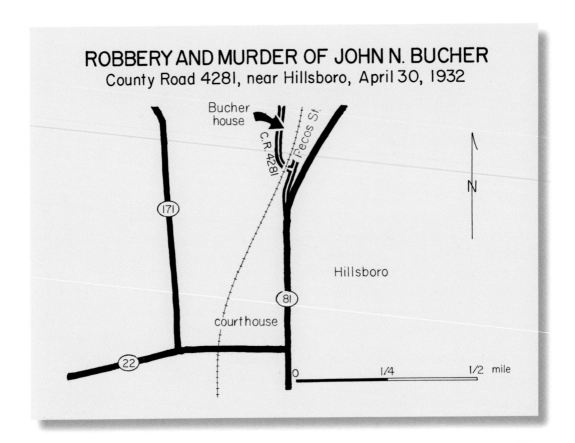

ROBBERY AND MURDER OF JOHN N. BUCHER
County Road 4281, near Hillsboro, April 30, 1932

Bucher house

C.R. 4281

Pecos St.

171

N

Hillsboro

81

courthouse

22

0   1/4   1/2 mile

The dwelling that has remained at the site of John N. Bucher's combination jewelry store and residence, where Ted Rogers murdered the businessman during a nighttime robbery staged with assistance from Clyde Barrow and a companion just north of Hillsboro, Texas, on April 30, 1932. Photograph by the author, 2006.

44

WHARTON AMBUSH, U.S. HIGHWAY 59 BRIDGE
AND APPROACH, WHARTON, AUGUST 15, 1932

Traveling in two cars, Clyde Barrow, Bonnie Parker, and Raymond Hamilton through quick action avoided apprehension at a law officers' ambush near a 1930 overhead truss bridge across the Colorado River on the south edge of Wharton on the Gulf Coastal Plain. Although a second, modern bridge has been built parallel with the old one associated with the incident, the crime scene otherwise has changed little since the 1930s.

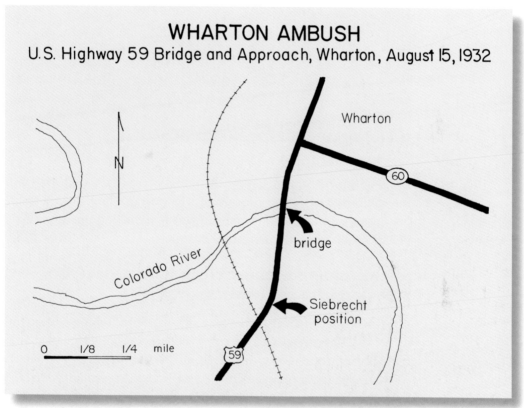

To reach the location, drive south on U.S. Highway 59 (South Richmond Road) from the central commercial district of Wharton, Wharton County, to the two bridges spanning the Colorado River at the south edge of downtown. The historic 1930 bridge that City Marshal W. W. Pitman planned to block with his car today carries southbound traffic across the river. Proceed across the bridge and drive about 0.2 mile to a slight bend in the highway toward the south-southwest. It was in the ditch at the east side of the road at this curve where Deputy Sheriff Carl Siebrecht stood as the two stolen cars approached and where he exchanged gunshots with both Barrow and Hamilton. Roadside parking is possible but dangerous in the area of the curve. Safe parking is available

The slight bend in U.S. Highway 59 leading to the Colorado River bridge on the south edge of Wharton, Texas, where Deputy Sheriff Carl Siebrecht participated in an unsuccessful ambush of Clyde Barrow, Bonnie Parker, and Raymond Hamilton on August 15, 1932. Photograph by the author, 2004.

at a municipal park just west of the north end of the 1930 bridge, but the span itself offers no pedestrian walkway and fast-moving traffic presents a considerable hazard to anyone on foot. The situation surely must have been equally dangerous in 1932.

MURDER OF DOYLE JOHNSON, 606 SOUTH THIRTEENTH STREET, TEMPLE, DECEMBER 25, 1932

After botching the armed robbery of a store in Temple, Texas, on Christmas Day, 1932, Clyde Barrow and W. D. Jones also bungled a car theft in front of a nearby residence at 606 South Thirteenth Street. As they attempted to make off with a Ford roadster people emerged from the house, and in the ensuing ruckus Barrow fired two bullets into automobile owner Doyle Johnson.

To reach the crime scene, leave Interstate 35 at exit 301 in Temple, Texas, at its intersection with Texas Highway 53 (West Central Avenue) and drive 1.0 mile east in the direction of the downtown business district. At Texas Spur 290 (North Third Street), turn south (right) and proceed 0.5 mile. Continue straight in a southerly direction on South Third Street when Texas Spur 290 veers to the left. At the intersection of South Third Street with West Avenue G, turn west (right) and proceed five blocks on West Avenue G to its juncture with South Thirteenth Street. Turn north (right) on South Thirteenth Street and drive half a block to the crime scene. The former Doyle Johnson residence at

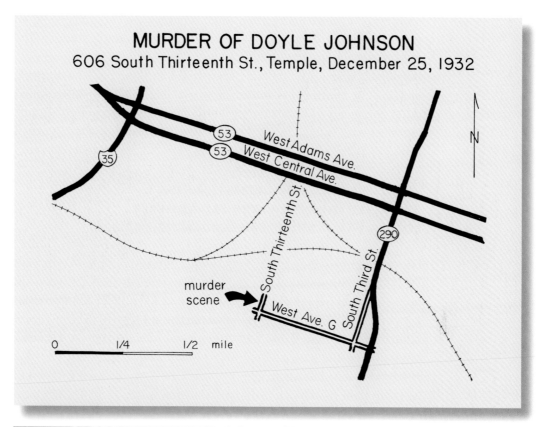

MURDER OF DOYLE JOHNSON
606 South Thirteenth St., Temple, December 25, 1932

The bungalow home at 606 South Thirteenth Street, Temple, Texas, in front of which Clyde Barrow fatally shot Doyle Johnson in a bungled car theft on Christmas Day 1932. Photograph by the author, 2002.

606 South Thirteenth Street is a single-story wooden bungalow painted gray with white trim, and it has a front dormer window. It stands at the west side of the street near the middle of the block. The area along West Avenue G, where Barrow and Jones failed in their robbery attempt, remains lined with 1920s and 1930s tourist courts, filling stations, and other commercial structures, while the neighborhoods on either side are filled with bungalow homes from the first third of the twentieth century.

AMBUSH AT LILLIAN MCBRIDE'S HOUSE, 3111 NORTH WINNETKA AVENUE (FORMERLY 507 COUNTY AVENUE), DALLAS, JANUARY 6, 1933

On the night of January 6, 1933, Clyde Barrow, Bonnie Parker, and W. D. Jones stumbled into a Dallas police ambush that had been set up for another person at the home of one of Raymond Hamilton's sisters, Lillian McBride. The location was in the old West Dallas neighborhood that all of them knew well. When two officers unexpectedly came around from the back of McBride's house, Barrow shot one of them dead and escaped down an alley into the darkness, meeting Parker and Jones in their car a block and a half away to escape.

The crime scene is located in West Dallas just off Singleton Boulevard (formerly Eagle Ford Road). To reach the location, leave Interstate 30 at exit 44A and drive north 0.8 mile on Sylvan Avenue (crossing Fort Worth Avenue and West Commerce Street) to Singleton Boulevard. Turn west (left) on Singleton and proceed four blocks to the intersection with Winnetka Avenue. Turn north (right) on Winnetka Avenue

The well-preserved former residence of Lillian McBride in West Dallas, where Clyde Barrow on the night of January 6, 1933, unexpectedly walked into an ambush planned for another criminal and subsequently killed Dallas deputy sheriff Malcolm Davis. Photograph by the author, 2009.

CHAPTER ONE

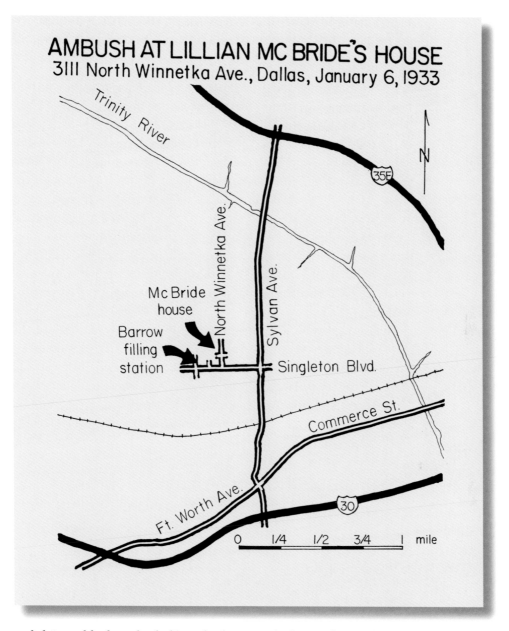

AMBUSH AT LILLIAN MC BRIDE'S HOUSE
3111 North Winnetka Ave., Dallas, January 6, 1933

Trinity River

35E

N

McBride house

Barrow filling station

North Winnetka Ave.

Sylvan Ave.

Singleton Blvd.

Commerce St.

Ft. Worth Ave.

30

0   1/4   1/2   3/4   1   mile

and drive a block and a half to the house, which stands on the west side of the street next to a red-brick Methodist church. The single-story wooden dwelling with a porch across the front is painted white. Alternatively, leave Interstate 35E at exit 340B and drive south on Wycliff Avenue (which becomes Sylvan Avenue) 1.7 miles (crossing the Trinity River) to Singleton Boulevard. Turn west (right) onto Singleton Boulevard and follow the directions above to Lillian McBride's house. The turn from Singleton Boulevard onto Winnetka Avenue is only two blocks east of Henry Barrow's Star Service Station, home of the Barrow family.

THEFT OF ROSBOROUGH V-8 FORD CONVERTIBLE SEDAN, 202 ROSBOROUGH STREET, MARSHALL, MARCH OR APRIL 1933

After Buck Barrow received a pardon on March 22, 1933, he and wife Blanche planned a vacation trip to Missouri with Bonnie Parker, Clyde Barrow, and their companion, W. D. Jones. On the way there, Clyde or W. D. stole an almost new 1932 Ford convertible sedan belonging to Robert F. Rosborough from the driveway in front of his family's home at 202 Rosborough Street in Marshall, Texas. On the way to Joplin, the party gathered at a roadside and took snapshots of each other, many of them in front of the newly stolen vehicle. Following a gunfight at Joplin on April 13, 1933, lawmen found a camera with unprocessed film, which turned out to be the pictures made at the roadside gathering. These photographs, some of the most famous showing Bonnie and Clyde, also included the license plate on Rosborough's car, connecting its theft to the Barrow Gang.

To visit the crime scene, from the intersection of U.S. Highway 80 and U.S. Highway 59 in Marshall, Texas, drive west on U.S. 80 (West Grand Avenue) and drive 1.2 miles to its intersection with Farm to Market Road 1997 (North Grove Street). Turn south (left) on North Grove Street and drive one block to its junction with West Burleson Street. Turn west (right) on West Burleson Street and drive two blocks

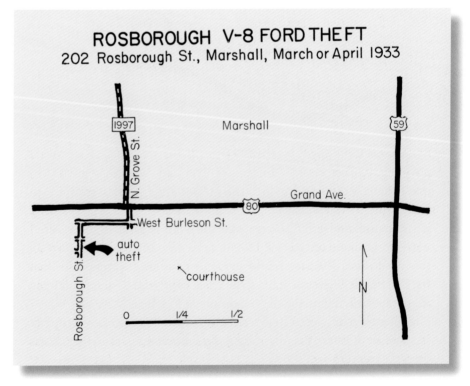

ROSBOROUGH V-8 FORD THEFT
202 Rosborough St., Marshall, March or April 1933

The concrete driveway in front of the red-brick bungalow at 202 Rosborough Street in Marshall, Texas, from which Clyde Barrow in March or April 1933 stole the 1932 Ford V-8 convertible sedan that appears in many photographs showing members of the gang. Photograph by the author, 2007.

to its intersection with Rosborough Street. Turn south (left) onto Rosborough Street and drive one block to a pair of almost identical red-brick-with-white-trim single-story 1920s brick bungalows at the east side of the street. The house at 202, the more southern of the two similar dwellings, is the one where the Rosborough family resided. The driveway in front of the house from which the V-8 Ford was taken is still marked by two narrow strips of concrete paving. The quiet setting a few blocks west of the courthouse, dominated by a nearby two-story red-brick high school building, has changed little since 1933.

SALT FORK OF THE RED RIVER AUTOMOBILE CRASH, WELLINGTON VICINITY, JUNE 10, 1933

By summer 1933, Clyde Barrow, Bonnie Parker, and W. D. Jones were planning another family rendezvous with Buck and Blanche Barrow, this time in western Oklahoma. The three desperadoes took a circuitous route by way of the eastern Texas Panhandle that unexpectedly led them into an area of road construction on U.S. Highway 83 north of Wellington. There on the night of Saturday, June 10, 1933, at considerable speed they left the roadway and crashed into the bed of the Salt Fork of the Red River, wrecking the car and injuring Clyde, W. D., and most especially Bonnie.

Although today more modern bridges carry U.S. Highway 83 across the Salt Fork of the Red River, significant remains survive from the former structure that stood at the site in 1933. To reach the scene of

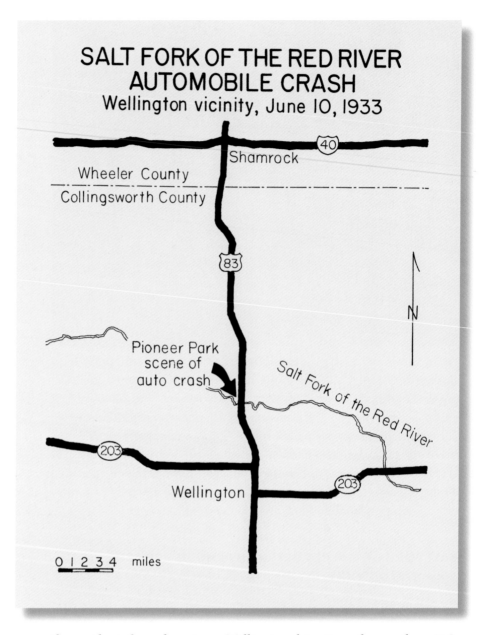

SALT FORK OF THE RED RIVER AUTOMOBILE CRASH
Wellington vicinity, June 10, 1933

Shamrock

40

Wheeler County
Collingsworth County

83

N

Pioneer Park
scene of
auto crash

Salt Fork of the Red River

203

203

Wellington

0 1 2 3 4 miles

the accident, from downtown Wellington drive 6.5 miles north on U.S. Highway 83, or alternatively from Interstate 40 at Shamrock drive 19.4 miles south to Collingsworth County Pioneer Park, located on the north bank of the Salt Fork of the Red River at the west side of U.S. Highway 83. Enter the park area, which offers free day use, and drive to the area along the river, where one may view scattered wooden timbers in and along the riverbed. These timbers supported the roadway of the former highway bridge. On either side of the river, aligned with the wooden members, stand remnants of the concrete abutments from the roadway approaches to the earlier structure. It was in the vicinity

The concrete abutment from the north end of the former timber bridge across the Salt Fork of the Red River north of Wellington, Texas, at which Clyde Barrow, Bonnie Parker, and W. D. Jones were involved in a single-vehicle wreck in which Bonnie received serious burns and other injuries on the night of June 10, 1933. Photograph by the author, 2002.

of this previous bridge that the Barrow vehicle crashed and burned. A state historical marker near the current 1939 northbound bridge on U.S. Highway 83 recounts the events of June 10, 1933.

AMBUSH AT ESTERS ROAD, IRVING, NOVEMBER 21, 1933

Of all the places where lawmen attempted to ambush members of the Barrow Gang, probably none has easier access or has been so modified as the scene of the trap set by Dallas County sheriff Richard Allen "Smoot" Schmidt near Esters Road between Dallas and Fort Worth on November 21, 1933. It has been transformed from bucolic pastures to shopping centers in the modern city of Irving. Clyde Barrow and Bonnie Parker escaped from the snare, though both were wounded by gunfire, and their family members avoided any injuries.

In 1933 unpaved Texas Highway 15, known locally as the North Fort Worth Pike, was one of several east-west routes linking Dallas with Fort Worth. Esters Road intercepted it about sixteen miles west of downtown Dallas. The ambush took place on Highway 15 just east of its intersection with Esters Road. To reach the scene from downtown Dallas drive 14.0 miles west-northwest on Texas Highway 183/Interstate 35E, remaining on Texas Highway 183 (known locally as the Airport Freeway) westbound as it separates from the interstate. Follow signs toward the south entrance to the Dallas/Fort Worth International Airport. Exit from Texas Highway 183 at Esters Road and proceed via the access

On the night of November 21, 1933, Dallas County sheriff R. A. "Smoot" Schmidt staged an ambush on Clyde Barrow and Bonnie Parker at the intersection of Esters Road with the North Fort Worth Pike, today Texas Highway 183. The site of the formerly quiet unpaved country road has been transformed through suburban growth in Irving, Texas, into a freeway surrounded by shopping areas. Photograph by the author, 2009.

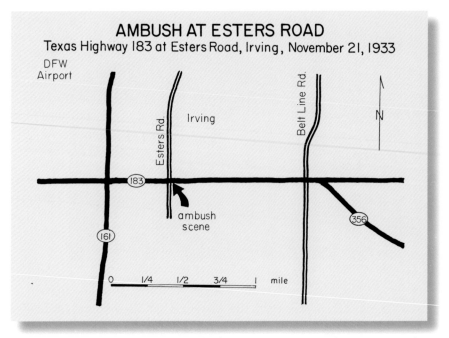

AMBUSH AT ESTERS ROAD
Texas Highway 183 at Esters Road, Irving, November 21, 1933

DFW Airport

Irving

Esters Rd.

Belt Line Rd.

N

183

ambush scene

161

356

0   1/4   1/2   3/4   1   mile

road to its overpass across the highway. The present-day Texas Highway 183 lies on top of the former Texas Highway 15. The best view of the ambush site is eastward from the pedestrian walkway on the east side of the Esters Road overpass across Texas Highway 183. Short-term parking is available in the shopping areas on either side of Texas Highway 183. Try to imagine how this built-up urban landscape appeared when it consisted only of open fields and pastures where "Smoot" Schmidt and his men tried to waylay Bonnie and Clyde.

BURGLARY OF RANGER NATIONAL GUARD ARMORY, 221 SOUTH RUSK STREET, RANGER, FEBRUARY 19, 1934

After Clyde Barrow and Bonnie Parker recovered from the gunshot wounds they received at the Esters Road ambush in November 1933, they proceeded to follow through on Clyde's long-held ambition to stage a raid on the Eastham Prison Farm. After freeing several convicts from the facility, Clyde and some of the fugitives felt that they needed additional military-style automatic weapons for their criminal activities. This situation led Barrow and Raymond Hamilton to break into the National Guard armory in Ranger, Texas, to steal guns and ammunition on the night of February 19, 1934.

To reach the crime scene, leave westbound Interstate 20 near Ranger at exit 354 and drive west 3.1 miles on Texas Loop 254 to its intersection with Main Street. There a preserved historic steel oil derrick stands as a landmark. Alternatively turn off eastbound Interstate 20 at exit 349 and drive northeast on Texas Loop 254 a distance of 2.2 miles to

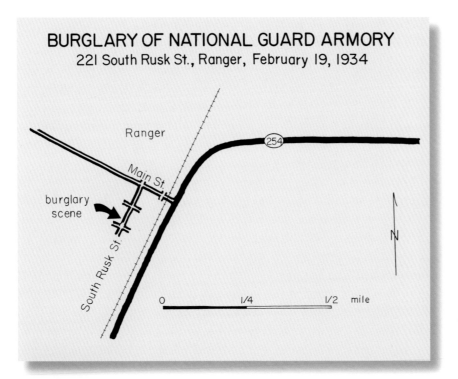

BURGLARY OF NATIONAL GUARD ARMORY
221 South Rusk St., Ranger, February 19, 1934

Ranger

254

Main St.

burglary
scene

South Rusk St.

N

0   1/4   1/2   mile

*Part of the walls
and the floor that
survive from the
National Guard
armory in Ranger,
Texas, that Clyde
Barrow and
Raymond Hamilton
burglarized for
automatic weapons
and ammunition
on the night of
February 19, 1934.
Photograph by the
author, 2010.*

the intersection with Main Street. In either instance, turn northwest onto Main Street toward downtown Ranger, crossing railroad tracks, and drive two blocks to the intersection with South Rusk Street. Turn southwest (left) onto South Rusk Street and proceed two blocks to a two-story brick Masonic lodge building on the corner at Elm Street. The site immediately northeast (to the right) of the lodge at 221 South Rusk Street features the floor and remaining walls of the former National Guard armory where Barrow and Hamilton forced entry.

ROBBERY OF R. P. HENRY AND SONS BANK,
224 EAST MAIN STREET, LANCASTER, FEBRUARY 27, 1934

Only a week after Clyde Barrow and Raymond Hamilton burglarized the armory in Ranger, Henry Methvin joined them in robbing the R. P. Henry and Sons Bank in Lancaster, a small town just south of Dallas. They successfully got away with about four thousand dollars, a small fortune at a time when a new car could be purchased for only about five hundred dollars.

To reach the robbery scene, drive south from Interstate 20 on the south side of Dallas on Texas Highway 342 (Lancaster Road) a distance of 4.2 miles to its intersection with East Main Street in downtown Lancaster. Turn east (left) on East Main Street, loop halfway around a traffic circle at the town square, and proceed one short block east to the intersection of East Main and South Henry Street. The historic bank that the trio robbed stood at the southwest corner of this intersection, 224 East Main Street, until 1994, when a tornado swept it away together with all the other historic buildings on the south side of the town square. Even though the walls and roof disappeared, the original floor and outline of the vault remain. Even today visitors can walk across the same white tile and concrete traversed by the thieves.

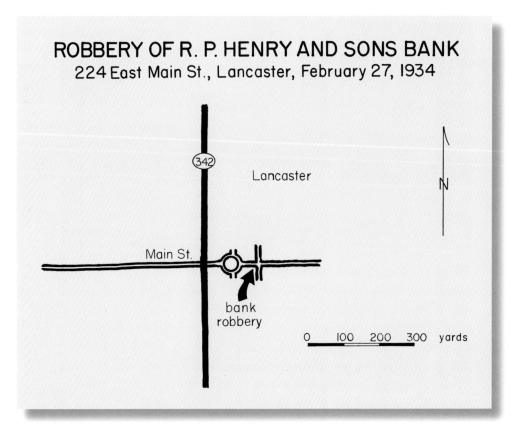

ROBBERY OF R. P. HENRY AND SONS BANK
224 East Main St., Lancaster, February 27, 1934

The black-and-white tile floors and foundations from the R. P. Henry and Sons Bank just off the town square in Lancaster, Texas, that Clyde Barrow, Henry Methvin, and Raymond Hamilton robbed at gunpoint on February 27, 1934. Photograph by the author, 2009.

MURDER OF TWO HIGHWAY PATROL OFFICERS, 500 BLOCK OF WEST DOVE ROAD, SOUTHLAKE (NEAR GRAPEVINE), APRIL 1, 1934

On Easter Sunday morning, April 1, 1934, Clyde Barrow and Henry Methvin shot and killed two unsuspecting Texas highway patrol officers on Dove Road, a rural lane just off Texas Highway 114 northwest of Grapevine. The murders did more than anything else to turn public attitudes against the Barrow Gang. Although the easy-to-access area now in the municipality of Southlake has become one of the suburbs northwest of the Dallas/Fort Worth International Airport, it still retains some of the rural character that it had during the 1930s.

To reach the murder scene, leave Interstate 35W north of Fort Worth at exit 70 and drive 7.6 miles southeast on Texas Highway 114, crossing U.S. Highway 377 at Roanoke, to the intersection with West Dove Road. Turn east (left) onto West Dove Road and proceed about one hundred yards to a gray granite marker on the south side of the road. The widow of one of the slain officers erected this memorial to both men. The shootings took place on the north side of the rural lane, which today has been transformed into a four-lane thoroughfare. Opposite the marker stands a modern unmarked sprawling brick office and maintenance facility for a communications company. A preserved section of old Dove Road as a country lane may be seen just 0.3 mile east of the monument, where the pavement veers northeast past a short portion of the old un-

Modern-day cyclists pedaling west along Dove Road in Southlake, Texas, in the immediate vicinity where Clyde Barrow, Bonnie Parker, and Henry Methvin were parked on Easter Sunday, April 1, 1934, when they murdered two highway patrol officers. Photograph by the author, 2009.

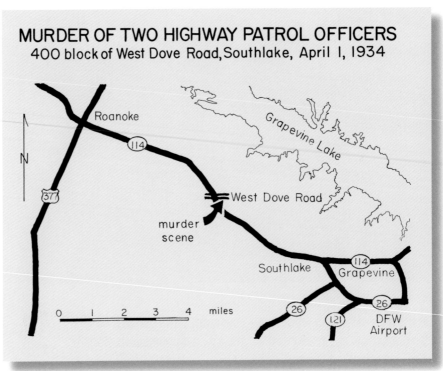

MURDER OF TWO HIGHWAY PATROL OFFICERS
400 block of West Dove Road, Southlake, April 1, 1934

paved road to intercept White Chapel Road near a large City of South-lake water tower. An alternative approach from the area of the Dallas/Fort Worth International Airport is on Texas Highway 114 from its junction with Texas Highway 26 in Grapevine. From this intersection drive 5.9 miles northwest on Texas Highway 114 to its juncture with West Dove Road and proceed a hundred yards east to the monument and nearby crime scene.

FUNERAL AND GRAVE OF CLYDE BARROW, DALLAS, MAY 25, 1934

After lawmen ambushed and killed Clyde Barrow and Bonnie Parker near Arcadia, Louisiana, on May 23, 1934, their remains were transferred to mortuaries in Dallas. The two families decided to have individual funerals and to bury the bodies separately. Clyde's service came first, at the Sparkman-Holtz-Brand Funeral Home in downtown Dallas. His own father closed the doors after unruly crowds surged in to view Clyde's remains. Following the service, a cortege of motor cars proceeded to the Barrow family plot in the Western Heights Cemetery, on the southwest side of the city, where Clyde's remains were interred next to those of his brother, Marvin I. "Buck" Barrow, where they both lie to this day. Mature crepe myrtles flank the burial place.

The funeral home occupied the former residence of Colonel A. H. Belo (founder of the *Dallas Morning News*) at 2101 Ross Avenue in downtown

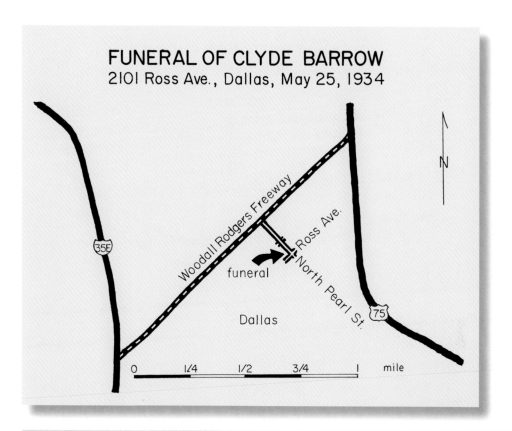

FUNERAL OF CLYDE BARROW
2101 Ross Ave., Dallas, May 25, 1934

35E

Woodall Rodgers Freeway

Ross Ave.

North Pearl St.

75

funeral

Dallas

N

| 0 | 1/4 | 1/2 | 3/4 | 1 | mile |

The Belo mansion in downtown Dallas in 1934 was a funeral home where the memorial service was held for Clyde Barrow on May 25. Photograph by the author, 2009.

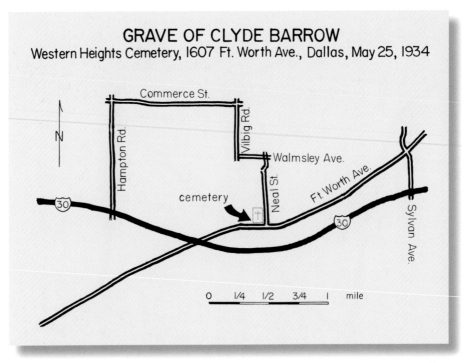

GRAVE OF CLYDE BARROW
Western Heights Cemetery, 1607 Ft. Worth Ave., Dallas, May 25, 1934

Dallas. Located near the area that would later be home to the Dallas Museum of Art, the Nasher Sculpture Center, and the Dallas Center for Performing Arts, the mansion became the headquarters for the Belo Foundation, and it retains that role today. To reach the historic house, from Interstate 35E northbound, take exit 429A toward U.S. Highway 75/McKinney (the Woodall Rodgers Freeway) and proceed northeastward 1.0 mile to the exit for North Pearl Street. Drive 0.2 mile southeast on North Pearl Street to its intersection with Ross Avenue, where the two-story beige brick building with white columns stands. Alternatively, from Interstate 35E southbound, take exit 429B toward Interstate 45/Houston (the Woodall Rodgers Freeway link) and proceed 1.0 mile on the expressway to the exit for North Pearl Street. Proceed as already noted to the funeral site at the Belo mansion. Commercial parking and street-side metered parking are available in the immediate area.

The Western Heights Cemetery, location of the Barrow family burials, lies at 1607 Fort Worth Avenue on the southwest side of Dallas. From Interstate 30 westbound, take exit 43A, which is marked for Sylvan Avenue. Turn north (right) onto Sylvan Avenue and proceed one block to an intersection with Fort Worth Avenue. Turn west (left) onto Fort Worth Avenue and drive 0.7 mile to the cemetery, on the north side of the street at 1607 across from a used car lot. The Barrow family plots are in the southwest corner of the former country cemetery, which is filled with hackberry, elm, and juniper trees. Because the gates to the little-used cemetery are often locked even during daylight hours,

it may be necessary to cross over the low black metal fence at the south side to view individual graves. Free street-side parking is available on Neal Street at the east side of the cemetery.

A more circuitous route is required to reach the Western Heights Cemetery from Interstate 30 eastbound. Leave the interstate at exit 42, which is marked for Hampton Road. Drive north on Hampton Road 0.5 mile to its junction with Commerce Street. Turn east (right) onto Commerce and proceed through a warehouse district 0.4 mile to Vilbig Road. At Vilbig turn south (right) and drive 0.2 miles into a residential neighborhood to the junction with Walmsley Avenue opposite the Dallas Police Department automobile impoundment yards. Turn east (left) on Walmsley and go one long block to Neal Street. At Neal turn south (right) and drive three blocks to the cemetery on the right at Fort Worth Avenue.

The burial place of Clyde Barrow and Marvin I. "Buck" Barrow in the family plot in the Western Heights Cemetery on the southwest side of Dallas. Photograph by the author, 2009.

FUNERAL AND GRAVE OF BONNIE PARKER, DALLAS, MAY 26, 1934

Bonnie Parker's funeral followed that of Clyde by one day. The memorial service took place at the McKamy-Campbell Funeral Home on Forest Avenue, followed by interment next to two of her sister's children in the historic Fishtrap Cemetery in West Dallas. A year after Bonnie's mother passed away in 1944, the family reinterred the young woman's

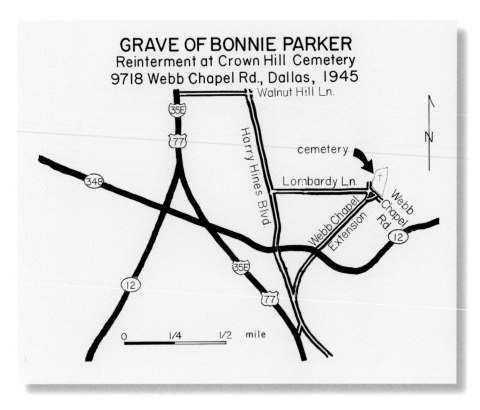

GRAVE OF BONNIE PARKER
Reinterment at Crown Hill Cemetery
9718 Webb Chapel Rd., Dallas, 1945

remains next to those of her mother at the Crown Hill Cemetery, 9718 Webb Chapel Road, north of Dallas Love Field airport.

Freeway construction obliterated the historic McKamy-Campbell Funeral Home, but the site of Bonnie Parker's 1945 reinterment at the Crown Hill Cemetery may be viewed. To visit the location, leave Interstate 35E northbound at exit 435, which is marked for Harry Hines Boulevard. Turn left onto Harry Hines northbound and drive 0.2 mile north. At a fork in the road, bear northeast (right) at an intersection with Webb Chapel Extension. Proceed northeast on Webb Chapel Extension a distance of 1.2 miles. Just after a curve to the left, at a stoplight turn east (right) onto Larga Drive. Stay on Larga Drive 0.2 mile as it bows around to the northeast and comes to an intersection with four-lane Webb Chapel Road. Turn northwest (left) and drive a quarter block past the Hughes funeral home to the entrance gate to the Crown Hill Cemetery on the right. From Interstate 35E southbound, leave the freeway at exit 438 for Walnut Hill Lane. At Walnut Hill, turn east (left) and drive 0.7 mile to the intersection with Harry Hines Boulevard. At Harry Hines, turn south (right) and proceed 1.0 mile to Lombardy Lane. At Lombardy Lane turn east (left) and drive 1.0 mile to the junction with Webb Chapel Road and the entry to the burial ground on the left just after the intersection. This difficult left turn back to the cemetery gate is quite sharp. The awkward junction of Webb Chapel

Extension, Webb Chapel Road, and Lombardy Lane tends to confuse first-time visitors.

On entering the comparatively modest cemetery, take the left fork in the paved roadway in front of the cream-colored mausoleum and park. Begin looking for a long, dark green hedge with interspersed cedar trees that extends north-south up the middle of the west side of the grounds. Bonnie Parker's bronze burial marker, as well as that for her mother, may be found on the west edge of this hedge about fifty feet from its south end. Often fresh flowers or other tokens adorn the grave.

Abilene Daily Reporter (Abilene, Tex.), February 20, 1934, p. 1.
Barrow, Blanche Caldwell. *My Life with Bonnie & Clyde.* Edited by John Neal Phillips. Norman: University of Oklahoma Press, 2004.
Celina Record (Celina, Tex.), April 21, 1932, p. 1; April 28, 1932, p. 1; August 18, 1932, p. 1; August 24, 1932, p. 1.
Dallas Morning News (Dallas, Tex.), March 12, 1930, sec. I, p. 16; March 25, 1930, sec. I, p. 10; April 15, 1932, sec. I, p. 1; April 16, 1932, sec. I, p. 1; April 20, 1932, sec. I, p. 1; April 22, 1932, sec. I, p. 1; April 23, 1932, sec. II, p. 8; April 25, 1932, sec. II, p. 6; August 2, 1932, sec. I, pp. 1, 2; December 15, 1932, sec. I, p. 4; December 16, 1932, sec. I, p. 1; January 7, 1933, sec. I, pp. 1, 2; January 8, 1933, sec. I, pp. 1, 4; January 9, 1933, sec. I, p. 8; January 22, 1933, sec. II, pp. 1, 12; January 26, 1933, sec. I, pp. 1, 8; April 14, 1933, sec. II, p. 10; June 12, 1933, sec. I, pp. 1, 3; November 23, 1933, sec. I, pp. 1, 3; November 24, 1933, sec. I, pp. 1, 14; November 25, 1933, sec. I, p. 3; November 26, 1933, sec. I, pp. 1, 7; December 2, 1933, sec. I, p. 9; December 22, 1933, sec. II, p. 5; January 17, 1934, sec. I, pp. 1, 12; January 18, 1934, sec. I, pp. 1, 12; sec. II, p. 4; February 17, 1934, sec. I, pp. 1, 12; February 28, 1934, sec. I, pp. 1, 10; March 1, 1934, sec. I, pp. 1, 3, 5; sec. II, pp. 1, 3; March 21, 1934, sec. I, p. 2; April 2, 1934, sec. I, pp. 1, 3; April 3, 1934, sec. I, pp. 1, 5, 6; April 4, 1934, sec. I, pp. 1, 12; April 7, 1934, sec. II, pp. 1, 12; April 8, 1934, sec. I, pp. 1, 8, 10; sec. II, p. 1; April 9, 1934, sec. I, pp. 1, 8; April 10, 1934, sec. I, pp. 1, 14; April 17, 1934, sec. I, p. 7; April 18, 1934, sec. II, p. 1; May 2, 1934, sec. II, pp. 1, 10; May 12, 1934, sec. I, pp. 1, 12; sec. II, p. 1; May 16, 1934, sec. II, pp. 1, 12; May 19, 1934, sec. I, p. 3; May 22, 1934, sec. I, pp. 1, 12; May 24, 1934, sec. I, pp. 1, 10, 11; sec. II, pp. 2, 6; May 25, 1934, sec. I, pp. 1, 4; sec. II, p. 10; May 26, 1934, sec. II, pp. 1, 6; May 27, 1934, sec. II, pp. 1, 14; June 1, 1934, sec. I, p. 10; August 14, 1934, sec. I, pp. 1, 2; September 6, 1934, sec. I, pp. 1, 2; September 7, 1934, sec. II, p. 1; October 13, 1934, sec. II, p. 5; January 29, 1935, sec. II, pp. 1, 10; April 22, 1948, sec. I, p. 7; June 24, 2007, sec. B, p. 2.
Denton Record-Chronicle (Denton, Tex.), April 21, 1932, p. 1; April 22, 1932, p. 1; April 23, 1932, p. 1; April 25, 1932, p. 4.
Electra News (Electra, Tex.), April 14, 1932, p. 1; April 21, 1932, p. 1; April 28, 1932, p. 1; May 19, 1932, p. 1; June 2, 1932, p. 3.
Fort Worth Press (Fort Worth, Tex.), April 2, 1934, pp. 1, 5; April 3, 1934, pp. 1, 7.
Fort Worth Star-Telegram (Fort Worth, Tex.), February 27, 1934, evening ed., p. 1; April 2, 1934, evening ed., pp. 1, 4; April 3, 1934, evening ed., pp. 1, 4; May 7, 1934, evening ed., p. 16; May 23, 1934,

evening ed., pp. 1, 4; May 24, 1934, evening ed., pp. 1, 6, 20; May 25, 1934, evening ed., pp. 1, 8; May 26, 1934, evening ed., pp. 1, 2, 5; May 31, 1934, evening ed., pp. 1, 4, 10, 11; June 14, 1934, evening ed., p. 8.

Guinn, Jeff. *Go Down Together: The True, Untold Story of Bonnie and Clyde.* New York: Simon & Schuster, 2009.

Hillsboro Evening Mirror (Hillsboro, Tex.), May 2, 1932, pp. 1, 4; May 3, 1932, p. 1; May 4, 1932, p. 1; May 6, 1932, p. 1.

Hinton, Ted. *Ambush: The Real Story of Bonnie and Clyde.* Dallas: Southwestern Historical Publications, 1979.

Jones, W. D. "Riding with Bonnie & Clyde." *Playboy* 15, no. 11 (November 1968): 151, 160, 162, 164–65.

Kaufman Weekly Herald (Kaufman, Tex.), April 21, 1932, p. 1; April 28, 1932, p. 2; May 19, 1932, p. 1.

Loud Speaker (Ranger, Tex.), February 23, 1934, p. 1.

Mabank Weekly Banner (Mabank, Tex.), April 20, 1932, p. 1; April 28, 1932, pp. 1, 4.

Marshall News Messenger (Marshall, Tex.), March 10, 1985, sec. A, pp. 1, 12.

McKinney Daily Courier-Gazette (McKinney, Tex.), April 21, 1932, pp. 1, 4; April 23, 1932, pp. 1, 6; April 24, 1932, pp. 1, 6.

McKinney Weekly Democrat-Gazette (McKinney, Tex.), April 21, 1932, sec. 1, p. 8; April 28, 1932, sec. 2, p. 1.

Phillips, John Neal. *Running with Bonnie and Clyde: The Ten Fast Years of Ralph Fults.* Norman: University of Oklahoma Press, 1996.

Ramsey, Winston G. *On the Trail of Bonnie & Clyde Then and Now.* London: Battle of Britain International, 2003.

Ranger Times (Ranger, Tex.), April 16, 1934, p. 1; March 20, 1934, p. 1; May 6, 1934, p. 1.

Temple Daily Telegram (Temple, Tex.), December 27, 1932, pp. 1, 2; December 28, 1932, p. 1; December 29, 1932, p. 1; December 30, 1932, p. 1.

Veit, Richard J. "The Waco Jailbreak of Bonnie and Clyde." *Waco Heritage and History* (Waco, Tex.), 20, no. 2 (December 1990): 3–20.

Victoria Advocate (Victoria, Tex.), August 15, 1932, p. 1; August 16, 1932, p. 1; September 19, 1932, pp. 1, 2.

Wellington Leader (Wellington, Tex.), June 15, 1933, pp. 1, 10.

Wharton Spectator (Wharton, Tex.), August 19, 1932, p. 1.

Wichita Daily Times (Wichita Falls, Tex.), April 14, 1932, pp. 1, 2; April 15, 1932, pp. 1, 15; May 11, 1932, p. 1.

Wichita Falls Record News (Wichita Falls, Tex.), April 15, 1932, pp. 1, 2; May 12, 1932, p. 4.

Wichita Falls Times (Wichita Falls, Tex.), May 7, 1961, magazine section, p. 21.

2 FOUR BROTHERS IN CRIME: THE NEWTON BOYS, EXPRESS CAR AND BANK ROBBERS OF UVALDE

Growing up in rural West Texas during the early twentieth century, the four sons of Jim and Janetta Newton would have been expected to grow up to be cotton farmers or cattle ranchers. Instead they became one of the most successful teams of professional bank and express car robbers in the United States. Resembling railway baggage cars, express cars transported high-value freight and usually had armed guards. The Newton Boys' career ended in 1924 with a spectacular express car heist at Rondout, Illinois, that netted them an unbelievable three million dollars but ended with their arrests and imprisonment.

Willis Newton headed the criminal enterprise, with brothers Jess and Joe providing most of the muscle. Doc Newton, who grew up mentally slow because of a childhood coyote bite, typically drove the getaway cars. Willis had several early encounters with the law, being imprisoned first for the theft of a bale of cotton and then again for burglary. While incarcerated, he learned from other convicts the fine art of blowing open safes with nitroglycerine. Once freed in 1919, he perfected his skills and then recruited his brothers to join in what became a family enterprise.

Willis's first experience in taking money from banks came at Winters, Texas, early on the morning of Wednesday, March 5, 1919. A friend named Frank recruited him into a group that included Walter Harris (alias "Frenchy" Leneaus, Slim Edgerton, and John R. McFadden) and safecracker Allen Hindglass Inman (also known as Alora E. Enman). About 3:00 AM the four men cut the telephone wires out of the town and then let themselves into the two-story Winters State Bank through the rear door. They proceeded to the vaults, not realizing that they had "trapped" a young woman operator upstairs at the second-floor telephone exchange. A professional in the use of nitroglycerine, Inman blew the door loose from a vault containing safe-deposit boxes, though he was unable to open the safe holding cash. The thieves systematically dumped the contents of safe-deposit boxes on the floor, removing the negotiable World War I Liberty bonds and war savings stamps. On finishing their work, the thieves fled town in a Hudson Super Six sedan that Harris and Inman had stolen in Wisconsin. As they fled south from Winters in the dark, they missed a road intersection and ended up driving into such deep sand near Buffalo Gap that they got bogged down and the car's drive shaft snapped. With daylight approaching, the criminals had little choice but to retreat into the brush in the rough country of the nearby Callahan Divide. There they hid out all day.

Under cover of darkness on the evening of March 5, the four fugitives, with Inman carrying the stolen bonds and stamps, made their way into the little town of Buffalo Gap. There about eleven o'clock they spotted a 1917 Ford Model T in a shed at the home of the school superintendent and hand pushed the car a couple of blocks down the street to a location in front of the Nazarene church. There Inman was in the process of cranking its engine when a car bearing three lawmen drove up. The officers asked the four men whether they needed any help, and when the group declined the officers drove on a short distance. Then Winters police officer Chris Kornegay declared, "It was four men we were after. Let's go back and investigate." No sooner had the officer inquired where the strangers were from than a gunfight broke out. The two parties exchanged about eighteen shots, one of them striking the safecracker in the torso, while the other three outsiders melted into the darkness, each going a different direction. The lawmen took injured Inman into custody and the next morning captured Walter Harris at a farm midway between Buffalo Gap and Merkel. Willis Newton made his way to Abilene, where he connected with friend Jack "Red" Johnson. On the morning of Thursday, March 6, a railway conductor reported two unidentified men leaving his freight train at Eskota, west of Abilene. That very morning, lawmen working on that tip arrested Newton and Johnson and conveyed them to the Runnels County sheriff's department at Ballinger. There they found Harris already in jail and learned that Inman had died from his gunshot wound. Newton's friend Frank had escaped, but in Abilene his companion, Jack Johnson, ended up being arrested for a crime he did not commit.

While the grand jury in Ballinger considered indictments against the three suspected bank burglars, the men themselves plotted an escape. They made their move in the early hours of Sunday, March 16, 1919. Observing the boilerplate steel ceiling detached in places above the misdemeanor room on the second floor of the jail where they were held, they pried some of the metal sheets loose with a heating stove poker. Then they broke a piece of flat iron from one of the cots and heated it red hot in the coal- and wood-fueled stove. With Willis standing on the shoulders of one cellmate, the third handed him the red-hot piece of iron, with which he gradually scorched a hole through two-by-six timbers forming the ceiling. In the meantime one of the inmates tore up blankets and tied the strips together to form a makeshift rope.

Once Willis had burned a large enough opening in the ceiling, cellmates boosted him high enough to get through the hole into the attic, and then from above he aided the other two in scrambling through. Once in the loft they found a rickety old eight-foot ladder, which two men held upright while Willis clambered up to let himself through a hatch onto the roof. He then draped the "rope" back down inside so the other two could climb up to the roof. Finally they tied their handmade rope to a chimney and one by one let themselves down from the second story to the ground. Willis was the first out, and he remembered, "I don't think there was a time in my life that I felt better than I did right then. Sitting back there looking at that bright moon and them coming down. I was home free!" They walked to the other side of town, stole a Model T Ford, and drove themselves through the night to San Antonio to make a clean escape.

Having benefited from Inman's practical introduction to safe-cracking, Willis Newton joined with other criminals in breaking into business premises. He gradually recruited his brothers to join him in creating their own ring of bank burglars and robbers who, when opportunities presented themselves, also occasionally robbed trains. For the first two years, the gang typically undertook night burglaries of small-town banks. During the summertime they traveled across the Great Plains and Midwest, sometimes crossing into Canada, casing potential banks, noting exit routes from towns, and finding out whether there were night watchmen. Then weeks or months later in the cold of winter, when residents were bundled into their homes for warmth, the Newton brothers returned late at night. Their first step was to sever the telephone wires to prevent communications in and out of town. Then they forced their way into the banks and used nitroglycerine to blow the doors from safes and vaults. Then there was little more to do than to scoop up money, bonds, and valuables into cloth bags. Willis claimed that it took only about five minutes to "grease" a safe, that is, to pour liquid nitro around its door and blow it off, so a carefully planned nighttime burglary required only about fifteen minutes. By then the Newton Boys were back in their car on the way out of town.

After doing their work, often hundreds of miles away from home, the four brothers typically returned to Texas to enjoy the proceeds of their efforts. After a profitable season of burglary, "Then we come on down to San Antone for the winter, where we stayed at the St. Anthony Hotel most of the time," Willis remembered. "Sometimes me and my wife would get an apartment. The boys would stay at them big hotels." Joe Newton described with relish the high-life pleasures he enjoyed as a successful criminal. "When you went into a barbershop, there was always a good-looking manicurist in there, and in the café there was al-

ways good-looking girls waiting on you," he said, adding, "when you're young and got some money in your pocket and a hundred-dollar suit on, why you can always find somebody that'll go out and have something to eat with you anyway. Yeah."

Even though the Newton Boys operated mostly outside the Lone Star State, occasionally they took advantage of opportunities closer to home. In one such instance they made a bargain with W. A. Boyd, a veteran detective for the Texas Bankers Association, paying him for a list of the banks in the state that had old-time square safes with doors that could easily be blown with nitroglycerine. "He give us the names of fifteen or twenty, told us where they was at," Willis remembered. As part of the deal, Willis said, "we give him three thousand dollars and if anything happened, he was going to protect us." Over the years the gang put that list to good use.

The first known Texas bank that the Newton Boys as a group burglarized was the Boerne State Bank in Boerne, thirty miles north of San Antonio. On the night of Tuesday, February 8, 1921, they made a preliminary visit to the town, accosting local resident Gilbert Norman and questioning him about Paul Menn, the private security

officer whom local merchants employed to watch over their properties at night. They returned the next night, after a bitterly cold norther had blown in, kidnapped Menn off the street, and then drove to an alley alongside the bank. While two gang members held the town watchman at gunpoint, the others used heavy crowbars and a pick first to break through the iron bars of a window and then to burrow into the brick side of the vault inside. There they rifled through safe-deposit boxes, taking an estimated seven thousand dollars worth of negotiable Liberty bonds and a small amount of cash. They exited south out of town, eventually releasing Menn unhurt. Joe Newton recalled, "But he was a real nice old fellow. Down towards San Antone, we took him out in the hills there and give him a blanket, told him to build up a fire because it was real cold."

The next Texas "bank job" for the Newton brothers was just west of San Antonio in the town of Hondo, but there they did something unusual. Instead of burglarizing one bank, they broke into two during the same night. Having finished most of their winter's work, the four brothers were wintering in San Antonio but decided that they did not have quite enough money to maintain the lifestyle they liked. According to Joe Newton, "We was running short and decided to rob a bank in Hondo" that they had been thinking about for some time. Because of their family connections in nearby Uvalde, the brothers knew the night watchman, "a big fat fella." After cutting the telephone wires in and out of Hondo early in the morning of Sunday, March 9, 1921, they located the watchman sitting in the heated Southern Pacific passenger depot. "It was a pretty cold night and we thought he'd sit tight," Joe remembered. While he kept an eye on the officer from a doorway across the street, the other three brothers first pried an opening through the iron bars on the last window away from the street at the Hondo State Bank. After squeezing inside they found that the bankers had not even locked the vault, so they hastily helped themselves to securities, money, and other valuables in the safe-deposit boxes. Because the work had gone so quickly, one of the brothers suggested, "Well, we've got lots of time, why don't we go over and try the other one?" After forcing entry to a storeroom behind the First National Bank that did not lead into the bank proper, they moved around to the front, only sixty yards from the depot and night watchman, and forced their way through the front doors. Once inside they jimmied the vault door and helped themselves to more negotiable bonds. They consciously left behind jewelry and old coins that might have been traceable, leaving two feet of loose papers, objects, and other debris on the floors of the vaults. Quietly the thieves departed town, leaving no clues to their identity. The magazine published by the Texas Bankers Association in grudging recognition of the

The front of the Hondo State Bank in Hondo, Texas, as it appeared about the time when it was burglarized by the Newton Boys on March 9, 1921. Courtesy of Frances Miller and UTSA's Institute of Texan Cultures, image 096-0477.

Interior of the Hondo State Bank, showing the vault that protruded from the wall behind the tellers' cages. After they forced entry to the bank early on the morning of March 9, 1921, the Newton Boys found the door to this vault unlocked, so they easily helped themselves to the contents. Courtesy of Frances Miller and UTSA's Institute of Texan Cultures, image 096-0476.

Newton Boys' efficiency pronounced in its next issue, "If there had been three banks in the town, no doubt they would have robbed it too."

On Thursday, August 25, 1921, the Newton Boys undertook the first of two late summer/early autumn train heists in Texas. They planned the first to coincide with an expected registered mail shipment of bank notes from the Federal Reserve Bank in Dallas to member banks. Willis Newton and occasional accomplice Brent Glasscock jumped through the open door of the express car on the northbound Missouri-Kansas-Texas Katy Limited passenger train as it slowed down to cross the tracks of the Texas and Pacific Railway at Bells in east-central Grayson County, Texas, just after midnight. According to the schedule, the train was fourteen minutes away from a planned stop in Denison. The robbers met three armed clerks inside, got the drop on all of them, and then began unsuccessfully looking for distinctive square canvas sacks with brass padlocks that typically carried Federal Reserve money shipments. Finding only ordinary registered mail instead, they tossed out the one sack of this as the train approached town. Jess Newton was waiting with a car to pick it up, and then he rendezvoused with his confederates, who jumped from the train after they pulled the emergency stop cord, which brought it to a stop on a gentle curve half a dozen blocks south of the Denison depot.

Frustrated at having "missed the big money" on the Katy Limited, the Newton Boys pulled a follow-up railroad job, this time south of Texarkana. Already they had been observing movements at the Texarkana train station, where regularly they observed "a man come from Shreveport . . . with a big express box." It could only be filled with money or other valuables, and "he'd take it to the express office there in Texarkana." The gang members decided that if they had taken only small pickings on the Missouri-Kansas-Texas at Denison, they could do better on the Kansas City Southern. Accordingly about eight o'clock on the night of Wednesday, September 7, 1921, the gang boarded the northbound KCS Number 2 passenger train at Bloomburg, just on the Texas side of the Arkansas state line, secreting themselves in the dark in the space between the locomotive tender and the express car. As the train approached the long wooden trestle across the bottoms of the Sulphur River, Jess and Willis Newton climbed up and over the tender to the cab of the locomotive. Engineer F. Woodson saw the two young men with pistols and heard the words, "Take it easy. Don't make any fuss. Do as we tell you and you won't get hurt." He followed orders to stop the train so that the passenger cars on the end would remain over the trestle, leaving the engine and the express car on the earthen approach at the far end of the bridge.

At this point, taking the engineer with them, the robbers went back to join partner Brent Glasscock at the express car. Holding Woodson at gunpoint, they ordered the clerks inside the express car to open up, threatening to shoot the engineer if they disobeyed. Hiding with drawn pistols beneath piles of mail bags, clerks John B. Cheatham and Anthony N. Johns said nothing. Then the robbers broke the glass above the door and through the opening tossed a vial of formaldehyde, claiming that it was poison gas. With eyes burning and throats choking from the fumes, the two guards shortly thereafter unbolted the sliding door and surrendered their arms. "We want that black box containing money shipped from Shreveport," barked one of the robbers. "If we don't find it in here we are going to kill you." To their great dismay, one of the clerks declared, "Mister, it didn't come tonight. You can look this car over all you want." Indeed the box was not there. Disconnecting the passenger cars on the bridge from the rest of the train, one of the thieves took engineer Woodson back to the locomotive and ordered him to proceed toward Texarkana with only the express car in tow. In the meantime the other two robbers slit open the bags containing registered mail and filled a sack of their own with all the items that appeared to have any value. On approaching the outskirts of Texarkana, the robbers ordered the engineer to stop the train and on threat of death to back the locomotive the fifteen miles he had just traversed to the Sulphur River bridge to pick up the rest of his train that had been left behind. "We hit the woods and went over to where we had our place ready," Willis Newton remembered. They spent the next twenty-four hours in a hiding place deep in the thickets that they had already provisioned with food and water and waited for Jess Newton to pick them up in the car. Years later Willis grumbled, "We got a pretty good bunch of bonds and stuff, but we missed that box."

Six months passed before the Newton Boys perpetrated another crime in Texas, and this time they broke with their typical procedure of staging nighttime bank burglaries. During the midday lunch hour on Friday, March 10, 1922, the four Newton Boys descended on the New Braunfels State Bank, on the plaza in the ethnic German community northeast of San Antonio. According to some witnesses, two of the brothers were seen minutes earlier sipping coffee at the café in the Plaza Hotel on the north side of the square. They parked a seven-passenger 1921 Buick touring car crosswise in front of the bank entrance at 451 North Plaza a couple of doors down from the hotel, and Willis and Jess stepped inside the front door, where they found four employees and no customers. Jess advanced to bank president F. G. Blumberg at a teller's window, while Willis stepped over a low rail and pulled a revolver on the other three members of the staff. "The two men compelled us to lie on the floor face down," Blumberg reported. Willis remembered that he "talked real rough to them," adding, "That's the way to do it, and then you don't have to hurt nobody." In only three or four minutes Willis entered the open vault, and there, in his words, "I stuffed the cash in the sack endways and then a big row of Liberty Bonds. Then I come out." In the meantime bookkeeper Harold Adams came back into the bank from an errand, followed by Doc Newton, who had observed him from the car. Blumberg reported to the press, "When the men had got the money and bonds they pushed all five of us into the vault and locked the door." The three robbers then returned to the waiting getaway car and drove out of town half a dozen miles to a pre-arranged site in a particularly brushy cedar pasture, where they hid their car and quietly waited all day and all night, heading out for San Antonio and a successful escape just before dawn on March 11.

The Newton Boys staged one more bank job in the state, but it was a more customary nighttime burglary. As usual, they waited until the early morning hours of an especially cold and windy Saturday, January 5, 1924, when they expected most law-abiding people in San Marcos, Texas, would be closed up in their homes. Willis Newton recalled that "a cold norther was just a-blowin.'" Systematically gang members severed the telephone lines in and out of the town and also disabled a streetlight outside the First State Bank and Trust Company, on the northwest cor-

Interior of the New Braunfels State Bank as it appeared at midday on March 10, 1922, when the Newton Boys staged a successful daylight robbery. Bookkeeper Harold Adams (left) and *cashier Kermit Kloepper* (wearing suit coat) *were both on duty when the gang struck. Courtesy of Sophienburg Museum and Archives, New Braunfels, Texas.*

ner of the courthouse square. They even cut the rope to the fire alarm gong at city hall. After removing a plate-glass window from the front door, two of the burglars forced entry to the bank, leaving the other two as lookouts along the street approaches. Starting at 3:30 AM, the inside men set off seven consecutive nitroglycerine charges. The vault had "a pretty heavy drum door," Willis recalled, adding, "I put about six ounces of grease in it and blowed the door plumb through the window and over to the other side of the street on the sidewalk." The blasts tore furnishings, business machines, and tellers' cages into shambles. The force of the last explosion strewed coins and shreds of bank notes throughout the bank and out into the street. While the two robbers worked inside for close to an hour, outside the others turned back the

The porter polishing brass outside the entry to the First State Bank and Trust Company in San Marcos, Texas, in March 1940. Sixteen years earlier the Newton Boys blew the exterior doors from the building when they used too much nitroglycerine to gain access to the contents of a safe inside. Courtesy of Farm Security Administration/Office of War Information Collection, Library of Congress, Washington, D.C., image LC-USF34-035599-D.

handful of townspeople who ventured to approach. Then, carrying two gunnysacks filled with loot, the party quietly departed on foot, and an accomplice in a car picked them up. As part of the careful plans, the driver delivered the burglars to a field of corn stalks not far outside town. They retreated into the middle of the field, where the dried plants gave the men complete cover while they waited for about twenty-four hours in the cold. The next night the driver returned, flashed his headlamps, and picked up his confederates and their loot, which amounted to approximately twenty-four thousand dollars in cash plus an estimated eighteen thousand dollars in government bonds.

The Newton Boys went on to commit the largest express car robbery in the United States. They took more than three million dollars from a train near Rondout, Illinois, on June 12, 1924. In the course of the heist, one of the thieves accidentally shot Doc Newton, and his brothers took him to a physician in Chicago for treatment. This act led to their arrest, prosecution, conviction, and eventual imprisonment at the Leavenworth federal penitentiary. On release they returned home but then faced prosecution in other states for crimes there. Eventually the four brothers returned to their home in Uvalde, where they resided for the remainder of their lives.

Writers Claude Stanush and David Middleton interviewed Willis and Joe Newton as old men about their careers in crime. Willis described his feelings this way: "Sometimes people ask me if I'm sorry that I ever robbed banks and trains. . . . But no, I'm not sorry. . . . I might never have robbed any banks, though, if I hadn't gotten in with those bank robbers in the state pen. When I heard that banks were covered by insurance, that settled it for me. . . . Robbing banks is hard work. There's no fun to it. I never done it for the excitement. I done it only for the money."

WINTERS STATE BANK BURGLARY, 100 WEST DALE STREET, WINTERS, MARCH 5, 1919

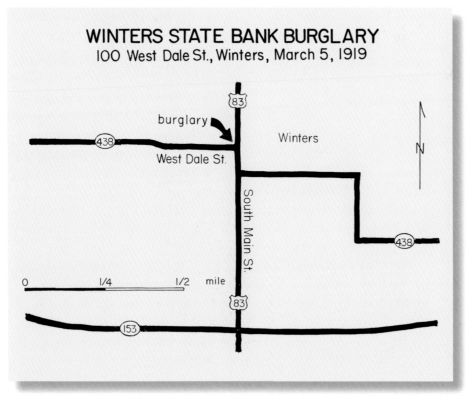

The Winters State Bank building in Winters, Texas, showing its rear side, where the burglars forced entry during the early morning hours of March 5, 1919. Photograph by the author, 2006.

In the early morning hours of a very cold March 5, 1919, Willis Newton and three others broke into the Winters State Bank and took valuables from safe-deposit boxes. The two-story masonry bank building still stands, today housing an insurance agency at the northwest corner of Main and Dale streets in downtown Winters. Though its façade was modernized over the years, the rough limestone rear of the building remains virtually unchanged since the gang members forced their way through the back door decades ago.

To reach the crime scene, from the intersection of U.S. Highway 83 and Texas Highway 153 on the south side of Winters drive north seven blocks (0.5 mile) to the juncture with Texas Loop 438 West (West Dale Street). The former Winters State Bank stands at the northwest side of the intersection and bears an official Texas historical marker. This commercial district is so well preserved that on the concrete curb and sidewalk across West Dale Street from the bank building there is still a steel horse hitching ring.

BUFFALO GAP SHOOT-OUT, SOUTHEAST CORNER OF OAK AND MULBERRY STREETS, BUFFALO GAP, MARCH 5, 1919

After escaping with valuables from safe-deposit boxes at the Winters State Bank, the burglars hid out in the rough, thickly wooded Callahan Divide and in the evening made their way on foot to the little town of Buffalo Gap. There they stole a car from the school superintendent and were in the process of starting it in front of the Nazarene church when a posse of lawmen stopped to investigate. Gunfire broke out, and lawmen fatally wounded one of the thieves.

To reach the site of the shooting from the intersection of Farm to Market Roads 89 and 613 on the south side of the village of Buffalo Gap, drive six blocks north (on Litel Street). Then at a sharp right bend in the road proceed one block east (at the curve the road becomes Vine Street) to the intersection with Mulberry Street. Turn north (left) on Mulberry and drive one block to its juncture with Oak Street. The gunfight in 1919 took place on Mulberry Street in front of the west-facing Nazarene church at the southeast corner of this intersection, where today a modern residence stands. In 1977 the historic Nazarene church was relocated five blocks north to the Buffalo Gap Historic Village, where it now may be viewed.

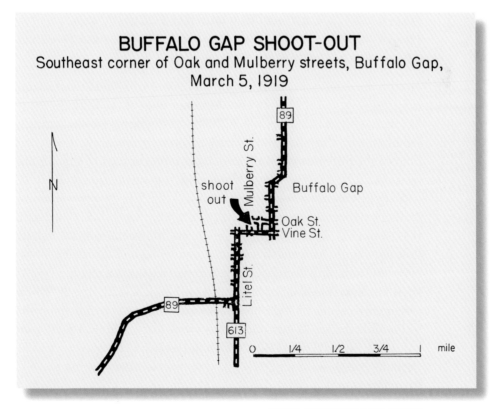

BUFFALO GAP SHOOT-OUT
Southeast corner of Oak and Mulberry streets, Buffalo Gap,
March 5, 1919

BALLINGER JAIL BREAK, OLD RUNNELS COUNTY JAIL (COURTHOUSE ANNEX), 602 STRONG AVENUE, COURTHOUSE SQUARE, BALLINGER, MARCH 16, 1919

During the early hours of Sunday, March 16, 1919, Willis Newton and his confederates, incarcerated on the upper floor of the Runnels County Jail, made good their escape. Although the building has been greatly modified over the years and its upper story was removed, the ground floor of the historic stone building still survives as part of a larger masonry building constructed on three sides of it during the 1930s.

To reach the crime scene, drive one block southeast on U.S. Highway 83 (South Seventh Street) from its intersection with U.S. 67 (Hutchings Avenue) in downtown Ballinger. At the intersection of U.S. 67 with Strong Avenue, turn northeast (left) on Strong and drive two blocks along the side of a rectangular courthouse square to a stone county sheriff's department office building fronting on the avenue at the extreme east corner of the square. The current 1930s building known as the Courthouse Annex was built around three sides of the historic stone jail, one exterior wall of which is visible on the northwest side, opposite the three-story brick 1920s county jail that took its place as the calaboose.

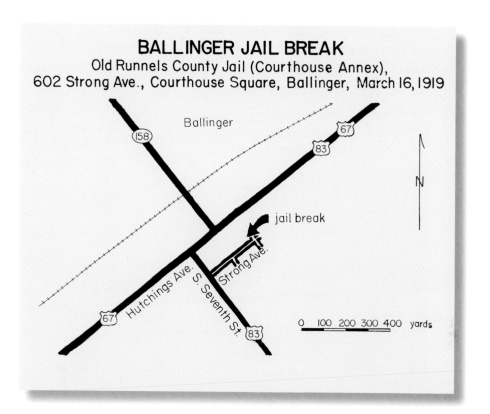

BALLINGER JAIL BREAK
Old Runnels County Jail (Courthouse Annex),
602 Strong Ave., Courthouse Square, Ballinger, March 16, 1919

Ballinger

158

67

83

jail break

Hutchings Ave.

S. Seventh St.

Strong Ave.

67

83

N

0   100 200 300 400   yards

*The rear side of the former Runnels County Jail in Ballinger, Texas, from which Willis
Newton and his partners escaped early on the morning of March 16, 1919. During the
1930s the upper floor of the jail was removed and rooms added to three sides of the old
building, leaving only this portion of its original construction visible. Photograph by the
author, 2010.*

ST. ANTHONY HOTEL, WINTER SEASON RETREAT OF THE NEWTON BOYS, 300 EAST TRAVIS STREET, SAN ANTONIO, 1921–1924

The luxurious St. Anthony Hotel in San Antonio was one of the favored retreats for the Newton Boys after they became successful bank thieves. The century-old hotel continues to be a favorite base of operations for out-of-town visitors to the Alamo City.

The St. Anthony Hotel in San Antonio, the luxurious winter season retreat for the Newton Boys during the early 1920s. Photograph by the author, 2007.

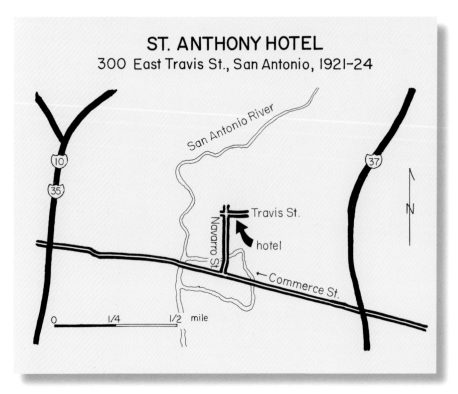

To reach the hotel, leave Interstate 37/U.S. Highway 281 on the east side of downtown San Antonio at exit 141 northbound or exit 141A southbound for Commerce Street. Once at Commerce, turn west and drive 0.6 mile through the central business district to its intersection with Navarro Street. At the junction with Navarro, turn north (right) and drive five blocks (0.2 mile) to the hotel, on the right side of Navarro at East Travis Street facing on Travis Park.

HONDO STATE BANK AND FIRST NATIONAL BANK DOUBLE BURGLARY, 1711 AVENUE M AND 1114 EIGHTEENTH STREET, HONDO, MARCH 9, 1921

Although the bank that the Newton Boys burglarized in Boerne in February 1921 no longer stands, both of the banks they struck in Hondo later in the spring are preserved to this day. They first broke into the Hondo State Bank, where they found the vault unlocked, and then had so much time left that they went around the corner and made their way into the almost adjacent First National Bank as well.

The single-story brick building that housed the Hondo State Bank in 1921 stands at 1711 Avenue M. To reach the crime scene, turn north from U.S. Highway 90 in downtown Hondo onto Farm to Market Road 462 (Avenue M) and drive one and a half blocks, crossing the Southern Pacific Railroad tracks. The commercial building fronts on Avenue M,

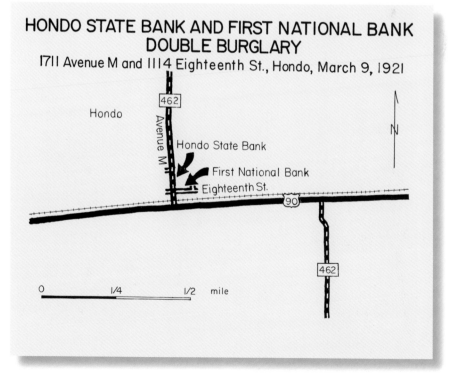

HONDO STATE BANK AND FIRST NATIONAL BANK
DOUBLE BURGLARY
1711 Avenue M and 1114 Eighteenth St., Hondo, March 9, 1921

The commercial building that housed the Hondo State Bank, the first of two banks burglarized by the Newton Boys in Hondo, Texas, on the night of March 9, 1921. Photograph by the author, 2006.

Site of the former First National Bank, the second of two banks burglarized in Hondo, Texas, by the Newton Boys the night of March 9, 1921. The historic bank occupied the west (left) half of the present structure that today houses the Hondo National Bank. Photograph by the author, 2006.

with its south side lying on an east-west alley. It was at the eastern-most barred window in the building on this alley that the Newton Boys forced their entry.

The rear of the two-story Hondo First National Bank is only a few feet away on the other side of the same alley. It was here that the burglars unsuccessfully attempted to break into this second bank on the same night. Frustrated at the rear door, they went around to the front of the building at 1114 Eighteenth Street and easily got in there. To reach this second crime scene, from the old Hondo State Bank building walk or drive half a block south on Farm to Market Road 462 (Avenue M) to its intersection with Eighteenth Street. Turn east (left) on Eighteenth and go half a block to the front entry. Today the Hondo National Bank operates at the site. In 1921 the First National Bank conducted business in the west (left) side of the present bank building, which today has a modern pink granite and cream-colored masonry façade.

BELLS-DENISON EXPRESS CAR ROBBERY BOARDING POINT, BROADWAY STREET RAILWAY GRADE CROSSING, BELLS, AUGUST 25, 1921

Shortly after midnight on August 25, 1921, the Newton Boys staged the first of their two express car robberies in Texas. Willis Newton and gang member Brent Glasscock hoisted themselves through the open door of the express car on the northbound Katy Limited passenger train of the Missouri, Kansas, and Texas Railway when it slowed down to cross the intersecting tracks of the Texas and Pacific Railway at Bells in eastern Grayson County. The Katy tracks northward from Bells to Denison, where the passenger train traveled, were taken up in the 1980s, leaving behind the earthen roadbed, crossties, and industrial debris. Although the site has changed substantially, one can still find the place where the tracks crossed.

To reach the crime scene drive 1.7 miles south into the town of Bells on U.S. Highway 69 from its intersection with U.S. Highway 82. Just after passing beneath a set of railway tracks, turn east (left) on the first paved street, North Street. This turn is one block before reaching an intersection with east-west Texas Highway 56. Drive east one block on North Street to its juncture with Broadway Street. Turn north (left) on Broadway and proceed one block to a railway grade crossing, where limited free street-side parking may be found. Be sure to park well back from the actively used rail line. From this location look about 150 feet eastward along the old Texas and Pacific tracks to a historic and rather tall wooden telegraph pole. Its cross arms once supported east-west telegraph wires for Texas and Pacific company communications, as well

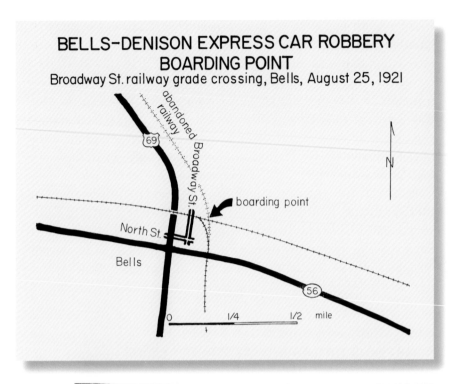

BELLS–DENISON EXPRESS CAR ROBBERY
BOARDING POINT
Broadway St. railway grade crossing, Bells, August 25, 1921

Curving railroad track just west of the point where tracks of the Missouri, Kansas, and Texas Railway crossed those of the Texas and Pacific Railway at Bells, Texas, where Willis Newton and Brent Glasscock entered the express car of the northbound Katy Limited passenger train just after midnight on August 25, 1921, to rob the car of its valuables. Photograph by the author, 2010.

as north-south wires for use by employees of the Missouri, Kansas, and Texas Railway. It marks the site of the former railway junction near which Newton and Glasscock jumped into the northbound express car. Because parts of this railway line remain in active use, take every precaution to avoid being surprised and/or injured by moving locomotives or rail cars.

BELLS-DENISON EXPRESS CAR ROBBERY ESCAPE, 600 BLOCK OF SOUTH LAMAR AVENUE, DENISON, AUGUST 25, 1921

By the time that Willis Newton and Brent Glasscock had taken what they wanted from the registered mail in the express car on the northbound Katy Limited during its quarter-hour run from Bells northward into Denison, the train was pulling into the southeast edge of Denison. The robbers pulled the emergency stop cord that signaled the locomotive engineer to bring the train to a halt. It drew to a stop about half a dozen blocks south of the Denison depot, in the vicinity of the 600 block of South Lamar Avenue. In the dark, the robbers alighted with their loot, and another gang member picked them up in a car. Although the steel rails have been removed, the site remains well preserved.

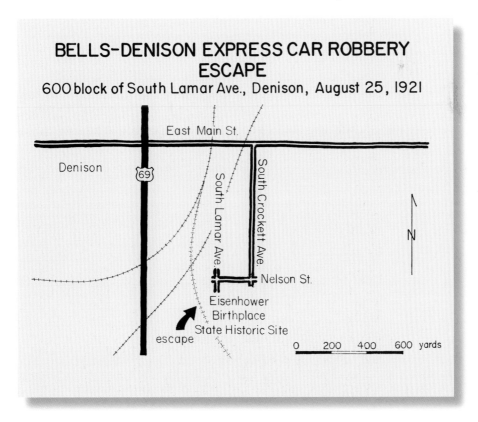

BELLS-DENISON EXPRESS CAR ROBBERY ESCAPE
600 block of South Lamar Ave., Denison, August 25, 1921

When the northbound Katy Limited passenger train pulled into Denison, Texas, early on the morning of August 25, 1921, express car robbers Willis Newton and Brent Glasscock pulled the emergency stop cord, the engineer stopped it in the vicinity of the 600 block of South Lamar Avenue (near a house with three front gables where future U.S. president Dwight D. Eisenhower had been born in 1890), and the two thieves escaped to a waiting automobile. Photograph by the author, 2010.

To reach the crime scene, turn east from U.S. Highway 69 onto East Main Street in downtown Denison. Proceed east three blocks, crossing multiple railway tracks and passing the Katy railway depot, to the intersection with South Crockett Avenue at the historic three-story Travelers Hotel. Turn south (right) on South Crockett and drive six blocks to its juncture with Nelson Street. Turn west (right) on Nelson to drive one block to a juncture with South Lamar Avenue. Turn south (left) into the parking area for the Eisenhower Birthplace State Historic Site. The earthen roadbed for the Missouri, Kansas, and Texas railway line, where the Katy Limited stopped the night of the robbery, can be accessed directly west of the parking lot. A public walking path lies atop this embankment where visitors may view the roadbed, historic telegraph poles, and concrete bases for former railway signals. Care should be taken to avoid the poison ivy that abounds alongside the footpath. At the time of writing, access to this park area was free, although a modest admission fee was charged for entry to the Dwight D. Eisenhower birthplace house museum, in front of which the Katy tracks formerly passed.

SULPHUR RIVER EXPRESS CAR ROBBERY
BOARDING POINT, NEAR WEST MAIN STREET RAILWAY
GRADE CROSSING, BLOOMBURG, SEPTEMBER 7, 1921

On the night of September 7, 1921, Willis Newton and Brent Glasscock robbed the northbound Kansas City Southern Number 2 passenger train between Bloomburg and Texarkana. Although the scene of the actual robbery near the Sulphur River bridge is not accessible, it is possible to see the area of the former Bloomburg depot, where the two bandits boarded the train.

To reach the crime scene, drive two blocks north in the village of Bloomburg on Farm to Market Road 3129 (Arkansas Avenue) from its intersection with Farm to Market Road 74 (Cypress Street). At the junction of Farm to Market Road 3129 with Main Street, turn east (right) on Main and drive one block to the railway tracks. Free street-side parking is available in the immediate area. According to local residents, the Bloomburg station, in front of which the train stopped on the night of September 7, 1921, stood west of the tracks north of this street crossing in the area just east of a present-day modern beige frame building with brown asphalt shingles. Because the railway line remains in active use, visitors should take care to avoid any moving trains.

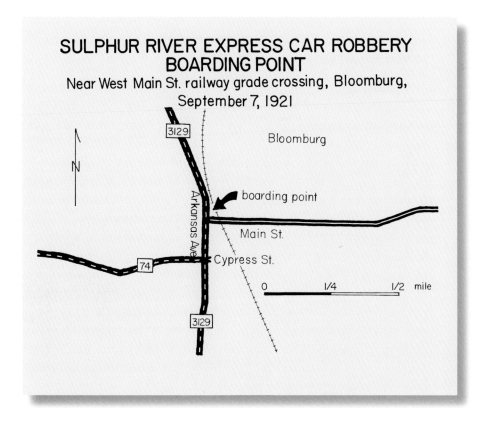

SULPHUR RIVER EXPRESS CAR ROBBERY
BOARDING POINT
Near West Main St. railway grade crossing, Bloomburg,
September 7, 1921

When the Newton Boys on September 7, 1921, robbed their second express car in Texas, they boarded the Kansas City Southern Number 2 when it stopped for passengers in this area near the former station just north of the intersection of the tracks with West Main Street in Bloomburg, Texas. Photograph by the author, 2006.

NEW BRAUNFELS STATE BANK ROBBERY, 451 MAIN PLAZA, NEW BRAUNFELS, MARCH 10, 1922

At midday on Friday, March 10, 1922, the Newton Boys staged a daring daylight robbery of the New Braunfels State Bank, on the Main Plaza in the German-settled town of New Braunfels, Texas. After locking the employees in the vault, the criminals made a clean escape.

To reach the crime scene in the town of New Braunfels, leave Interstate 35 at exit 187 marked for Farm to Market Road 725. At the intersection with Farm to Market Road 725, turn northwest onto South Seguin Avenue and drive 1.2 miles to the Main Plaza at the center of the town. Follow the one-way traffic around the plaza to its northwest side, looking for the prominent white, two-story Plaza Hotel, and stop in one of the free street-side diagonal parking spaces on the west side of the square. Some witnesses reported seeing two of the thieves sipping coffee at the hotel immediately prior to the 1922 robbery. A cream-colored 1937 art deco terra cotta façade survives from the building that housed the New Braunfels State Bank southwest of the Plaza Hotel. The bank in 1922 occupied the west half of the area now marked by the larger, more recent building front.

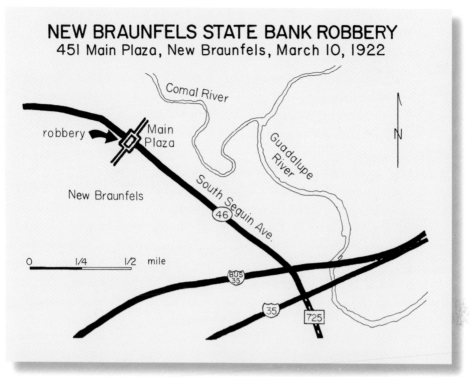

NEW BRAUNFELS STATE BANK ROBBERY
451 Main Plaza, New Braunfels, March 10, 1922

Comal River

robbery → Main Plaza

Guadalupe River

New Braunfels

South Seguin Ave.
46

N

0   1/4   1/2   mile

BUS 35

35   725

The cream-colored terra cotta façade of a later bank marks the site just west of the two-story white Plaza Hotel in New Braunfels, Texas, where the Newton Boys took money and bonds from New Braunfels State Bank at midday on March 10, 1922. Photograph by the author, 2010.

SAN MARCOS FIRST STATE BANK AND TRUST COMPANY BURGLARY, 100 WEST HOPKINS STREET, SAN MARCOS, JANUARY 5, 1924

With a cold norther howling during the early hours of Saturday, January 5, 1924, the Newton Boys burglarized the First State Bank and Trust Company on the courthouse square in San Marcos, Texas. Blasts of nitroglycerine used to open the safes wrecked the interior of the bank as the yeggmen helped themselves to money and securities. Today a restaurant operates in the historic building, and diners enjoy meals inside the very vault that the Texas bank burglars looted.

To reach the crime scene, leave Interstate 35 at its intersection with Texas Highway 80 on the east side of San Marcos. Drive 1.3 miles west on Texas Highway 80 to the courthouse square (intersection with Texas Highway 82). The two-story brick First State Bank and Trust Company building, now housing a restaurant, stands at the northwest corner of the square at 100 West Hopkins Street, where free street-side parking is available.

The First State Bank and Trust Company on the courthouse square in San Marcos, Texas, the scene of the Newton Boys' last bank robbery in the Lone Star State perpetrated during the early hours of January 5, 1924. Photograph by the author, 2009.

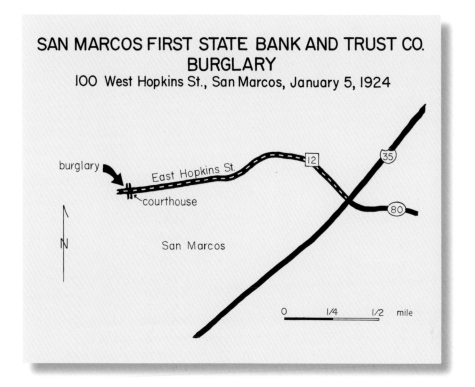

SAN MARCOS FIRST STATE BANK AND TRUST CO. BURGLARY
100 West Hopkins St., San Marcos, January 5, 1924

BURIAL PLACES FOR THE NEWTON BOYS, HILLCREST MEMORIAL CEMETERY, 1300 BLOCK OF U.S. HIGHWAY 90 WEST (WEST MAIN STREET), UVALDE

The four Newton brothers with their family members lie near each other in the Hillcrest Memorial Cemetery on the west side of Uvalde, Texas, the town where they resided most of their later years. This is a traditional burial ground with handsome scattered oak, mesquite, and pecan trees.

To find the burials drive west 1.7 miles on U.S. Highway 90 West (West Main Street) from its intersection with U.S. Highway 83 at the center of Uvalde. Enter Hillcrest Memorial Cemetery at the main gate on the north side of the highway and then turn west (left) at the first cemetery street intersection. Drive west to the next cemetery street intersection, turn north (right), and park at the side of the roadway. The remains of three of the brothers, Willis, Jess, and Wylie (Doc), lie beneath markers along the east side of this pavement. The fourth brother, Joe, is buried beside his wife, Mildred, on the other side of the cemetery street in the fifth row to the west at the eighth grave marker to the north of an aged mesquite tree. Across U.S. Highway 90 to the south in the City of Uvalde Cemetery is the grave of John Nance Garner, who served as the nation's vice president from 1933 to 1941.

The graves of Willis, Jess, and Wylie "Doc" Newton in the foreground with that of Joe Newton in the fifth row on the other side of the paved street in the Hillcrest Memorial Cemetery at Uvalde, Texas. Photograph by the author, 2006.

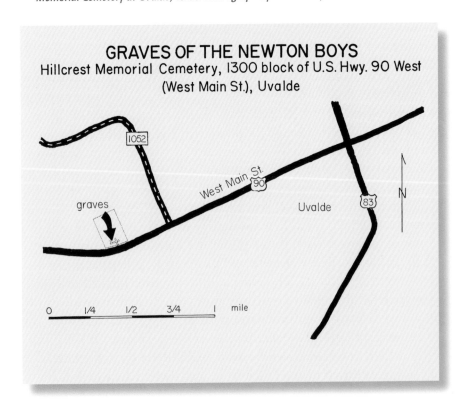

GRAVES OF THE NEWTON BOYS
Hillcrest Memorial Cemetery, 1300 block of U.S. Hwy. 90 West (West Main St.), Uvalde

1052

West Main St.
90

graves

Uvalde

83

N

0   1/4   1/2   3/4   1   mile

Abilene Daily Reporter (Abilene, Tex.), March 6, 1919, pp. 1, 3; March 7, 1919, pp. 1, 8; March 9, 1919, p. 2; March 10, 1919, pp. 1, 6; March 11, 1919, p. 5; March 17, 1919, pp. 1, 3; March 19, 1919, p. 6.

Ballinger Daily Ledger (Ballinger, Tex.), March 5, 1919, p. 1; March 6, 1919, p. 1; March 7, 1919, p. 1; March 8, 1919, pp. 1, 2, 3; March 10, 1919, p. 1; March 11, 1919, p. 1; March 12, 1919, p. 1; March 13, 1919, p. 1; March 17, 1919, p. 1; March 18, 1919, p. 1; March 20, 1919, p. 2.

Banner-Ledger (Ballinger, Tex.), March 7, 1919, p. 1; March 14, 1919, pp. 1, 4; March 21, 1919, p. 1.

Daily Texarkanian (Texarkana, Ark.), September 7, 1921, pp. 1, 4; September 8, 1921, p. 1.

Dallas Morning News (Dallas, Tex.), March 6, 1919, p. 4; March 9, 1919, part 1, p. 11; January 11, 1921, p. 1; February 9, 1921, p. 2; August 26, 1921, p. 13; September 8, 1921, pp. 2, 14; March 11, 1922, p. 1; January 6, 1924, sec. 1, p. 4; January 7, 1924, sec. 2, p. 11; February 1, 1924, sec. 2, p. 17; March 1, 1924, sec. 4, p. 8; June 21, 1924, sec. 1, p. 2; August 18, 1924, sec. 1, p. 7; November 26, 1924, sec. 1, p. 1; December 12, 1924, p. 1; January 20, 1926, sec. 1, p. 12; February 5, 1926, sec. 1, p. 3; March 23, 1935, sec. I, p. 7.

D'Hanis Star (D'Hanis, Tex.), January 14, 1921, p. 3.

Fort Worth Press (Fort Worth, Tex.), September 7, 1921, pp. 1, 2.

Fort Worth Star-Telegram (Fort Worth, Tex.), March 6, 1919, p. 1; March 8, 1919, p. 1; March 9, 1919, sec. 2, p. 21; March 17, 1919, p. 1; August 25, 1921, p. 1; March 10, 1922, p. 1.

Four States Press (Texarkana, Ark.), September 8, 1921, p. 2; September 9, 1921, p. 1.

"Good Morning! Has Your Bank Been Robbed?" *Texas Bankers Record* (Dallas, Tex.), 10, no. 5 (January 1921): 41.

Hondo Anvil Herald (Hondo, Tex.), January 15, 1921, [pp. 2, 5].

New Braunfels Herald (New Braunfels, Tex.), March 17, 1922, p. 1.

Newton, Willis, and Joe Newton. *The Newton Boys: Portrait of an Outlaw Gang.* Edited by Claude Stanush and David Middleton. Austin: State House Press, 1994.

San Angelo Daily Standard (San Angelo, Tex.), March 6, 1919, p. 1; March 10, 1919, p. 2; March 8, 1919, p. 1; March 14, 1919, p. 3; March 17, 1919, pp. 1, 4.

San Antonio Evening News (San Antonio, Tex.), January 10, 1921, p. 1; January 12, 1921, p. 1; March 11, 1922, pp. 1, 2; March 13, 1922, pp. 1, 2; January 5, 1924, pp. 1, 3; January 7, 1924, p. 12.

San Antonio Express (San Antonio, Tex.), January 10, 1921, p. 1; January 11, 1921, p. 1; January 12, 1921, p. 2; February 9, 1921, pp. 1, 2; February 10, 1921, p. 3; February 11, 1921, p. 9; February 12, 1921, p. 4; March 11, 1922, pp. 1, 2; March 12, 1922, pp. 1, 2; March 13, 1922, pp. 1, 2; March 14, 1922, p. 9; January 6, 1924, sec. I, p. 11.

San Antonio Light (San Antonio, Tex.), March 11, 1922, pp. 1, 2; March 12, 1922, pp. 1, 2; March 14, 1922, pp. 1, 2; January 5, 1924, pp. 1, 2; January 7, 1924, p. 1.

San Marcos Record (San Marcos, Tex.), January 11, 1924, pp. 1, 3, 4, 10; January 25, 1924, p. 1; September 30, 1927, p. 1; February 21, 1930, p. 1.

Uvalde Leader-News (Uvalde, Tex.), July 11, 1924, [pp. 4, 6]; July 18, 1924, [p. 7].

3 THE SOUTHERN PACIFIC PAYROLL ROBBERY IN EL PASO
AN ATTEMPTED HEIST, THE MURDER OF AN INNOCENT MAN, AND AN INTERNATIONAL PRISONER EXCHANGE

El Paso judge Ballard Coldwell looked up from his desk to see a pretty thirteen-year-old girl in a pink dress walking into his office. The year was 1932. From beneath a fashionable soft-brimmed hat, she immediately declared, "I want you to get my father out of jail."

Barely a teenager, the visitor was Antonia Carrasco, and Judge Coldwell knew all about her daddy. Six years before, he had participated in one of the most daring holdup attempts in the history of El Paso, a fatal try on the Southern Pacific Railroad payroll. "I was interested immediately," the judge later said, adding, "She was so plain and straight about it, I promised to do what I could." Coldwell advised Antonia to come back to his court every week, and that she did for many months, almost always wearing the same pink dress, no doubt her best. She kept reminding the judge of his pledge.

The events that led Antonia Carrasco to Judge Ballard Coldwell's legal chambers began in March 1924. Manuel Villareal gathered several men at La Punta Bar across the river in Juarez, Mexico, to plan a major heist in El Paso. One of their number, José Carrasco, Antonia's father, had worked in the repair shops of the Galveston, Harrisburg, and San Antonio Railway, part of the Southern Pacific system, and he was aware of its pay schedule. He also knew that armed guards brought large sums of money from the American Trust and Savings Bank to the Van Noy Lunchroom, which was adjacent to the yard office in the shop area, so that employees could conveniently cash their checks. The thieves made plans to steal the cash by force of arms on the next payday, Tuesday, March 18, 1924. Joining Villareal and Carrasco were Adrian Sanchez, Alejo Minjárez, and Agapito Rueda. Carrasco had long engaged in smuggling illegal alcohol across the international border and was known among U.S. customs officers as "the Submarine" because of his swimming abilities. Rueda had been back only two weeks after his release from Leavenworth, where he had been imprisoned on a liquor conviction. The five were all men hardened by crime and desperate for a haul of money.

On the morning of Tuesday, March 18, one of the gang members stole a Dodge touring car from a Juarez taxi service, picked up the other men, and a little before eleven o'clock headed across the Rio Grande on the Santa Fe Street Bridge. According to some sources, one or two of the criminals had already joined the railway employees gathering at the Van Noy Lunchroom to cash paychecks. In the meantime a second car bearing two bank tellers, two armed guards, and $14,447 in cash was headed toward the same café from downtown. Driving north on Octavia Street, the bandits arrived first, making a U-turn and parking on the west side of the street opposite the eatery in the 400 block. They had barely pulled into place when, according to José Carrasco, "We saw the pay automobile about 15 or 20 feet before it stopped. As soon as the pay car arrived, our driver got off the car, left his engine running, and told us to jump out." The time was about 11:05 AM.

The robbers rushed the bank car. To their surprise, an unsuspecting member of the crowd cried out in greeting, "Carrasco!" That unfortunate twenty-one-year-old railway car worker, Anastacio López, paid for recognizing his friend by getting a bullet in the heart. This shot led to a melee of firing. Bank guard Charles Bitticks was standing at the rear of the bank vehicle when he first heard firing. He saw the other guard, William H. "Bill" Meers, run around to the front of the car, where one of the robbers shot him down in the street. "He did not get an opportunity to fire a shot," his friend declared. Bitticks then stepped back around the end of the vehicle and started firing at the thieves while trying to avoid hitting bystanders.

In the meantime bank teller W. L. Laird moved from the car onto the sidewalk. "A Mexican stepped up and, placing a gun in my face, demanded that I throw up my hands," he reported. When Laird complied, "I dropped the sacks containing the money to the ground and ran around the corner of the restaurant." Bank teller George H. Reed was not so lucky; one of the robbers shot him in the chest. Mrs. W. G. Davis was working inside the Van Noy Lunchroom when he staggered through the door exclaiming, "My God! Mrs. Davis[,] I'm shot three times." He fell in his own blood on the floor. Terrified bystander Robert Kirk ran out the rear of the restaurant and along its north side. "Everybody seemed to be shooting," he reported to the press. "One of the officers was standing on the east side of the pay car firing at the bandits, who were running toward their machine across the street." This officer was guard Bitticks, who despite a gunshot wound in the groin, put up such a stout defense of the money that the bandits retreated.

As the gang drove away, they left behind a scene of carnage. Security guard Bill Meers and bystander Anastacio López lay dead, while teller George H. Reed and guard Charles A. Bitticks suffered grievous wounds from which they eventually recovered. In the confusion of the failed robbery, the bandits left in the street the three bags of money Laird had dropped.

The gunfight continued as the bandits retreated. After seeing distinctively curly-haired Agapito Rueda shoot twice at Bill Meers, Charles Bitticks reported, "I shot at him and missed him. Then he turned and shot at me. I shot at him again and he stumbled and fell as he tried to get in the car." Then as the Dodge touring car pulled out, another of the robbers ran toward it, jumped onto the back bumper, and held onto the rear-mounted spare tire, a pistol in one hand. Bitticks remembered, "He was shooting at me and I was shooting at him." From the back seat of the Dodge, José Carrasco also saw the last bandit leap onto the moving vehicle. "I told him that I was wounded and he told me that I didn't have anything on him, that he was wounded, too." U.S. revenue agent Emmett Dawson saw the bandit car fleeing the scene southbound on Tays Street. He assumed from its bullet-shattered windshield and high speed that the vehicle held bootleggers, so he gave chase. The driver hastily turned around and sped back northward, losing the pursuer.

Within half an hour law officers reached the crime scene, which by then was swarming with hundreds of railway workers and locals. Neighborhood resident Salvador Ballinas joined the crowds, later remembering, "We went to the scene of the shooting and saw the front window glasses with bullet holes." In the meantime officers blanketed the southern residential district of the city, where they suspected that the thieves had headed. Captain Joe E. Stowe, a longtime police officer, declared, "There is greater safety for them in south El Paso than in Juarez. . . . Once a criminal loses himself in the lower end of the city, every Mexican resident becomes his friend and protector." This is indeed what happened, as the robbers melted away into the predominantly Hispanic neighborhood.

Most of the criminal party escaped, but the two who had been wounded were unable to avoid apprehension. Law officers first located the bullet-punctured getaway car with its bloody upholstery in a north-south alley in the block bounded by St. Vrain and Hills streets and Third and Fourth avenues. While this party located the bandits' Dodge, other officers tracked down the only robber whose name they knew, José Carrasco. Railway pay records showed his address in South El Paso, but when lawmen rushed the house they found it empty. A detective then checked with the El Paso post office, which reported Carrasco's mailing address had been changed to 607½ Tornillo Street. Six police officers then converged on the small house along an alley. Carrasco's mother met them at the door, saying that there was no man in the house. Having thrown a cordon around the dwelling, Captain Joe E. Stowe and Sergeant Mike Snyder pushed themselves inside and in a back room found an aged woman lying on a bed. Carrasco's mother begged them not to disturb the ill female, but Stowe peered underneath the couch to find a heap of rugs and rags. Moving the bed away from the wall and drawing back the covering, he found a bloody leg belonging to José Carrasco. Covering him with pistols, officers dragged the criminal from his hiding place. Arresting the injured man, they took him to a hospital for treatment of a gruesome gunshot wound caused by a bullet that shattered the bone in his lower right limb. That night a surgeon amputated the leg at the knee.

Still more lawmen converged on South El Paso in hopes of apprehending additional robbers. The press reported that officers searched every house in the district. At midday on Wednesday, the day following the bloody events, they knocked on the door of a residence at 410 South St. Vrain Street, no more than a hundred yards from where they had found the abandoned getaway car. Inside the dwelling they found the curly-haired robber, Agapito Rueda, also with a severe gunshot. One of guard Charles Bitticks's bullets had broken the bone in the upper left leg, though the wound eventually healed.

While officers searched for the attackers, families made plans for funerals in remembrance of Anastacio López and William H. Meers. López's remains went to his home at Valentine, Texas, where his sister and brother-in-law planned his interment. Many local merchants, bankers, and law officers attended services held for Meers at the Trinity Methodist Church and at Evergreen Cemetery in El Paso. He was survived by his wife of twenty-five years; son William Jefferson "Jeff" Meers, a senior at El Paso High School; and a daughter. "He never had a chance or this thing would not have happened," his widow told a reporter. The thoughts that passed through teenaged Jeff Meers's mind went unrecorded.

Legal proceedings moved forward against José Carrasco, Agapito Rueda, and Adrian Sanchez, a third robbery suspect apprehended later. Carrasco's murder trial came first, in September 1924, and he received a death sentence that his attorney appealed. Next Agapito Rueda went to trial in November 1924, also receiving a guilty verdict and death sentence. The press reported, "Mrs. Meers and her son, Jeff, . . . were in the courtroom when the verdict was read. They have been in constant attendance during the trial." Justice for Rueda came just over a year later, when he was executed in the electric chair at the state penitentiary in Huntsville on January 9, 1926. Adrian Sanchez died from tuberculosis in the El Paso County Jail before he could be tried.

Four years passed, and most people not immediately associated with the robbery attempt forgot about it. Jeff Meers, son of one of the victims, graduated from El Paso High School, went to work as a clerk for Pacific Fruit Express, and married Elizabeth Kenton. Despite Jeff's seemingly normal life, his mother realized that "the death of his father made a deep impression on him. He would be reading a book, and . . . I would watch him and he would be, almost unconsciously, betraying . . . that he felt duty-bound to avenge his father. He would grit his teeth and his jaws would steel in determination." She also knew that in early summer 1930 Jeff had become obsessed by reports that robbery mastermind Manuel Villareal had been seen just across the Rio Grande in Juarez.

On Wednesday, June 18, 1930, Jeff Meers crossed the river into Juarez with a journalist friend named Jack Shafer. The latter was seeking material for a short story. Each carried a concealed sidearm. "We went to the office of a Juarez newspaper and to the police station and inquired about the rurales, the organization in which Shafer was particularly interested," Meers reported. That evening the two Americans went to the Owl Bar, taking seats in the rear. When Jeff asked one of the bartenders if he knew Manuel Villareal, the man quipped, "Sure I know him." Then in jest he pointed toward a forty-year-old waiter named Antonio Visconte, saying, "That's Villareal standing over there with a tray in his hand." Meers took the joke seriously, believing that he saw facial resemblance between the waiter and pictures of Villareal. He and Shafer ordered two beers, and when Visconte brought them to the booth, Jeff invited the server to have a seat. As soon as he did so, Meers pulled out a .38-caliber pistol and pumped six bullets into the blameless man's chest, killing him instantly. In the confusion that ensued, no one told Meers whom he had actually shot. "I did not know I had killed Visconte, an innocent man, until I was in a cell in the Juarez jail," Meers said. "His face looked like Villareal's to me. There was no doubt in my mind."

Jeff Meers's rash act led him into a legal nightmare that he could never have imagined. First, while in the city jail, he became the subject of demonstrations by hundreds of members of the Juarez bartenders' union and other labor organizations, all demanding that the American pay the maximum penalty for the unprovoked murder of their colleague. The central government even sent soldiers with rifles and bayonets to lend protection. Shifting the twenty-seven-year-old American to the state prison in Chihuahua, the judicial system tried him for the murder, finding him guilty and sentencing him to life behind bars. Then Meers suffered a tough break from being at the wrong place at the wrong time.

During the early morning hours of Monday, June 8, 1931, three college students drove southward on U.S. Highway 77 from St. Benedict's College in Atchison, Kansas, headed home to their families in Mexico. They had paused at the side of the road in Ardmore, Oklahoma, when a local sheriff's department vehicle approached. Two officers emerged from the car, frightening the young men, two of whom darted into the darkness. Deputy Sheriff William Guess called out in English for them to halt, to no avail, and then he shot repeatedly. Both students fell to the ground dead. One was a cousin of Mexican president Pascual Ortíz Rubio. In the murder trials held for both of the Oklahoma officers, local juries found the defendants not guilty. Although authorities in Mexico claimed there was no connection between the Juarez case and the two acquittals in Oklahoma, they changed Jeff Meers's sentence from life in prison to death before a firing squad.

Jeff Meers's and José Carrasco's families never gave up hope of securing freedom for their loved ones in the Chihuahua and Texas state prisons. They wrote the men regular letters that buoyed them through the hardest times. José later reported that his wife "wrote to me every week. . . . She told me how my little Antonia and my little Carlos were growing up. She kept me cheered while I worked in the sweaty penitentiary boiler room." Jeff's family members and American authorities worked to ease his life on murderers' row at the state prison in Chihuahua. Sheriff's deputy Allen G. Falby made regular trips into Mexico to retrieve stolen automobiles, and each time that he went to Chihuahua he would stop by the prison to check on Meers and another American prisoner, on the pretext of delivering them fresh clothing. "I became so well acquainted with those officers that they let me take them to the Palacio Hotel," Falby recalled, "and I would let them eat two or three steaks at a time." Mrs. Elizabeth Meers also made prison visits to see her husband before his sentence was changed to the death penalty. In time Jeff's predicament became a cause célèbre in El Paso legal circles.

Partly because of teenaged Antonia Carrasco's efforts through Judge Ballard Coldwell, lawyers, jurists, consuls, and even state governors began considering a swap of prisoners—Carrasco for Meers. Officials declared publicly that laws prohibited such exchanges, but behind the scenes people on both sides of the border worked to effect the trade. Talk changed to action in July 1932, when two Texas Rangers speedily drove José Carrasco by automobile from the Huntsville penitentiary to the El Paso County Jail, but then plans to release him in exchange for Meers fell through. That fall Chris P. Fox was elected sheriff of El Paso County, and he inherited the messy situation. "When I took over as sheriff, it was placed in my lap. . . . We had Carrasco in our bastille and I wanted to get rid of him." After a false start in January, the deal was

Jeff Meers and José Carrasco shake hands in a press photograph at the international boundary at the middle of the Santa Fe Street Bridge in the early morning hours of April 20, 1933, as authorities from the United States and Mexico exchange them as prisoners. Courtesy of the University of Texas at El Paso Library Special Collections Department.

struck, and on April 19, 1933, Mexican authorities and a prison guard quietly departed the Chihuahua prison by car with Jeff Meers. They planned to meet the Americans with Carrasco to make a trade at the middle of the Santa Fe Street international bridge between Juarez and El Paso.

On the evening of April 19, 1933, American attorneys, family members, reporters, and lawmen gathered in the El Paso sheriff's office to await news of Meers's arrival in Juarez. Carrasco remained in his jail cell, fully dressed and with his cork leg attached. A telephone call came about three o'clock on the morning of April 20. Fox remembered, "I told the person who was talking to me to use extreme caution, as we'd be keeping things under wraps as we didn't want to have Meers hijacked over in Juarez by members of the family and friends of the man he had mistakenly killed." About 3:10 AM four automobiles left the El Paso courthouse bearing lawmen, José Carrasco, Meers family members, and newspaper reporters, and the convoy arrived at the American end of the Santa Fe Street Bridge about ten minutes later. They waited a while, and then according to Fox, "At the other end, lights flashed, and our U.S. Customs boys, who had been acting as liaison, gave the word that they were approaching; so we went to the middle of the bridge." Fox broke the silence, calling out, "Hello, Jeff." José Carrasco then walked up, a wide smile across his face. He reached his hand out for Meers's and asked him, "Did you learn to speak Spanish?" "Yep, I sure did," the happy American replied, adding, "I learned to swear in Spanish just like the other boys." Then from the darkness emerged Elizabeth Meers with the exclamation, "Oh, Jeff!" After an embrace the two parties headed back to their respective sides of the river.

Soon a celebration began in Juarez. Antonia Carrasco got her father back. It was José's intention to move with his family to his home state of Quintana Roo in the south of Mexico. In the 1970s former sheriff Chris P. Fox, however, wrote to a friend, reporting that "the last I heard, Joe Carrasco, still sporting his wooden leg, was running a little cantina in Juarez." By that time, according to Fox, William H. Meers's widow had passed away and son Jeff had moved "somewhere out in California." All of the participants in the prisoner exchange, in Fox's words, had driven "away into the dawn of another day, and another life."

VISIT THE CRIME SCENES

SANTA FE STREET BRIDGE, 1100 BLOCK OF SOUTH SANTA FE STREET, EL PASO, INBOUND ROUTE OF ROBBERS ON MARCH 18, 1924, AND SCENE OF PRISONER EXCHANGE ON APRIL 20, 1933

When the would-be thieves entered the United States in their stolen Dodge automobile on March 18, 1924, they did so by crossing from Juarez into El Paso on the Santa Fe Street Bridge. When U.S. and Mexican authorities exchanged José Carrasco for Jeff Meers on April 20, 1933, they made the swap midway across the same viaduct. Though rebuilt, the Santa Fe Street Bridge remains one of the two active crossing points over the Rio Grande in downtown El Paso, today carrying north- and southbound pedestrians and northbound motor traffic.

To reach the scene, leave Interstate 10 on the north side of the El Paso business district at exit 18B eastbound or exit 19B westbound, both of which are marked for the Downtown Convention Center. Where the

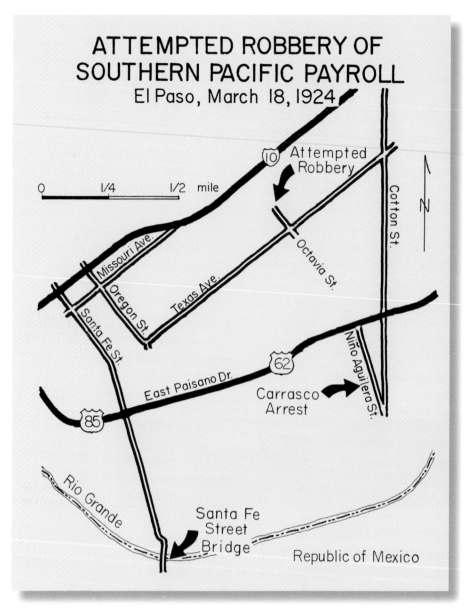

ATTEMPTED ROBBERY OF SOUTHERN PACIFIC PAYROLL
El Paso, March 18, 1924

0   1/4   1/2   mile

Attempted Robbery

Missouri Ave.

Oregon St.

Texas Ave.

Octavia St.

Cotton St.

Santa Fe St.

East Paisano Dr.

Carrasco Arrest

Niño Aguilera St.

Rio Grande

Santa Fe Street Bridge

Republic of Mexico

N

eastbound ramp intersects North Santa Fe Street, turn south (right). From the westbound ramp merge onto East Missouri Street, drive 0.5 mile on Missouri to its intersection with North Santa Fe Street, and turn south (left) onto Santa Fe. Proceed 0.8 mile south on Santa Fe Street (which becomes Texas Loop 375) to its terminus at the international bridge. Metered street-side parking and commercial parking are both available in the immediate vicinity of the bridge. This area typically has traffic congestion. Even though this bridge has been reconstructed since the historic events, it is possible to approach the vicinity of the 1933 prisoner exchange by walking to the international boundary marked by U.S. and Mexican flags near the middle of the bridge.

Note that doing this requires possession of valid passports, payment of modest cash tolls, and legal formalities with both Mexican and U.S. border control officers. If one wishes to view the international border area at the middle of the viaduct, it is necessary to proceed all the way across to the Mexican end of the bridge and pass through international border control there before being permitted to return to the American side.

South toward the Santa Fe Street Bridge across the Rio Grande between El Paso and Juarez. This modern structure stands in the general area of the historic cross-border viaduct that carried the inbound Southern Pacific payroll robbers on March 18, 1924, and served as the neutral location for the Jeff Meers–José Carrasco prisoner exchange on April 20, 1933. Photograph by the author, 2006.

ATTEMPTED ROBBERY OF SOUTHERN PACIFIC PAYROLL, 400 BLOCK OF NORTH OCTAVIA STREET, EL PASO, MARCH 18, 1924

The attempted robbery of the Southern Pacific payroll in El Paso took place in front of the wood-frame Van Noy Lunchroom inside the railway yards of the Southern Pacific and the El Paso & Southwestern companies immediately northeast of downtown El Paso. The area remains an active railroad staging yard to this day. In 1924 vehicles traversing Octavia Street could bounce across multiple railway grade crossings from one side of the yard to the other, but for years the thoroughfare has been closed. The eating place catering to railyard workers stood just over one city block into the now closed railway yards beyond the point where Octavia Street now abuts against the southeast side of the tracks.

To reach the crime scene from Interstate 10 eastbound, take exit 19 immediately north of the El Paso business district. The ramp merges

Northwest on North Octavia Street from Texas Avenue in El Paso, showing the cul-de-sac where the street formerly passed across the tracks in the Southern Pacific maintenance shop and staging yards. The March 18, 1924, attempted payroll robbery took place on what now is closed private property about a block and a quarter into the still-active railway yards. Photograph by the author, 2006.

quickly into West Wyoming Avenue, which serves as the eastbound freeway access road at this point. Drive northeast 0.1 mile on West Wyoming to its intersection with North Oregon Street. At North Oregon, turn southeast (right) and drive five blocks to its juncture with Texas Avenue. Turn northeast (left) on Texas and proceed 0.6 mile to North Octavia Street. At Octavia turn northwest (left) and drive one and a quarter blocks to its dead end at the railway yards.

To reach the crime scene from Interstate 10 westbound, take exit 19B northeast of downtown. The exit ramp merges onto East Missouri Avenue as the westbound access road for this portion of the freeway. Drive 0.6 mile southwestward on Missouri to its intersection with North Cotton Street. Turn south (left) on Cotton and proceed 0.3 mile by way of an overpass across the Southern Pacific tracks to its intersection with Texas Avenue. At Texas Avenue, turn southwest (right) and drive 0.4 mile through a wholesale warehouse district to the intersection with North Octavia Street. At Octavia turn northwest (right) and drive one block and a quarter to its terminus at the tracks.

The Van Noy Lunchroom, in front of which the attempted robbery took place, stood about a block farther into the railway yards. Today this industrial property with frequently moving remote-controlled locomotives does not have public access, though it may be viewed from the end of the street. The current cul-de-sac area on Octavia Street was traversed by the bank pay car, the robbers, and the lawmen on the morning of March 18, 1924.

ARREST SITE FOR JOSÉ CARRASCO, 607 NIÑO AGUILERA STREET (FORMERLY TORNILLO STREET), EL PASO, MARCH 18, 1924

On the afternoon following the attempted robbery, lawmen converged on a little house at the rear of 607 Tornillo Street, today Niño Aguilera Street, on the south side of El Paso. There they found José Carrasco hiding under a pile of rags beneath a bed. Today a historic brick house stands on the front part of the lot where officers made the arrest.

To reach the arrest scene, follow the directions already given from Interstate 10 east- and westbound to North Santa Fe Street and the Santa Fe Street Bridge. At the intersection of North Santa Fe Street with U.S. Highways 62 and 85 (East Paisano Drive), turn east (left) instead of continuing southward to the international bridge. Proceed eastward on East Paisano Drive 0.9 mile through a built-up commercial area to the intersection with Niño Aguilera Street. At Niño Aguilera, turn south (right) and drive two and a half blocks to the modest brick residence behind a stone and metal fence, the third house on the right in this block.

The historic brick residence at 607 Niño Aguilera Street, behind which law officers arrested the badly wounded José Carrasco following his participation in the attempted payroll robbery on March 18, 1924. Photograph by the author, 2006.

Ballinas, Salvador. "The View from the Second Ward." *Password* (El Paso, Tex.) 28, no. 3 (fall 1983): 125–29.

Dallas Morning News (Dallas, Tex.), March 19, 1924, sec. I, p. 1; June 27, 1925, sec. I, p. 2; October 8, 1925, sec. I, p. 5; January 9, 1926, sec. II, p. 14; June 23, 1930, sec. I, p. 1; June 9, 1931, sec. I, pp. 1, 3; June 12, 1931, sec. I, pp. 1, 2; June 30, 1931, sec. I, pp. 1, 7; July 4, 1931, sec. I, p. 1; November 23, 1931, sec. I, p. 7; January 12, 1933, sec. I, p. 3; January 15, 1933, sec. I, p. 1; April 21, 1933, sec. I, p. 1.

El Paso Herald (El Paso, Tex.), March 18, 1924, p. 1; March 19, 1924, pp. 1, 2, 4; March 20, 1924, pp. 1, 2; March 21, 1924, p. 1; March 22–23, 1924, pp. 1, 11; November 10, 1924, p. 1; November 13, 1924, p. 1; January 9, 1926, p. 1; June 19, 1930, pp. 1, 8; June 20, 1930, pp. 1, 2; June 21, 1930, p. 1.

El Paso Herald-Post (El Paso, Tex.), January 11, 1933, pp. 1, 7; January 12, 1933, p. 1; January 13, 1933, p. 5; April 21, 1933, pp. 1, 5; April 22, 1933, p. 1; September 27, 1972, sec. B, p. 9.

El Paso Times (El Paso, Tex.), March 19, 1924, pp. 1, 3, 10; March 20, 1924, pp. 1, 12; March 21, 1924, pp. 1, 2, 4; March 22, 1924, p. 12; March 23, 1924, p. 2; March 25, 1924, p. 3; November 13, 1924, p. 12; November 14, 1924, pp. 1, 2; January 9, 1926, pp. 1, 10; June 19, 1930, p. 1; June 20, 1930, p. 1; June 21, 1930, p. 3; June 23, 1930, pp. 1, 2; January 12, 1933, p. 3; April 20, 1933, pp. 1, 3; April 21, 1933, pp. 1, 3; April 22, 1933, pp. 1, 3; April 23, 1933, p. 1.

Falby, Allen G., Chris P. Fox, Mrs. Callie Fairley, Tony Trujillo, and E. A. "Dogie" Wright. "Oral History: Law Enforcement in El Paso." *Password* 22, no. 1 (spring 1977): 3–16.

Fox, Chris P. "The Exchange." *Password* 18, no. 1 (spring 1973): 17–20.

———. Letter to Murray Neal, September 14, 1972. File 7, Box 28, Chris P. Fox Papers. C. L. Sonnichsen Special Collections Department, University Library, University of Texas at El Paso, El Paso, Tex.

Porter, Eugene O. "The Attempted Payroll Robbery." *Password* 18, no. 1 (spring 1973): 14–16.

4 BECKY ROGERS, THE FLAPPER BANDIT

Bank cashier Frank Jamison thought very little about the slight young woman, looking to be only seventeen or eighteen, who came into the Farmers' National Bank in Buda, Texas, on Saturday morning, December 11, 1926. She told him that she worked as a reporter for the *Beaumont Enterprise*, and she spent the morning talking to local farmers about cotton crops, prices, and government policies, jotting down their comments in a loose-leaf binder. Politely she had asked permission to use a typewriter inside the tellers' cages. As lunchtime approached and business slowed down, Jamison stepped inside the walk-in vault for something. "As I came out she was standing five or six steps away with a gun pointed at me," he said. The petite robber with a blue automatic pistol then ordered, "Stay where you are." Within a week newspapers across the nation were describing the thief, Rebecca Bradley Rogers, as the Flapper Bandit. During the 1920s "flapper" in popular slang referred to a young woman who showed disdain for conventional dress and behavior.

Becky, as her friends knew her, was born in Texarkana, Arkansas, about 1905. She moved with her parents to Fort Worth at age six and attended elementary schools and the old Central High School in the city. It was there that she met Otis Rogers, who had been born in Chillicothe in West Texas and whose family also had relocated to Fort Worth. They were high school sweethearts, and upon graduation they both went to the University of Texas in Austin. Despite a stormy courtship, they married secretly at the courthouse in Georgetown on October 25, 1925. He eventually earned a law degree and became an attorney. Not even the bride's widowed mother knew of the vows.

Rebecca Bradley Rogers worked her way through studies toward a bachelor's degree in history at the university. Having a three-hundred-dollar annual student loan in addition to income from part-time jobs, she managed to pay her tuition, fees, and living expenses. Things appeared to be going smoothly until her mother lost a seemingly secure job in Fort Worth and moved to Austin to live with her, placing additional strain on her daughter's resources. Rebecca began working even longer hours as a clerk in the State Capitol and as an assistant to uni-

111

versity professor Charles W. Ramsdell, who managed business affairs for the Texas State Historical Association.

The co-ed, who now had begun work toward a master's degree, needed still more money to cover living expenses for both mother and herself. Secret husband Otis Rogers had no means with which to assist her, for he was completing his own studies and then attempting to establish a legal practice in Amarillo. Professor Ramsdell planned a summer away from Austin in 1926, leaving the financial affairs of the state historical association in Rebecca's hands. Perhaps not understanding the implications of the decision, he agreed that his student assistant could have $1.40 from the $3.00 dues collected for each new member that she brought into the organization. With the professor away, Rogers employed several dozen part-time stenographers to write membership solicitations to several thousand people, some of the names and addresses being gleaned from *Who's Who* directories. She used her own funds to pay for wages and office supply expenses, mixing her own and association funds. In the haste of the effort, Rogers often deposited funds received without recording membership details. She also added names and addresses for members and put her own money in the accounts to pay their dues. The financial books of the association became an absolute jumble. A few months later the professor penned to a friend, "The girl was undoubtedly suffering from some sort of a psychosis last year. . . . Many of the records were entirely gone, and others had not been kept at all." In the end she owed the Texas State Historical Association an estimated $1,200, which at the time was enough money to buy two new automobiles.

In the meantime Rogers left the historical association to become a stenographer in the office of Dan Moody, attorney general and soon to be governor of the state. Not making enough money there to pay her debts, she mortgaged a house in Fort Worth for which ownership papers were in both her and her mother's names to satisfy some creditors and to take a promised trip with her mother. The mortgage money was not enough. Somehow she needed to raise more. The newspapers at the time were filled with reports of the epidemic of bank robbery that plagued the country during the 1920s, so Rebecca decided that she too would take some money from a bank.

Her target was the Farmers' State Bank in Round Rock, just north of Austin. As early as Wednesday, December 8, 1926, Rebecca Rogers, using the alias Grace Loftin, began driving her Ford Model T coupe to the town in order to visit with locals. She posed as a writer for the Waco newspaper and asked people about cotton crops. Each day she came to the lobby of the bank, conferring with customers and employees as she supposedly gathered information for her newspaper report. Her real goal was gaining access to the bank when there were no customers and few employees, thus making it easier to force access to the vault. Frustrated for the first two days, she decided to stage a diversion to draw people away from the bank. Finding a vacant residence not far from the bank, on Friday, December 10, she prowled around inside. Then she purchased matches and coal oil at a local store, returned to the empty house shortly before bank closing time, and set the building alight. A next-door neighbor, Mrs. Willie Walsh, saw the young woman enter the house for about ten minutes and then drive rapidly away; shortly thereafter the residence burst into flames. Running into the bank, Rebecca shouted an alarm, but none of the employees left to investigate. "I told them I was sure I saw a house afire up the street, but they didn't seem to be paying any attention to it," she complained. Even this ploy failed. For a while she stood in the bank lobby until an end-of-day time lock automatically closed the vault door.

The frustrated Becky Rogers returned to Round Rock the next morning, Saturday, December 11, 1926, but then left as soon as locals suspiciously began asking her about the previous day's fire. She headed back to Austin and then drove a few miles farther south on the San Antonio highway, pausing in sleepy little Buda. There she spotted the cream-colored brick Farmers' National Bank, one of several commercial buildings on the west side of the street across from the railroad tracks. It showed promise as a stick-up site. Using the same strategy she had employed in Round Rock, the petite new graduate of the university again presented herself as a journalist interviewing local farmers, merchants, and the two bankers about cotton crops. In this way she made her way behind the tellers' windows in order to pull her gun on employees Frank Jamison and J. R. Howe.

Ordering the men to open the safe that was inside the bank vault, she demanded, "Dig that money out." Rebecca helped herself to two stacks of bank notes that turned out to total about a thousand dollars. Placing the money in her handbag, she asked the bankers if there would be enough air inside the vault for them to last half an hour. Locking them inside, she calmly stepped out the door to her car and quietly headed north out of town on the Austin highway. Within ten minutes the bankers had jimmied the vault lock from the inside with a screwdriver and released themselves, whereupon they telephoned alarms to law officers in all directions, giving them the automobile license number, 810–863, that locals had observed on the bandit's vehicle.

Although alert lawmen were watching the roads, Rebecca made her way into Austin. Her only problem was getting stuck on a muddy road and having to ask a farmer to pull her out. On the way back into the city she bought a box of sweets. Removing the contents, she placed the

The front of the
Farmers' National
Bank in Buda on
the afternoon after
it was robbed by
Rebecca Bradley
Rogers on
December 11, 1926.
Courtesy of San
Antonio Light
Collection, UTSA's
Institute of Texan
Cultures, image
L-0725-A.

pistol and the cash inside the box and went to Scarbrough's department store to have it wrapped. Next she headed to the main Austin
post office. "I told the man at the window it was an iron. Some women
would call the gun an iron, so you see I didn't yarn about it. I addressed
the package to the university station because I didn't want to get it
back too soon," she said. Rogers then made the mistake of taking her
car to a local garage to have the mud from the day's drive washed off.
It was there, at the corner of Fifth and Brazos streets, that an alert
Austin police officer spotted the vehicle with license number 810–863
reported from Buda. Three officers waited at the shop to arrest Rebecca
Rogers when she returned to pick up the car at 5:30 PM. Already the
evening *Austin Statesman* newspaper was carrying a headline describing the daring robbery.

Events moved quickly over the next twenty-four hours. Austin authorities turned Rogers over to Hays County sheriff George M. Allen. After the young woman gave Allen the receipt for her registered mail, he went to the main post office and retrieved the box. "I got the package about 2:30 Sunday morning. . . . It was addressed to 'Miss Rebecca Bradley, University Station,'" he reported, adding, "There was $910 in bills, a money purse and a .32 automatic in the box. The gun had a cartridge in the chamber but its magazine was gone." (Becky said that she thought that the gun was unloaded when she robbed the bank.) Allen transported the young woman to the Hays County Jail in San Marcos, where friends and family members made her bail at 6:00 AM on Sunday, December 12. That same day Otis Rogers informed the press in Amarillo that he had learned of the robbery and was leaving for Austin to assist in any way he could.

Not only had Becky robbed a bank, been arrested, spent the night in jail, and then been released on bail, but she also experienced her secret marriage being revealed to the world in newspaper print. This was only the start. During the next days her story would be read across the nation in headlines from "Girl with Pistol Robs Bank in Texas" in the *New York Times*, to "Boy Orator to Defend Bandit Wife" in the *Havre Daily News-Promoter* in Montana. In one day the Texas Flapper Bandit had become a national news phenomenon.

The wheels of justice began moving. Legal authorities first tried Rebecca Rogers for arson. In January 1927 a grand jury in Williamson

County indicted her for burning the vacant house as a diversion in her unsuccessful attempt to rob the bank in Round Rock. After several delays, the case came to trial at Georgetown in late September 1927. The jurors could not agree on conviction or acquittal, so the trial ended with no decision, and the case was continued. Next came a trial on the charge of robbery by firearm. Originally scheduled for San Marcos, it shifted to La Grange in Fayette County after the granting of a change in venue. There on December 17, 1927, a jury found Rogers guilty and sentenced her to fourteen years in the state penitentiary.

Up to this time Otis Rogers had been only an observer in the legal proceedings. After the conviction, however, he became an official member of the defense team that appealed the guilty decision to the Texas Court of Criminal Appeals in Austin. There he alone argued the

case, and as a result, on January 23, 1929, the appeals court reversed the conviction because of improper arguments by the district attorney. This meant that Rebecca would be tried again for the armed robbery of the bank. The second robbery trial began in La Grange on May 13, 1929. This time the judge stopped the proceedings, declaring that he could not secure an unbiased jury in Fayette County. He transferred the case to New Braunfels in Comal County. This third trial for Rebecca Bradley Rogers for robbery by firearms began on September 9, 1929, with twenty-seven-year-old Otis Rogers representing his wife and gaining assistance from two of his University of Texas law school class-mates, twenty-eight-year-old J. H. Schleyers and twenty-eight-year-old Leo Brewster. The press declared them the "youngest ever" defense team "to try a capital case in Texas." Arguing that Rebecca Bradley Rogers was insane at the time of the robbery, they convinced nine out of twelve jurors that she should be acquitted. Three jurors held out for conviction, so the trial ended in a hung jury. Thus Rebecca Rogers was tried four times for either arson or armed robbery. The editor of the

New Braunfels Herald observed that there "seems to be a very widespread sentiment that failure in four attempts to convict probably means a conviction can never be secured," concluding, "it would seem that justice tempered with mercy might well apply here." This is just what happened. Williamson County authorities in September 1929 quashed the arson charges, while Hays County officials dismissed robbery by firearms charges in October 1933. Rebecca Bradley Rogers was a free woman.

The news that robbery charges had been dismissed reached Otis and Rebecca Rogers the day before she bore their first child, a daughter. Even during the last of the trials, the couple had moved to Fort Worth, where Otis pursued a legal career. For years Rebecca served as his legal secretary. In time they had two more children, and the diminutive Otis gained a reputation as the "little giant" among Fort Worth attorneys who "always got in the last word." They lived and worked together until Rebecca's death in 1950 followed by his the next year.

In time most people forgot about the Flapper Bandit and the Buda bank robbery, but the memories lingered in Hays County. Sheriff George M. Allen reported that after he and Rebecca passed through Buda on the way to the county jail in San Marcos after her arrest on the day of the heist, "she burst out laughing and said, 'I have a whole lot to live down, but not as much as those men back there who let a little girl hold them up with an empty gun.'"

VISIT THE CRIME SCENE

ROBBERY OF FARMERS' NATIONAL BANK, BUDA, DECEMBER 11, 1926

The historic Farmers' National Bank, robbed by Rebecca Bradley Rogers on December 11, 1926, today houses an antique and gift shop in the 300 block of North Main Street in Buda, Texas.

To reach the crime scene most easily from Interstate 35 southbound, take exit 221 marked for Main Street in Buda and proceed south on the access road to a stoplight intersection at Main Street. From Interstate 35 northbound, take exit 220 marked for Farm to Market Road

The historic Farmers' National Bank building in Buda, Texas, robbed by Rebecca Bradley Rogers on December 11, 1926, today serves as a retail shop. Photograph by the author, 2010.

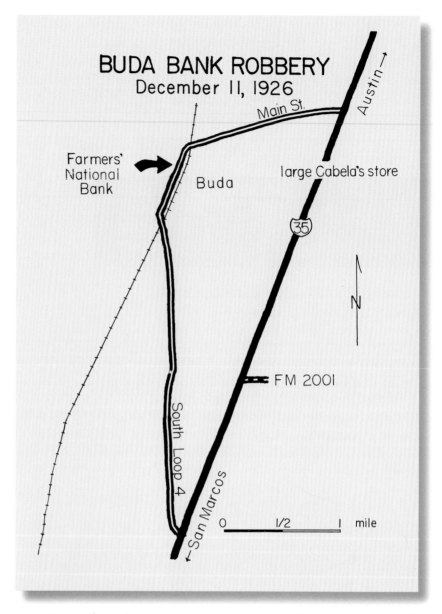

BUDA BANK ROBBERY
December 11, 1926

Main St.

Austin →

Farmers'
National
Bank

Buda

large Cabela's store

35

N

South Loop 4

FM 2001

San Marcos

0   1/2   1 mile

2001. Proceed northward on the access road to the intersection with FM 2001. After stopping at this juncture, proceed on straight northward on the access road another 0.7 mile to a stoplight intersection with Main Street. Both exits serve the large Cabela's outdoor outfitter on the outskirts of Buda. From the interstate turn west on Main Street and drive 1.6 miles generally westward on Main Street to the historic downtown commercial district, where the modest cream-colored brick building stands on the west side of North Main Street directly across from the Basil Anthony Moreau Memorial Library. The vault where Rebecca Rogers locked the two bankers now holds displays of retail merchandise in the store.

☞ JUDGE THE EVIDENCE FOR YOURSELF

Amarillo Daily News (Amarillo, Tex.), December 14, 1926, pp. 1, 9; December 15, 1926, pp. 1, 15.

Austin American (Austin, Tex.), December 13, 1926, pp. 1, 2; December 14, 1926, pp. 1, 10; December 15, 1926, pp. 1, 9; December 16, 1926, pp. 1, 10; September 28, 1927, p. 1; September 30, 1927, pp. 1, 2; December 6, 1927, p. 1; December 7, 1927, pp. 1, 2; December 8, 1927, p. 1; December 10, 1927, p. 1; December 13, 1927, p. 1; December 14, 1927, p. 1; December 15, 1927, pp. 1, 2; December 17, 1927, p. 1; October 18, 1928, pp. 1, 2; September 9, 1929, pp. 1, 2; September 12, 1929, p. 1; September 13, 1929, pp. 1, 2; September 21, 1929, p. 1.

Austin Statesman (Austin, Tex.), December 11, 1926, pp. 1, 2; December 13, 1926, pp. 1, 8; December 14, 1926, pp. 1, 2; December 15, 1926, pp. 1, 10; December 16, 1926, pp. 1, 8; September 26, 1927, pp. 1, 6; September 27, 1927, p. 1; September 30, 1927, pp. 1, 2; December 5, 1927, pp. 1, 10; December 7, 1927, pp. 1, 12; December 10, 1927, p. 1; December 12, 1927, p. 1; December 17, 1927, p. 1; October 17, 1928, p. 1; September 13, 1929, p. 1; September 16, 1929, p. 1; September 20, 1929, p. 1; September 23, 1929, p. 1.

Fort Worth Star-Telegram (Fort Worth, Tex.), August 9, 1950, p. 8; April 27, 1951, pp. 1, 8.

La Grange Journal (La Grange, Tex.), December 1, 1927, p. 7; December 15, 1927, p. 3.

New Braunfels Herald (New Braunfels, Tex.), September 13, 1929, pp. 1, 6; September 20, 1929, pp. 1, 5; September 27, 1929, p. 1.

San Antonio Express (San Antonio, Tex.), December 12, 1926, pp. 1, 2; December 13, 1926, p. 1; December 14, 1926, pp. 1, 12; December 7, 1927, pp. 1, 2; December 10, 1927, pp. 1, 2; December 11, 1927, pp. 1, 2; December 15, 1927, pp. 1, 4; December 17, 1927, pp. 1, 2; September 16, 1929, pp. 1, 2; September 21, 1929, pp. 1, 2.

San Marcos Record (San Marcos, Tex.), December 17, 1926, pp. 1, 8; January 21, 1927, p. 1; March 18, 1927, p. 1; July 15, 1927, p. 1; December 16, 1927, p. 2; December 23, 1927, sec. 2, p. 1; May 17, 1929, p. 11.

Sunday American-Statesman (Austin, Tex.), December 12, 1926, pp. 1, 2; December 19, 1926, p. 1; December 4, 1927, p. 6; December 11, 1927, p. 1; December 18, 1927, pp. 1, 4, 5; September 8, 1929, pp. 1, 8.

Williamson County Sun (Georgetown, Tex.), January 14, 1927, p. 1; March 25, 1927, p. 1; September 27, 1929, p. 1.

5 THE STANTON FRAME-UP
KILLING BLAMELESS MEN FOR A BOUNTY

On Thursday night, December 22, 1927, Walter Kelley, a farmer living about five miles west of Stanton, Texas, saw a campfire in Mustang Draw west of his house. He went out on the cold evening to investigate and found Calvin Cidney Baze, whom he had known for some time as a farmer and stock raiser in Glasscock County, south of Stanton. With him by the fire was Lee Smith, whom Baze introduced as a dairyman from Kermit. J. Hilario Nuñez, Norberto Diaz, and Victor Ramos, all Mexican farmworkers, stood around the fire trying to keep warm. Baze, who was bilingual, said they had hired the men in Odessa that evening and had brought them along to start grubbing mesquite from a field on his stock farm early the next morning. Many local people in Stanton knew Baze from his beautiful tenor voice as a gospel singer in the Church of Christ. Others were acquainted with him as a wrestler who liked to compete with the "pros" who worked with traveling circuses. A man of religious faith, thrift, and hard work, Baze had a solid reputation as a person who did everything that he could for his wife and five children.

After Kelley had returned home, the five men reluctantly left the warmth of their campfire and drove by truck into nearby Stanton. The three Mexican laborers may have felt woozy after drinking from a container of moonshine whiskey that Baze had passed around to help warm them up. As they entered town, with the Anglos in the cab of the truck and Mexicans in the back, they saw another fire, this time much larger. The First Christian Church, vacant because its congregation had disbanded in 1915, was ablaze, and for a few minutes the five men joined townspeople watching it burn. Then they got back into the vehicle and drove to a two-story brick building at the corner of St. Peter and Front streets, fronting on the Bankhead Highway just across from the Texas and Pacific Railway tracks. Victor Ramos remembered that the Anglos told the three workers to "get out of the truck and wait until we come back." It was sometime between three-thirty and five o'clock in the morning, well before daylight. The three men stumbled up onto the sidewalk at the south-facing front of the building that housed the Home National Bank.

About three minutes later the two Anglos returned, this time getting out of the truck with a .30–30 rifle and a Colt revolver. Calvin Baze yelled out, "*Vamos*," meaning "Let's go," as both men started firing the guns at the three intoxicated Mexicans. Baze later told his family that Lee Smith had ordered him, "'When I tell you to shoot, Cal, you shoot or I will.' . . . I turned, and I knew he would kill me, so I shot and killed one." By this time Baze realized that he had truly taken a man's life, and he screamed at Victor Ramos as he struck him repeatedly over the head with the revolver, "Go on, but if you return I'll kill you." Although wounded by gunshots in four places, the third man ran for his life. Then, still in the pre-dawn darkness, the two Anglos salted the remains of one of the two dead men with a cloth bag containing a two-foot fuse, a half pint of gunpowder, two chisels, two punches, and a brace with two drills—all safecracking tools—and one of them broke out a front window of the bank to make it look like there had been an attempted entry.

Why did Baze and Smith turn on their erstwhile employees two days before Christmas in 1927? The answer comes in events thirty-five miles to the west at Odessa just a month before. Early on the morning of November 25, lawmen shot and killed two men who appeared to be breaking into the Citizens National Bank building in the town. Only two weeks before, in response to an "epidemic" of bank robbery, the Texas Bankers Association had offered a five-thousand-dollar money

The south-facing walkway outside the Home National Bank in Stanton, where Lee Smith and Calvin Baze murdered two men in a frame-up attempt to secure the five-thousand-dollar-per-head "dead bank robber reward" offered by the Texas Bankers Association. Photograph by the author, 2005.

reward for every criminal killed in the process of robbing a bank that had membership in the association. If someone apprehended a bank robber alive, the capture did not qualify for the payment. The thief had to be killed in the act. Four lawmen shared equally the ten-thousand-dollar reward for killing the two Odessa bank robbers. Smith and Baze undoubtedly knew about the widely publicized shootings and hefty reward paid in the nearby town. They decided that if they could not kill bona fide bank robbers, they could frame up sham thieves to get the same reward anyway. With Nuñez and Diaz lying on the sidewalk in pools of blood and while the fire was still smoldering at the remains of the First Christian Church, the two criminals sought out Martin County sheriff V. Y. Sadler to report their shooting of "bank robbers."

For the next few hours Calvin Baze and Lee Smith were the toast of the town in Stanton. Even at the crime scene Smith boasted to night watchman Lee Richards, "I killed that _____," and then went on to say that he had used the same .30–30 Winchester the week before in "killing a coyote." Walter Kelley remembered seeing the two men at Tommie's Café about six o'clock in the morning of December 23 telling townspeople how they had foiled the bank robbery and how they hoped to spend their reward money. What the two killers did not know was that Victor Ramos had not only survived his grievous wounds but also that he had been telling the truth about what happened. The tables were about to turn.

After escaping from Baze and Smith, Victor Ramos ran blindly and encountered night watchman Lee Richards, who rendered first aid to his multiple wounds. Richards proceeded to the crime scene and then contacted Sheriff Sadler, next to arrive at the location of the bloody events. It is unclear whether the two killers had yet seen the sheriff. Once Sadler spoke with Victor Ramos and learned his side of the story, he concluded that he had a double murder rather than an attempted bank robbery on his hands, and he placed all three men—Baze, Smith, and Ramos—in the Martin County Jail for safekeeping. The sheriff contacted Justice of the Peace Jeff Watson to perform an inquest at the crime scene, which the judge completed that afternoon, pronouncing both Nuñez and Diaz killed by gunshots from Baze and Smith. The bodies of the two victims were transferred to the Reverend X. Gagnon, pastor of St. Joseph's Catholic Church, who conducted a brief ritual and buried them in the parish cemetery. Because "feeling was running high in Stanton" over the fire at the First Christian Church, which townspeople thought Baze and Smith had started, Sheriff Yates sent his prisoners to more secure jails for their own protection: Baze to Midland, Smith to Big Spring, and Ramos "to be held as a witness" back in Odessa. Baze and Smith were charged with murder.

On May 28, 1928, with Victor Ramos as a witness, a grand jury in Stanton formally indicted Lee Smith and Calvin Baze for the murder of J. Hilario Nuñez and Norberto Diaz. Legal proceedings began for the prosecution of the two killers. Calvin Baze's family employed Abilene attorney James P. Stinson to defend him in court, deeding 420 acres from their 580-acre stock farm to pay his fees. Then on the evening of Sunday, March 18, 1928, Calvin Baze and two other inmates of the Midland County Jail overpowered Deputy Sheriff D. E. Covington as he was handing them sandwiches. They forced him at gunpoint to release them and then accompany them by automobile to a point two miles north of town, where they left him bound and gagged. Years later Baze family members revealed that they had paid three thousand dollars for the Abilene lawyers to arrange Baze's escape and "make it look like a jail break." The fugitives made good their departure, though officers apprehended two of them north of Pyote, Texas, three days later. Calvin Baze, however, was never seen again by anyone who knew him from Stanton. His family never heard from him again. He seemed to have vanished into thin air.

Legal proceedings moved forward in the case of *State of Texas vs. Lee Smith*. Two trials eventually took place, the first in Abilene between April 30 and May 3, ending in the jury being divided, ten for conviction and two for acquittal. The proceedings then shifted from Abilene to nearby Baird, where on June 11–13, 1928, a second jury found Smith guilty of murder and sentenced him to life in the state penitentiary. Smith's attorneys filed an appeal, but on January 30, 1929, the Texas Court of Criminal Appeals reaffirmed the conviction. Lee Smith stayed in the penitentiary.

Years passed and no one heard anything more about fugitive Calvin Baze. Stanton residents gradually forgot about the heinous crime that took place in front of the Home National Bank. The building eventually became a hotel and then served other purposes. Then in July 1984 Martin County sheriff Dan Saunders, who was only two years old when the 1927 killings took place, received an unexpected telephone call.

Sheriff Saunders's caller from Oregon identified himself as Mallie Calvin. The lawman had known a Baze boy named Mallie, which is anything but a common name, and his father's given name was Calvin. The caller explained to Saunders that his father was named Baze Calvin and that the old man had told a story on his deathbed in 1966 that the son wanted to ask about. He proceeded to recount this story: "He told us that he got in trouble. That he had killed a Mexican. He was a deputy sheriff delivering a prisoner to Brown County, and two men jumped him, and he killed one . . . and . . . the sheriff told him he had better leave Texas."

At this point Sheriff Saunders interrupted the caller with three questions.

"Did your daddy like to sing?" he asked.

Mallie answered, "Yes, he loved to lead the church singing and loved religious songs."

"Was he athletic?" the lawman next queried.

"Yes, very much so," Mallie responded, adding, "even up until he got sick and was on his death-bed he loved to wrestle."

Saunders next asked the third question—the clincher: "Could he speak Spanish?"

"Yes," the son replied, "like a Mexican."

Then Dan Saunders knew it was time to explain: "Mallie, your father's name was Calvin Baze and yes, he did kill two people . . . and he went off and left his wife with five kids here and has never been seen by them since." Silence followed, and then more conversation.

For the first time the story of the fugitive's escape from Texas became known. Calvin Cidney Baze in 1928 assumed a new name, James Sidney Calvin, and made his way from Midland to the West Coast. There he farmed ninety acres in Washington State and for a time worked as a deputy sheriff. The killer remarried and had five children, giving them the same names as the offspring he had abandoned in Texas. One of these was Mallie Calvin, the man who made the phone call to Texas in 1984.

Through Sheriff Saunders, Mallie made contact by telephone with his half brothers and half sisters in Texas. From them he learned that after giving most of their stock farm to attorneys to pay for the legal defense of their father, the family barely made any living. "We went hungry nearly," explained daughter Mary Baze Herring of Midland. "We farmed. We borrowed from the bank to live on, and raised hogs, chickens, and cows . . . Oh, how the family suffered. Everybody, including myself, presumed he was dead." Because Baze had never communicated with his Texas family, he could not have learned that in 1961 papers were filed in Martin County to dismiss the charges against him due to insufficient evidence. He was a free man but never knew it.

Mallie Calvin and his brothers and sisters from the Pacific Northwest then planned a first-ever reunion with their half brothers and half sisters in West Texas. They gathered in Sheriff Saunders's office in Stanton, and, as the law officer remembered, "What a meeting it was. You didn't have any trouble telling they were half brothers and half sisters."

Reflecting on this unexpected solution to an almost forgotten murder case, Dan Saunders observed, "I was often thankful that I knew Martin County history when the son from Oregon called."

MURDER OF J. HILARIO NUÑEZ AND NORBERTO DIAZ, SOUTH FRONT OF FORMER HOME NATIONAL BANK, 106 NORTH FRONT STREET (BUSINESS INTERSTATE 20), STANTON, DECEMBER 23, 1927

Lee Smith and Calvin Baze murdered J. Hilario Nuñez and Norberto Diaz and assaulted Victor Ramos outside a two-story brick commercial building that housed the Home National Bank in Stanton, Texas. The location fronted onto the Bankhead Highway (an overland roadway that connected Washington, D.C., with San Diego), which paralleled the Texas and Pacific Railway adjacent to the business district in the town. Though it has had multiple uses over the years, the handsome brick structure remains intact to this day.

To reach the crime scene, leave Interstate 20 either east- or west-bound to take Business Interstate 20 through the town of Stanton. At

The brick building that housed the Home National Bank in Stanton, location of the murders in the 1927 Stanton Frame-up. Photograph by the author, 2005.

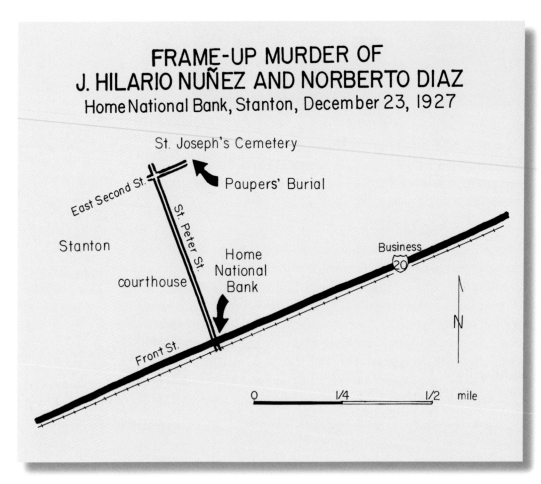

FRAME-UP MURDER OF
J. HILARIO NUÑEZ AND NORBERTO DIAZ
Home National Bank, Stanton, December 23, 1927

St. Joseph's Cemetery

Paupers' Burial

East Second St.

St. Peter St.

Stanton

Business 20

Home National Bank

courthouse

Front St.

N

0   1/4   1/2   mile

the south side of the business district, turn north from Business Interstate 20 (North Front Street) onto St. Peter Street, where the distinctive-looking former bank building stands at the right side of the intersection. Free street-side parking is readily available. The shootings took place on the sidewalk at the south side of the structure.

BURIALS OF J. HILARIO NUÑEZ AND NORBERTO DIAZ, ST. JOSEPH'S CEMETERY, ENTRANCE AT 200 BLOCK OF EAST SECOND STREET, STANTON, DECEMBER 23, 1927

After he completed the legal inquests into their deaths, Justice of the Peace Jeff Watson turned the bodies of J. Hilario Nuñez and Norberto Diaz over to Father X. Gagnon of St. Joseph's Catholic Church. The priest conducted a brief funeral service and supervised the burial of the two men in St. Joseph's Cemetery.

To visit the graveyard, from the Home National Bank building at 106 North Front Street (Business Interstate 20), drive seven blocks north

St. Joseph's Cemetery in Stanton, where the bodies of J. Hilario Nuñez and Norberto Diaz were buried following the murder of the two men on December 23, 1927. Photograph by the author, 2005.

on St. Peter Street to its intersection with East Second Street. Turn east (right) on East Second and drive two blocks into the entrance of the burial ground. The unmarked graves of Nuñez and Diaz lie in the paupers' section at the extreme north end of the cemetery. The graveyard is open daylight hours and offers free parking.

☞ JUDGE THE EVIDENCE FOR YOURSELF

Abbott, Ramsey. "Crime and Law Enforcement in Martin County: Three Bank Robberies." *Permian Historical Annual* (Odessa, Tex.) 27 (1987): 73–86.

Abilene Daily Reporter (Abilene, Tex.), December 23, 1927, pp. 1, 11; January 5, 1928, p. 1; March 19, 1928, p. 1; March 20, 1928, p. 1; March 21, 1928, p. 1; March 26, 1928, p. 1; March 29, 1928, p. 1; April 4, 1928, p. 1; April 10, 1928, p. 1; April 11, 1928, p. 1; April 12, 1928,

p. 2; April 17, 1928, p. 9; April 30, 1928, pp. 1, 3; May 1, 1928, pp. 1, 3; May 2, 1928, pp. 1, 8; May 3, 1928, p. 1; May 4, 1928, p. 1; June 11, 1928, p. 1; June 12, 1928, p. 1; June 13, 1928, p. 1; June 14, 1928, p. 1; January 30, 1929, p. 1.

Abilene Morning News (Abilene, Tex.), December 24, 1927, p. 1.

Abilene Morning Reporter-News (Abilene, Tex.), December 25, 1927, p. 1; January 8, 1928, sec. 2, p. 6; March 25, 1928, p. 1; June 10, 1928, sec. 1, p. 1; January 31, 1929, p. 1.

Big Spring Herald (Big Spring, Tex.), December 30, 1927, sec. 1, p. 1; February 17, 1928, sec. 1, p. 1; April 20, 1928, sec. 1, p. 1; sec. 2, [p. 9]; April 13, 1928, sec. 1, p. 1; May 11, 1928, sec. 1, [p. 3].

Dallas Morning News (Dallas, Tex.), December 24, 1927, p. 1; January 5, 1928, p. 10; February 8, 1928, p. 2; February 11, 1928, pp. 1, 12; February 14, 1928, p. 1; March 20, 1928, p. 1; April 4, 1928, p. 4; April 30, 1928, p. 5; May 1, 1928, p. 7; May 2, 1928, p. 24; May 3, 1928, p. 2; May 4, 1928, p. 1; June 14, 1928, p. 1; January 31, 1929, pp. 1, 8; June 11, 1961, sec. 3, p. 2.

Fort Worth Star-Telegram (Fort Worth, Tex.), December 24, 1927, evening ed., p. 2; March 19, 1928, evening ed., pp. 1, 4; March 21, 1928, evening ed., p. 1.

Martin County, Tex. District Court Case Records. Cause no. 212. Office of District and County Clerk, Martin County Courthouse, Stanton, Tex.

———. Justice of the Peace Inquest Records, vol. 1/2, pp. 16–19. Office of District and County Clerk, Martin County Courthouse, Stanton, Tex.

Midland Reporter and Gazette Examiner (Midland, Tex.), December 27, 1927, p. 1.

Midland Reporter-Telegram (Midland, Tex.), November 16, 1986, sec. 3, pp. 1, 2.

Odessa News (Odessa, Tex.), December 28, 1927, pp. 1, 6.

Saunders, Dan. *Trails and Trials of a Small Town Sheriff.* Lubbock, Tex.: Cotten Publishing, 1996.

6 THE SANTA CLAUS BANK ROBBERY

Alex Spears, cashier at the First National Bank in Cisco, Texas, was sitting at his desk visiting with local grocer Oscar Cliett and a friend, Marion Olson, who had just come home for the Christmas holidays from Harvard University. It was just before lunch on a Friday two days before Christmas in 1927. The three friends looked up to see a man in a St. Nicholas costume approaching them. "Hello, Santa," Spears greeted him, though he got no response. "Hello there, Santa Claus," he repeated, to which the white-bearded figure muttered, "Hello." He seemed annoyed that several children had followed him inside and wanted to speak. "About that time another man appeared, this one with a gun in his hand," Olson reported, "and commanded us to 'stick 'em up.'" These were the first actions in what became known in the annals of Texas as the Santa Claus Bank Robbery. The chain of events, however, began several weeks earlier in Wichita Falls.

The boardinghouse of Mrs. Josephine Herron in that North Texas city provided a haven for a number of punks and thugs living on the edge of the law, among them Marshall Ratliff, Henry Helms, and Robert Hill. Ratliff and others in 1926 had robbed the bank at Valera, Texas; Helms headed a gang of toughs who were involved in automobile theft, burglary, and narcotics; and Hill, an orphan who had grown up in the state reformatory, had recently been released from prison for stealing clothes from a tailor shop. In the first part of December 1927, Ratliff conceived the idea of robbing the national bank in Cisco, a town where he had spent some time because his mother had operated a café there. Counting Helms and Hill in for the planned heist, Ratliff wanted one more stick-up man. The trio recruited Helms's brother-in-law, Louis E. Davis, whose sister lived on an oil lease just a few miles northwest of Cisco. They decided that the bank would be full of money on December 23, the Friday before Christmas, so they started making plans to make a withdrawal at gunpoint. For his part Robert Hill stole a blue Buick sedan from the Wichita Falls residence of E. C. Long and hid it in preparation for the heist. Marshall Ratliff feared that someone in Cisco might recognize him, so when he saw Mrs. Herron sewing a red calico and cotton Santa Claus costume for use on Christmas, he insisted that she

Avenue D, now Conrad Hilton Avenue, the main commercial street of Cisco, Texas, as it appeared about the time of the December 23, 1927, robbery of the First National Bank. Courtesy of Fort Worth Star-Telegram *Collection, Special Collections, the University of Texas at Arlington Libraries, image FWST 1112 #13 3/1/1940.*

give it to him instead. On Thursday, December 22, he gave his landlady money to buy several tins of corned beef, some pork and beans, and other groceries. With that food they set out southward in the stolen sedan that afternoon. Late that night the party camped in a tent outside a two-room house on the Lash Oil Lease near Moran where Louis Davis's sister lived with her husband, Sam Fox. This overnight stop put them within easy striking distance of their destination.

The four men got up early the next morning and headed into Cisco, an Eastland County town of about six thousand people that had prospered from the discovery of oil in its vicinity between 1919 and 1921.

Marshall Ratliff drove into town and then cruised some of its streets to familiarize his companions with its general layout. Just before noon he stopped at the side of a street, left the car, and, wearing the Santa Claus outfit with a bearded mask, in the company of Louis Davis he started walking down the sidewalk toward the First National Bank. Henry Helms took the wheel and with Robert Hill drove to the bank. He parked the blue Buick, blocking the alley at its side, and the two men sauntered toward the bank entrance on Avenue D (today Conrad Hilton Avenue). All four robbers, unmasked with the exception of Ratliff, made their way inside the busy lobby. Several children trailed behind Ratliff, each one attempting to tell a disinterested Santa what he or she wanted for Christmas. The bandits apparently had not anticipated that a man wearing a St. Nicholas suit would attract such a following.

Once the four criminals had entered the bank and Marshall Ratliff in his costume had greeted Alex Spears and his friends, customers and employees heard men call out, "Stick 'em up!" While two of the gang members tried to corral the customers and employees, Mrs. B. P. Blasingame rushed her six-year-old daughter, Frances, toward the rear of the bank. Seeing the bandits' revolvers, "I was afraid they would start shooting and I wanted to get out of there as quick as I could," the mother said. In the confusion she and Frances opened a door into a back work area, passed two bookkeeping employees, and then exited into the alley by a side door. Turning left and rushing past the parked Buick, they ran diagonally across a vacant lot to the 1915 city hall building half a block away. There they alerted several police officers, including Chief G. E. "Bit" Bedford.

In the meantime back at the bank, Henry Helms took charge of the assistant cashier, Jewel Poe, while Marshall Ratliff headed for the vault by way of the rear bookkeeping room. He was the one who put twelve thousand dollars in cash plus paper securities into a jute potato sack. "Marshall . . . scooped up the dough," robber Robert Hill later stated. By this time law officers had run to the bank from city hall, joined by armed townspeople. Many of the locals were eager to take shots at the bank robbers in hopes of receiving the widely publicized five-thousand-dollar reward that the Texas Bankers Association had offered for anyone who killed a thief in the act of robbing a bank. No one knows who fired the first shots, though bandit Louis E. Davis reported that he stepped into the alley to shoot into the air to frighten away spectators. He immediately suffered gunshots in the side, back, and both arms. The bandits then began hustling terrified hostages toward the same exit. About this time the Reverend Thomas Lennox, pastor of the First Christian Church, observed, "Chief Bedford was at the east end of

The First National Bank in Cisco, Texas, the way that it appeared when it was robbed on December 23, 1927. Courtesy of Fort Worth Star-Telegram Collection, Special Collections, the University of Texas at Arlington Libraries, image FWST 1112 #2 3/1/1940.

Employees of the First National Bank in Cisco at the time of the Santa Claus Bank Robbery on December 23, 1927. From left to right: E. Jewel Poe, Vance Littleton, Freda Stroebel, George P. Fee, and Ethel McCann. Courtesy of Fort Worth Star-Telegram Collection, Special Collections, the University of Texas at Arlington Libraries, image FWST 1112 #5 3/1/1940.

The Cisco City Hall to which Mrs. B. P. Blasingame and her daughter carried news that the First National Bank was being robbed on December 23, 1927. Today the 1915 building houses the Lela Latch Lloyd Memorial Museum. Courtesy of Fort Worth Star-Telegram Collection, Special Collections, the University of Texas at Arlington Libraries, image FWST 1112 #8 3/1/1940.

the alley and he said, 'They're robbing the bank, get men and guns and block the street.'" The minister then saw the fifty-nine-year-old officer, shotgun in hand, being struck by gunfire. Another to fall was fifty-five-year-old police officer George W. Carmichael. Cisco postmaster J. W. Triplett heard the gunfire, ran into his office for his service pistol, and reached the alley in time to hear an officer call out, "Get back, they're bringing them all out."

At gunpoint the bandits hustled Harvard student Marion Olson and two little girls, ten-year-old Emma May Robinson and twelve-year-old Laverne Comer, toward the waiting Buick, using them as human shields. They forced all three into the car, though the wounded Olson managed to escape. Laverne Comer tried to run as well, but, as she reported, "Santa Claus jerked me by my wrist into the car." Once inside the children alternately lay on the floor and sat in the laps of bandits as bullets were flying. Postal clerk Will Coldwell had joined a crowd of townspeople who were exchanging shots with the thieves. He later said that as Robert Hill drove the Buick eastward out of the alley, "I fired

Woodrow Wilson Harris, the fourteen-year-old whose presence of mind prevented the theft of his family's Oldsmobile by the robbers of the Cisco First National Bank on December 23, 1927. Courtesy of Fort Worth Star-Telegram Collection, Special Collections, the University of Texas at Arlington Libraries, image FWST 1112 #6 3/1/1940.

five times, once at the gas tank and four times at the left rear tire." The sedan with at least one shot-out tire turned right onto Avenue D and headed south. As quickly as they could, locals piled into their cars in chase.

Robert Hill drove the crowded and partially disabled Buick out of downtown Cisco as fast as he could manage, and then he realized that the fuel tank was almost empty. They had added no gasoline since leaving Wichita Falls. After seven blocks, as the bandits approached the intersection with Fourteenth Street, they spotted possible salvation in the form of another vehicle. Fourteen-year-old Woodrow Wilson Harris of Rising Star, Texas, was driving his parents and grandmother into town in their old Oldsmobile sedan. Stopping the getaway car in front of the J. R. Burnett house at 1505 Avenue D, three of the bandits ran to the Harris car and demanded it. They had to assist eighty-year-old Mrs. S. E. Graves out before they could help badly wounded Louis Davis inside, Marshall Ratliff tossing the potato sack full of money and paper securities into the back seat. Then they discovered that teenaged Harris had taken the ignition key when he said, "Wait until I throw it out of gear." He and his family had already escaped out of sight. The bandits could not start the car, and by now a posse of townspeople in cars was approaching. Lester Hooker darted out of one of the vehicles and from behind the partial protection of a utility pole started shooting at the bandits with a high-powered rifle. Bullets landing all around them, the thieves left mortally injured Louis Davis in the Oldsmobile, piled back into their blue Dodge with Helms at the wheel, and continued south out of town. Robert Hill, wounded in the arm by one of Hooker's shots, from the back seat threw out big-headed roofing nails to puncture the tires of pursuers.

The bandits turned east on Twenty-fifth Street, at the southern edge of Cisco, and headed into the countryside. Passing Robert Quincy Lee's model diversified farm, they continued on and turned south onto a rocky road into a brushy pasture on the John Stubblefield farm about four miles from downtown. There the Buick stalled, with most of its tires flat, windows shot out, multiple bullet holes in the body, and the two little girls hunkered down in the back seat. Laverne Comer remembered Santa Claus asking his companions, "Where's the money?" to which one

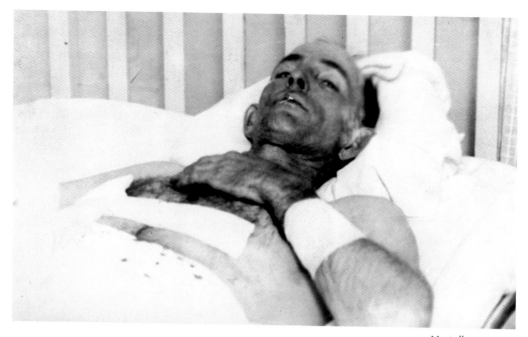

responded, "In the other car." The bandits had left the gunnysack full of loot in the Harris Oldsmobile on Avenue D. Their robbery had been for naught.

Two of the three remaining bandits carried wounds as they headed on foot into the brushy pasture, with the posse arriving just on their heels. The lawmen and townsfolk found the two girls unhurt inside the Buick, together with the abandoned Santa Claus costume. Sometimes leaving a trail of blood, the escaping robbers wandered through the pasture. After trudging about two miles, they left behind on the Irvin Finley farm a bloody overcoat, used bandages, and a small suitcase filled with first-aid supplies and tins of food, the last of what Josephine Herron had bought. Despite their physical condition, the three men made good their escape.

Having eluded the posse, Ratliff, Helms, and Hill gradually made their way undetected through the rangeland to a location south of town. Leaving badly injured Marshall Ratliff behind, Helms and Hill returned to Cisco in the early morning hours of Christmas Eve, Saturday, December 24. Prowling through the streets in darkness, they found a Ford Model T touring car parked in front of the home of Humble Pipeline Company employee Eugene S. Bell at 608 West Seventh Street. Since many of the Ford cars of this era all used the same basic ignition key, they had no trouble starting the car and driving back to pick up Ratliff. From there they then headed to the mesquite-covered ranching country west of Cisco. A cold front had blown in and they shivered in their open touring car, afraid that a campfire would give away their location.

In the early hours of Christmas morning Henry Helms, as the least wounded fugitive, drove the car with his partners to his sister-in-law's place between Putnam and Moran, where the party had camped before the robbery. Seeking relief from the cold, they entered the Sam Fox house, where they dressed Ratliff's and Hill's gunshot wounds. When Helms asked Ratliff whether he wanted a bullet cut out, the ringleader replied, "No, I have stood it this long and I will stand it now to the end." Mrs. Fox brewed coffee for the bandits and gave them a packet of chicken, dressing, and cake that she had prepared for her family's Christmas dinner. The fugitives then departed, heading into the rangeland to spend the remainder of the night.

After spending Christmas Day hiding out in the brushy pastures, about midnight the criminals drove to the isolated ranch home of R. C. Wylie north of Putnam. Saying that they had been in an accident, they requested a ride for medical help. Wylie replied, "My son, Carl, is away, but will return soon. He has the car." When the twenty-two-year-old came home from a Christmas party about two-thirty on the morning of Monday, December 26, the bandits forced themselves inside his vehicle at gunpoint and ordered him to begin driving. They had to take frequent detours to dodge approaching vehicles, stopping several times to try to siphon gasoline from cars parked at houses. When daylight beckoned, the fugitives sought cover in a place that Wylie believed to be the Brooks pasture, three miles from the Pueblo community in Callahan County, still generally west of Cisco. The group had only two oranges to eat, so the three fugitives consumed them, sharing nothing with their kidnapped driver. The bandits had a shotgun, a rifle, and about a dozen pistols, but no money and no food. Wylie remembered, "We stayed in a pasture . . . and nearly froze."

After twenty-four hours with young Carl Wylie as a driver, the robbers decided that lawmen surely had learned the description of the Dodge automobile in which they had abducted him. It was time to get different transportation. Being really confused about where they were, in the wee morning hours of Tuesday morning, December 27, the bandits had Wylie drive back into the outskirts of Cisco, which they mistakenly thought was Breckenridge. Leaving his two wounded compatriots with hostage Wylie, Henry Helms again walked the streets of the town looking for a likely car to steal. After trying several vehicles, he successfully started a 1924 Ford Model T roadster parked at 409 West Thirteenth Street, where barber Cecil Hibbert and his wife rented rooms. Helms returned to his companions, and they released Wylie in his car. Carl reached the Cisco city hall about five o'clock that morning to report his kidnapping and tell what he knew about the fugitives. Soon fresh telephone messages went out to alert officers in several counties.

The three men, crowded into the single-seated open roadster, headed north across Stephens and into Young County. Even though they had no money, at Eliasville they managed to get two loaves of bread from a storekeeper. The criminals continued on, hoping to cross the Brazos at the South Bend community. There law officers had barricaded the road from the south by the time that the robbers approached. The fugitives pulled up to a filling station, and then as Robert Hill reported, "We didn't see the officers until we got right at South Bend about a block from them." The bandits turned around and headed back south out of town, but one wheel on the car had lost its tire completely and they were running just on its rim. They could make only about twenty miles an hour. As Helms wrestled with the steering wheel to manage the Ford, Ratliff fired backward at the pursuing officers and Hill loaded the guns. At the county line Helms turned east from the main highway onto a county road in the direction of Oil City. The going was rough, and quickly the bandits abandoned their vehicle in hopes of seeking shelter in the brush around some nearby oil wells. The gunfire continued, with officers' rounds striking both Helms and Ratliff. A new wound in the thigh grounded the latter, whom officers arrested while Helms and Hill escaped once more. Hill recalled, "We run down [to] the Brazos River and got under a rock finally, and we stayed there all day." With Helms growing delirious with fever from his multiple gunshots, the two men evaded a manhunt involving about 150 lawmen and volunteers for two more days. Texas Rangers Manuel T. "Lone Wolf" Gonzaullas and Tom Hickman even used a federal government airplane fitted with machine guns to try to spot Helms and Hill from the air as they hid out in the rugged, wooded Brazos River breaks.

Hunger and Helms's fever finally drove the two men into Graham, the seat of Young County, about sixty miles north of Cisco. On the night of Thursday, December 29, Hill and Helms made their way into Graham, stumbling part of the way. Trying to find a friend staying at a place they thought was called the "Texan Rooms," they approached the residence of Mrs. Dee H. Harkey to ask its location, but the startled woman said she knew of no such place. They then ducked into a barn for the night. About breakfast time on Friday, December 30, they found the desired lodging, the Texan Hotel, and went inside to ask for a Mr. Fields. The clerk responded that there was no one registered by that name. He observed that one of the two men in soiled clothes was wearing a cartridge belt, so as soon as they left he called the sheriff's department.

Soon officers in automobiles began cruising streets in the neighborhood looking for two suspicious men. "As soon as we saw them we knew they were the bandits from the way they carried their wounded

The four lawmen who apprehended Robert Hill and Henry Helms in the 500 block of Fifth Street in Graham, Texas, on December 30, 1927. From left to right: E. Gentry Williamson, deputy sheriff of Young County; Walter Sikes, Amarillo real estate broker and former resident of Cisco; Elmer H. Little, deputy sheriff of Comanche County; and Jim Davis, city marshal of Graham. Courtesy of Fort Worth Star-Telegram Collection, Special Collections, the University of Texas at Arlington Libraries, image FWST 1112 #9 3/1/1940.

arms," said Comanche County deputy sheriff Elmer H. Little, one of the officers who arrested the last two Santa Claus bandits. Helms offered no resistance and even had to lean against a picket fence, but Hill made a teetering effort to run. "I figured we were going to be killed anyhow, on account of the bank reward, and I figured it was just as well to get killed running as with our hands up," he told the arresting officers. It was only a few days before the last two robbers joined Marshall Ratliff in the county jail in Eastland, the county seat just ten miles east of Cisco.

Lawmen and townspeople with Cisco bank robbers Robert Hill and Henry Helms outside the Young County Jail in Graham, Texas. Robert Hill is the man at the center of the front row wearing a dark jacket and hat with his left arm tucked inside the coat. Henry Helms stands to his left, looking toward the ground and wearing a long, heavy, unbuttoned overcoat. Courtesy of Fort Worth Star-Telegram *Collection, Special Collections, the University of Texas at Arlington Libraries, image FWST 1112 #7 3/1/1940.*

Trials took place in 1928 and 1929. All three of the surviving bandits were convicted in Eastland County for robbery with firearms. Henry Helms received a death penalty, while Marshall Ratliff and Robert Hill received ninety-nine-year terms. In subsequent trials juries found Marshall Ratliff guilty of the murders of Chief G. E. "Bit" Bedford and police officer George W. Carmichael, with sentences of death and ninety-nine years, respectively. When Henry Helms received his death penalty, he gamely remarked, "They poured it on me." He went to the electric chair at the state prison in Huntsville just after midnight on the morning of September 6, 1929. Since no family members claimed his remains, his body was buried on Peckerwood Hill, the cemetery for penitentiary inmates.

On October 23, 1929, in a final effort to save her son from the electric chair, Marshall Ratliff's mother filed an affidavit alleging that he had become insane since conviction and should not be executed. Two days later an Eastland judge issued a bench warrant to bring the defendant to Eastland from the state prison to be tried for the theft of the Harris Oldsmobile the day of the bank robbery. Huntsville and Eastland courts contended over which had jurisdiction, but other events decided the issue.

About eight-thirty on the evening of Monday, November 18, 1929, Marshall Ratliff attempted to escape from the Eastland County Jail. In the effort he shot and mortally wounded fifty-six-year-old Deputy Sheriff Thomas A. Jones. Jailer E. P. "Pack" Kilbourn recalled, "Both Jones and I had become convinced that Ratliff was blind, paralyzed[,] and crazy. We had put him through every sort of test, and he fooled us completely." Thinking he was mentally and physically incapacitated, the two guards left the door to Ratliff's second-floor cell open while they carried food to prisoners elsewhere on the floor. Seeing his opportunity, the bank bandit, as quick as a cat, stepped down the stairs to the office and tried all the doors, which were locked with keys. He then took a loaded pistol from the desk drawer and re-ascended the stairs, shooting Jones at point-blank range and ordering Kilbourn, "Give me them keys!" Ratliff kept firing, but Kilbourn threw himself down the stairs at the bandit, knocking both of them to the office floor, where he wrested the gun from the inmate. With assistance from others who came after hearing the gunshots, they returned Ratliff to his cell, where he again assumed the behavior of a docile madman.

Eastland County residents already resented the fact that Marshall Ratliff, the mastermind of the Santa Claus Bank Robbery, had managed to avoid the electric chair. After he had feigned insanity and then shot the popular deputy sheriff, resentment boiled over into anger. A night after Ratliff's abortive escape attempt, a crowd began building outside the county jail, just a block north of the courthouse in Eastland. In time an estimated one thousand men, women, and children gathered, some of them arguing with jailer "Pack" Kilbourn, the very man who had prevented the escape the night before. About nine o'clock a group of men started arguing with Kilbourn over Ratliff's fate, calling out, "Don't give him a chance to kill another good man!" and "We have waited long enough!" Several of them forced their way into the ground-floor office, took away Kilbourn's keys, and went upstairs to remove Ratliff from his cell. They roughly hauled him downstairs and outside to the waiting crowd.

The mob carried Ratliff, who had been stripped of his clothes, to a vacant lot at the southeast corner of West White and North Mulberry streets, diagonally across the street from the jail and behind a three-story commercial building and the Connellee motion picture theater.

From a telephone pole cable, the mob strung up Ratliff by the neck on a new grass rope. It broke, and men had to run for another before they successfully hanged him. The body dangled there for twenty minutes, illuminated by the headlamps of automobiles, with spectators reaching up to grab Ratliff's feet to turn him into the lights. A group of men hauled down the body and carried it two blocks to Barrow Furniture Company, the local casket maker and mortuary. After a mortician embalmed the remains, they were exhibited in the retail sales area of the store in order to accommodate the large number of people with a morbid wish to view the body. On the evening of November 20, the remains were transported to Fort Worth, Texas.

The modest memorial service for Marshall Ratliff took place at Shannon's Funeral Chapel on North Main Street in Fort Worth. As the doors were opened to the chapel for friends, family members, and curiosity seekers to seat themselves, a band unexpectedly marched past the front of the funeral home. The date was November 24, 1929, just after Thanksgiving, and a department store had sponsored the Christmas parade. Right behind the musicians strode a make-believe bearded Santa Claus in full red and white costume, waving to spectators along the street.

VISIT THE CRIME SCENES

ROBBERY OF FIRST NATIONAL BANK, 710 CONRAD HILTON AVENUE (U.S. HIGHWAY 183), CISCO, DECEMBER 23, 1927

Though substantially remodeled, the building that housed the First National Bank of Cisco still stands and until recent times accommodated Dixon's Auto Supply. In the 1960s the bank modernized its appearance and added a drive-up window in the opening in the masonry wall that

The First National Bank building in Cisco, Texas, as it appears today after a mid-twentieth-century remodeling as a modern bank and then subsequent adaptation as an automobile parts store. Photograph by the author, 2010.

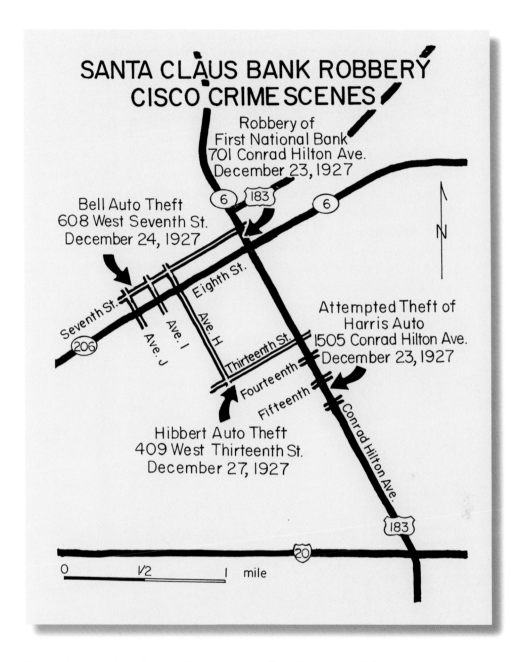

SANTA CLAUS BANK ROBBERY
CISCO CRIME SCENES

Robbery of
First National Bank
701 Conrad Hilton Ave.
December 23, 1927

Bell Auto Theft
608 West Seventh St.
December 24, 1927

Attempted Theft of
Harris Auto
1505 Conrad Hilton Ave.
December 23, 1927

Hibbert Auto Theft
409 West Thirteenth St.
December 27, 1927

N

Seventh St.
Eighth St.
Ave. I
Ave. J
Ave. H
Thirteenth St.
Fourteenth
Fifteenth
Conrad Hilton Ave.

206
6
183
6
183
20

0   1/2   1   mile

formerly served as the exit door into the alley, the scene of the heaviest gunfire during the 1927 robbery. Today the alley itself is little changed from its 1920s appearance.

To reach the crime scene, turn northwest from Interstate 20 onto U.S. Highway 183, now Conrad Hilton Avenue, and drive 1.0 mile to its intersection with Texas Highway 6/206. Proceed half a block farther northwest on U.S. Highway 183 to the former First National Bank building on the southwest (left) side of the street alongside the alley at the center of the block.

ATTEMPTED THEFT OF HARRIS FAMILY OLDSMOBILE, 1505 CONRAD HILTON AVENUE (U.S. HIGHWAY 183), CISCO, DECEMBER 23, 1927

The bandits tried to commandeer the Harris family's Oldsmobile sedan in front of J. R. Burnett's house at 1505 Avenue D, today Conrad Hilton Avenue. The house stood on the northeast side of the street about the middle of the block flanked by Fifteenth and Sixteenth streets. Marked by surviving concrete steps at street side, the lot today serves as a side yard for a two-story, gray-painted historic residence at 1507 Conrad Hilton Avenue.

To reach the crime scene, from Interstate 20 drive northwest on U.S. Highway 183, Conrad Hilton Avenue, eight blocks to the site midway between Fifteenth and Sixteenth streets. Alternatively, from Texas Highway 6/206 drive southeast on U.S. Highway 183, Conrad Hilton Avenue, eight blocks to the site, midway between Fifteenth and Sixteenth streets.

Site of the former J. R. Burnett residence, 1505 Conrad Hilton Avenue, Cisco, Texas, in front of which the Santa Claus bank bandits attempted to steal the Harris family Oldsmobile following the robbery on December 23, 1927. Photograph by the author, 2010.

THEFT OF EUGENE S. BELL'S FORD MODEL T TOURING CAR, 608 WEST SEVENTH STREET, CISCO, DECEMBER 24, 1927

Having spent their first night on the run following the robbery, Henry Helms, Robert Hill, and Marshall Ratliff desperately needed another getaway car. Leaving gunshot-disabled Ratliff hiding in the brush south of Cisco, Helms and Hill walked back into town under cover of darkness and in the early hours of Christmas Eve stole a convertible Model T touring car at the home of pipeline company clerk Eugene S. Bell at 608 West Seventh Street. The theft took place only half a dozen blocks away from the scene of the bungled bank heist. With daylight coming, the criminals drove out of town, picked up Ratliff, and set off for the brushy range country west of Cisco to hide from posse members. Days passed before Bell discovered what had happened to his vehicle.

To reach the crime scene drive six blocks southwest on West Eighth Street (Texas Highway 206) from Conrad Hilton Avenue (U.S. Highway 183) to its intersection with Avenue J. Turn northwest (right) on Avenue J and drive one block to its juncture with West Seventh Street. Turn northeast (right) on West Seventh Street and drive one-half block to the crime scene at the middle of the block on the northwest (left) side of the street. The white-painted wood frame bungalow with a porch across the front is the home where Eugene S. Bell resided and where the fugitives stole his car.

The former home of Eugene S. Bell at 608 West Seventh Street, Cisco, Texas, where Henry Helms and Robert Hill stole Bell's Model T Ford touring car early on the morning of December 24, 1927. Photograph by the author, 2010.

THEFT OF CECIL HIBBERT'S FORD MODEL T ROADSTER, 409 WEST THIRTEENTH STREET, CISCO, DECEMBER 27, 1927

The house that now stands at 409 West Thirteenth Street, Cisco, Texas, where the Santa Claus bank robbers stole Cecil Hibbert's Model T Ford roadster in the early hours of December 27, 1927. Photograph by the author, 2010.

Having abducted Carl Wylie with his Dodge sedan in the early hours of December 26, the bandits knew the next day that lawmen and posse members must have all received descriptions of the stolen car and its kidnapped driver. The time had come for them to get yet another car. In the early hours of Tuesday, December 27, they had Wylie drive to the outskirts of Cisco. They were so turned around by circuitous meandering to avoid lawmen that they mistakenly thought they were on the edge of Breckenridge. Leaving Hill and Ratliff in the vehicle to watch their hostage, Henry Helms tried to steal several cars, none of which would start. Finally he succeeded with a 1924 Ford roadster at the rented home of barber Cecil Hibbert at 409 West Thirteenth Street. After Ratliff and Hill transferred to join him in the single-seated convertible, they released Wylie in his sedan. The fugitives headed out of town, eventually taking a northerly track that would lead them toward a crossing of the Brazos River near South Bend in Young County.

To reach the crime scene, drive southeast on Conrad Hilton Avenue (U.S. Highway 183) five blocks from its intersection with West Eighth Street (Texas Highway 6/206). At the juncture with West Thir-

teenth Street, turn southwest (right) and drive four blocks on West Thirteenth. Cecil Hibbert's residence stood at the east corner of the intersection where this street intersects with Avenue H. Today the site of the Hibbert residence is occupied by a more recent brown-painted house with a metal roof.

SOUTH BEND ROADBLOCK, MAIN STREET, SOUTH BEND, DECEMBER 27, 1927

For days lawmen in all directions from Cisco had been on the lookout for the Cisco fugitives. Already they had learned of the Wichita Falls connections to the robbery, and authorities suspected that the fugitives might try to make for that city. Several lawmen and posse members gathered at South Bend in Young County, near a major bridge across the Brazos. On learning about the theft of the Hibbert roadster in Cisco, a handful of officers blocked Main Street in South Bend with two cars and were waiting on December 27, 1927, when three men in a Ford roadster pulled into view. "We didn't see the officers until we got right at South Bend about a block from them," reported fugitive Robert Hill. "We backed up quick as we saw them . . . , turning around and going as fast as we could." The lawmen pursued the car, which was

View northward on Main Street past the awning on the former post office in South Bend, Texas, toward the general area where law officers at a roadblock turned back Cisco bank robbers Marshall Ratliff, Henry Helms, and Robert Hill on December 27, 1927. Photograph by the author, 2009.

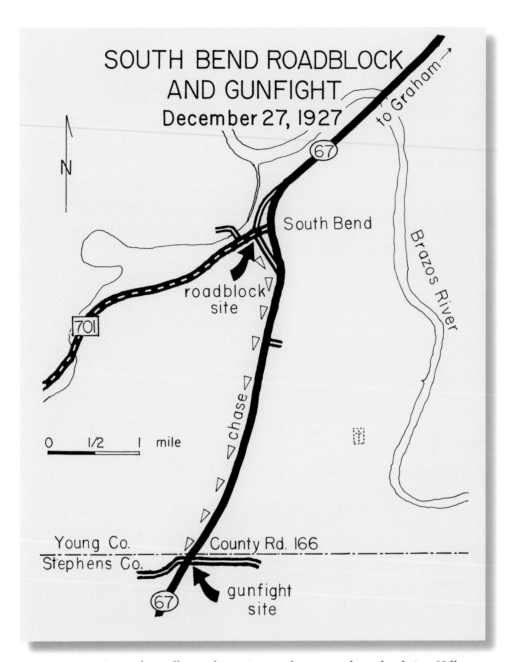

SOUTH BEND ROADBLOCK
AND GUNFIGHT
December 27, 1927

to Graham →

N

67

South Bend

Brazos River

roadblock
site

701

chase

0   1/2   1   mile

Young Co.
Stephens Co.

County Rd. 166

67   gunfight
site

running awkwardly on three tires and one wooden wheel rim. Hill continued, "Helms was driving. Ratliff shot at them and they returned fire, coming after us. I was reloading Marshall's guns."

To reach the scene of the events, exit Texas Highway 67 at its intersection with Ranch Road 701 in southern Young County and drive west 0.1 mile to its intersection with Main Street in the most built-up section of the scattered South Bend community. Turn south (left) onto Main Street and you will have reached the approximate site of the roadblock. The concrete commercial building on the west side of the street with a gas pipe flagpole was the post office. To follow the route of the running fight, drive south on Main Street to where it merges with Texas Highway 67 and continue southward on the state highway for about three and a half miles.

GUNFIGHT SOUTH OF SOUTH BEND, YOUNG/STEPHENS COUNTY LINE, VICINITY OF SOUTH BEND, DECEMBER 27, 1927

Law officers pursued the Cisco bank robbers south on the blacktop road from South Bend to the point where the pavement ended at the Stephens County line. There Henry Helms turned the Model T roadster east onto an unpaved road that led in the direction of a ford across the Brazos River and the community of Oil City on the other side. Quickly the three fugitives abandoned their car and made for the brush. As the robbers ran on foot, the lawmen's bullets took greatest effect, striking both Helms and Ratliff, the latter falling to the ground unable to rise. Hill helped Helms and the two escaped, while officers took Ratliff, with multiple wounds, into their custody. They carried him to the hospital for treatment of gunshot wounds and then safekeeping in the Young County Jail in Graham. From there he was transferred to Eastland County officers who had jurisdiction for the Cisco heist. In the meantime the other two escapees spent three more days hiding out in the recesses of the Brazos bottoms.

Unpaved Stephens County Road 166 (Duff Prairie Road), where Cisco bank bandits Marshall Ratliff, Henry Helms, and Robert Hill, followed by pursuing lawmen, turned east from the Graham-Breckenridge Road, abandoned their automobile, and engaged officers in a gunfight south of South Bend, Texas, on December 27, 1927. Photograph by the author, 2009.

To reach the crime scene, drive either north or south on Texas Highway 67 to its intersection with the Young/Stephens county line south of South Bend and north of Breckenridge. Just 0.1 mile south of the county line, the old gravel road to Oil City, now Stephens County Road 166 (known also as Duff Prairie Road), leads eastward. From the pavement turn east onto the gravel road and you will have reached the immediate vicinity of the running gunfight.

SURRENDER OF HENRY HELMS AND ROBERT HILL, 500 BLOCK OF FIFTH STREET, GRAHAM, DECEMBER 30, 1927

With Henry Helms becoming increasingly delirious from the effects of his gunshot wounds and both him and Robert Hill feeling cold, fatigued, and hungry, the last two fugitives made their way on foot into Graham, Texas, during the night of Thursday, December 29. They tried unsuccessfully to find lodgings, spent the night in a barn, and the next morning made their way to the Texan Hotel at 408 Elm Street. Manager E. H. Levein spotted pistols and a gun belt under one of their coats and telephoned to the sheriff's department a couple of blocks away to raise the alarm. Failing to locate a contact whom they had hoped to find at the hostelry, the two men in tattered and soiled clothes slowly walked a few steps north on Elm and then about half a block west on

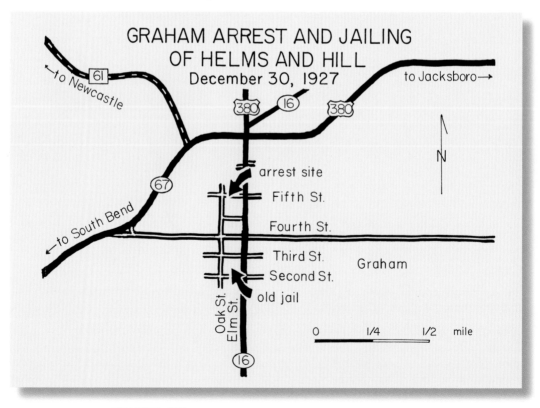

the south side of Fifth Street. Just after they passed the middle of the block, alongside the Clark W. Johnson house, four officers drove up and ordered the fugitives to raise their hands. Helms did so immediately, but Hill set off in a feeble run only to be stopped by four gunshots in the air. Officers escorted their captives two blocks south to the Young County Jail.

To reach the crime scene, drive south on Texas Highway 16 from its intersection with U.S. Highway 380 on the immediate north side of Graham, Texas. Proceed south two full blocks on Texas Highway 16 to its intersection with Fifth Street. Turn west (right) and drive just over half a block to the arrest site at the south side of the street. In 1927 this tree-shaded area now occupied by street-side parking for the Seven Oaks Dental Clinic was the location of a walk that ran alongside the Johnson home where law officers apprehended the last two Cisco bank robbers.

From this arrest site officers transported Hill and Helms a short distance south to the Young County Jail, where Marshall Ratliff had been temporarily housed following his capture three days earlier. There lawmen and locals gathered for a widely published photograph showing off their two bedraggled prisoners. To reach this calaboose, drive south two blocks on either Elm Street or Oak Street from the arrest scene to the south end of an oblong courthouse square. There the historic three-story brown-brick jail stands at 515 Second Street. Today the structure houses the Graham Area Crisis Center.

The historic Young County Jail in Graham, Texas, where officers initially held Marshall Ratliff, Henry Helms, and Robert Hill after their arrests in late December 1927. Photograph by the author, 2009.

PRISONER BURIAL OF HENRY HELMS, CAPTAIN JOE BYRD CEMETERY (PECKERWOOD HILL), HUNTSVILLE, AFTER EXECUTION ON SEPTEMBER 6, 1929

All three of the surviving bank robbers were convicted of crimes associated with the events in Cisco, with Henry Helms being sentenced to death. No family members claimed the body following his electrocution at the state penitentiary in Huntsville on September 6, 1929. Consequently the warden had his remains interred at the Texas prison cemetery, at the time unofficially called Peckerwood Hill and today known as the Captain Joe Byrd Cemetery.

To reach the burial site leave Interstate 45 at exit 116 for U.S. Highway 190/Texas Highway 30. Drive east on U.S. Highway 190/Texas Highway 30 (Eleventh Street) 1.8 miles, passing through the downtown business district of Huntsville, to a stoplight intersection at Sycamore Avenue. (This is the point where U.S. Highway 190 and Texas Highway 30 separate at a fork in the road.) Turn south (right) on Sycamore Avenue, a residential street, and drive 0.7 mile southward, passing the Sam Houston

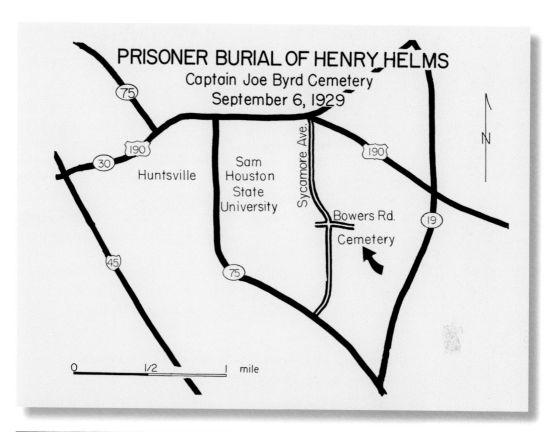

PRISONER BURIAL OF HENRY HELMS
Captain Joe Byrd Cemetery
September 6, 1929

75

190

30

Huntsville

Sam
Houston
State
University

Sycamore Ave.

190

Bowers Rd.

Cemetery

19

45

75

N

0   1/2   1   mile

Burial place of Cisco bank bandit Henry Helms in the Texas prison cemetery in Huntsville, Texas. Photograph by the author, 2010.

State University Athletic Complex and Stadium, to an intersection with a stop sign at Bowers Road. Turn east (left) on Bowers Road and drive 0.1 mile to the cemetery on the south (right) side of the street.

The grave of Henry Helms usually takes people a while to locate. The burial is marked by a prisoner-made concrete cross that bears only the inscription "9 6 29 X70." It lies between the tombstones marked more clearly for Jose Bosque (1929) and Earl B. Nice (1931) in the twenty-sixth row of graves (row E-F-3) eastward from the high end of the graveyard. The location is about 125 feet downhill from an ornamental wishing well. The crews that maintain this cemetery are inmates from the Walls Unit of the Texas Department of Corrections, only about a mile away. Penitentiary officials advise visitors not to enter areas where prisoner groundskeepers are actively working.

The electric chair used in the execution of Henry Helms in 1929 is preserved in the Texas Prison Museum. The museum has easy access via exit 118 from Interstate 45 on the north side of Huntsville.

ABDUCTION AND LYNCHING OF MARSHALL RATLIFF, DOWNTOWN EASTLAND, NOVEMBER 19, 1929

All of the surviving perpetrators of the Santa Claus Bank Robbery spent time incarcerated in the Eastland County Jail. The building also was the scene of the mob abduction of ringleader Marshall Ratliff followed by his illegal lynching in a vacant lot diagonally across the street on the night of November 19, 1929. Following the killing, participants in the events carried his lifeless body two blocks south to the Barrow Furniture Company store, which doubled as the mortuary in Eastland. There his body was embalmed and displayed to the public before its removal for burial in Fort Worth.

To reach the crime scene at the historic Eastland County Jail, drive one block west on Texas Highway 6 (Main Street) from its intersection with Texas Highway 112 (Seaman Street) at the east side of the Eastland County Courthouse. Turn north (right) onto North Lamar Street and drive one block to its juncture with West White Street. The two-story brick and stone jail stands at the northwest corner of the intersection. Tours of the interior are available through prior arrangement with the Eastland County sheriff's department. Visitors can see the cell where Marshall Ratliff was held and from which the rabble abducted him on the night of his death.

To see the scene of Marshall Ratliff's lynching, from the historic Eastland County Jail cross West White Street and walk one block west to its intersection with North Mulberry Street. A gray granite marker at the southeast corner of the street juncture recounts the events on

(opposite)
The historic Eastland County Jail in Eastland, Texas, where Marshall Ratliff, Henry Helms, and Robert Hill were all held and from which Ratliff was forcibly removed to be lynched on November 19, 1929. Photograph by the author, 2010.

The scene of the lynching of Marshall Ratliff in Eastland, Texas, on the night of November 19, 1929, in what at the time was a vacant area behind the three-story hotel building on the left and the light-colored brick theater with an elevated curtain loft. A tombstone-like gray stone marker at the street corner recounts the events. Photograph by the author, 2009.

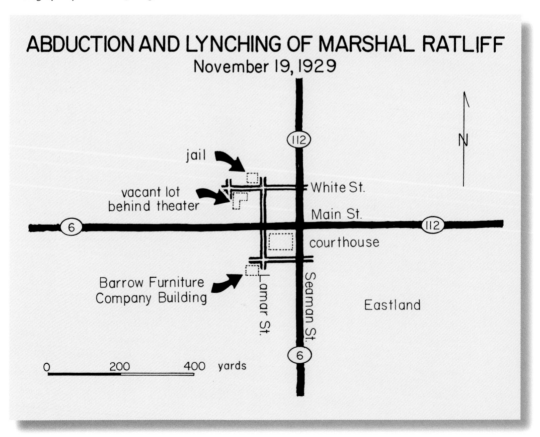

ABDUCTION AND LYNCHING OF MARSHAL RATLIFF
November 19, 1929

the night of November 19, 1929. The area of the lynching, at the time a vacant lot behind a brick building and a motion picture theater, remains mostly open today, though a recently built red and white motor vehicle garage with a metal roof occupies part of the site.

To visit the Barrow Furniture Company building, where Ratliff's mortal remains were embalmed and then displayed, return one block east on West White Street to North Lamar Street and go two blocks south to the courthouse square. The commercial building that housed the furniture store and mortuary stands at 201 South Lamar Street on the southwest corner of the square. At the time of research, it was the location of Allegro Mobility, a vendor of medical devices.

The downtown commercial building at 201 South Lamar Street in Eastland, Texas, that housed the Barrow Furniture Company, where the body of Marshall Ratliff was embalmed and exhibited to the public following his lynching on November 19, 1929. Photograph by the author, 2009.

👉 **JUDGE THE EVIDENCE FOR YOURSELF**

Abilene Daily Reporter, December 23, 1927, pp. 1, 11; December 27, 1927, pp. 1, 3, 12; December 28, 1927, pp. 1, 2, 3; December 29, 1927, pp. 1, 3, 6; December 30, 1927, pp. 1, 5; January 23, 1928, pp. 1, 9; January 24, 1928, pp. 1, 7; January 27, 1928, p. 1; January 31, 1928, p. 1; February 23, 1928, p. 1; February 27, 1928, pp. 1, 11; March 21, 1928, p. 11; March 22, 1928, p. 1; March 23, 1928, pp. 1, 4; March 27, 1928, pp. 1, 13; March 28, 1928, pp. 1, 13; March 29, 1928, pp. 1, 11; November 19, 1929, pp. 1, 3; November 20, 1929, pp. 1, 3.

Abilene Morning News, December 24, 1927, pp. 1, 4; December 27, 1927, pp. 1, 12; December 28, 1927, pp. 1, 3; December 29, 1927, pp. 1, 3; December 30, 1927, pp. 1, 4; December 31, 1927, pp. 1, 3; March 31, 1928, pp. 1, 4; November 20, 1929, pp. 1, 4.

Abilene Morning Reporter-News, December 25, 1927, sec. 1, pp. 1, 4; January 1, 1928, sec. 1, pp. 1, 2.

Cisco Daily News (Cisco, Tex.), December 23, 1927, pp. 1, 6; December 25, 1927, pp. 1, 2, 4; December 27, 1927, pp. 1, 5; December 28, 1927, p. 1; December 30, 1927, pp. 1, 6; February 24, 1928, pp. 1, 8; February 27, 1928, p. 1; March 23, 1928, p. 5; July 5, 1929, pp. 1, 4; September 6, 1929, p. 1.

Dallas Morning News, December 25, 1927, part I, pp. 1, 10; December 27, 1927, part I, pp. 1, 2; December 28, 1927, part I, pp. 1, 2; December 29, 1927, part I, pp. 1, 2, 5; December 30, 1927, part I, p. 1; December 31, 1927, part I, pp. 1, 2; January 1, 1928, part I, pp. 1, 2; January 8, 1928, part I, p. 1; November 21, 1929, part I, pp. 1, 2.

Eastland Telegram (Eastland, Tex.), September 6, 1929, pp. 1, 2; November 19, 1929, pp. 1, 2; November 20, 1929, pp. 1, 2; November 21, 1929, pp. 1, 6.

Fort Worth Star-Telegram, December 23, 1927, evening ed., pp. 1, 21; December 24, 1927, evening ed., pp. 1, 2; December 25, 1927, pp. 1, 2; December 27, 1927, evening ed., pp. 1, 4; December 28, 1927, evening ed., pp. 1, 2, 4; December 29, 1927, evening ed., pp. 1, 15; December 30, 1927, evening ed., pp. 1, 4; January 1, 1928, pp. 1, 2; January 2, 1928, evening ed., pp. 1, 6; January 23, 1928, evening ed., pp. 1, 4; January 24, 1928, evening ed., pp. 1, 4; March 23, 1928, evening ed., pp. 1, 8.

Graham Leader (Graham, Tex.), December 29, 1927, pp. 1, [8]; January 5, 1928, pp. 1, [8].

Greene, A. C. *The Santa Claus Bank Robbery.* New York: Knopf, 1972.

[Greene, A. C.] *The Santa Claus Bank Robbery.* Cisco, Tex.: First National Bank, 1958.

Ranger Times (Ranger, Tex.), December 23, 1927, p. 1; December 25, 1927, [sec. 1], pp. 1, 6; December 27, 1927, pp. 1, 2; December 29, 1927, pp. 1, 4; December 30, 1927, pp. 1, 8; January 20, 1928, p. 1; January 23, 1928, pp. 1, 2.

7 CAPTAIN CHARLIE AND THE RUM KING OF SAN ANTONIO

To say that Charlie Stevens and Lynn Stephens were antagonists would be an understatement. They were downright enemies. Each did all he could to oppose the other. Charlie Stevens directed liquor-law enforcement in Prohibition Era San Antonio, while Lynn Stephens headed the largest gang of moonshiners and bootleggers in the city. Members of the Anti-Saloon League in Bexar County fondly nicknamed the agent "Captain Charlie," while members of the criminal underworld knew their Mr. Stephens as "Boss."

In 1922 Charlie Stevens became a federal prohibition enforcement officer in the city, but his career began in the late 1880s when as a teenager he worked as a jailer for Bexar County. Over the years he served as constable, deputy sheriff, Texas Ranger, police captain, and customs inspector. His nemesis, Lynn Stephens, had been a retail liquor dealer prior to the beginning of statewide prohibition in Texas in 1918, but as soon as legitimate alcohol sales ended, he initiated illegal dealings. He earned the title "Rum King of San Antonio" from organizing a huge enterprise that ran its own factory-scale distilleries. The booze was distributed in trucks from the Broadway Garage, a "front" business operating just north of downtown.

For years the prohibition agent and the moonshiner played what seemed almost like a game of cat and mouse. While tall, broad-shouldered Lynn Stephens built his empire, modest Charlie Stevens, wearing horn-rimmed eyeglasses, chased him and his minions, as well as other liquor runners. Among the agent's raids was one on November 3, 1927, at a house at 236 Ridgewood Court that Lynn Stephens owned under the alias S. C. Norris. There authorities destroyed forty gallons of whiskey. This raid paled in scope next to one that Captain Charlie helped stage on the Comal Street Cooperage Company at 311 South Comal Street on May 25, 1929. There Martin Casbeer managed an illegal distillery for Lynn Stephens, and agents made a huge haul of alcohol, stills, and supplies. Captured financial records showed transactions totaling half a million dollars over the preceding three years.

The enforcement agent did not single out Lynn Stephens as his adversary but took on all moonshiners and bootleggers. In a tragic

Charlie Stevens
in October 1925,
after he had
become a federal
liquor agent
operating in San
Antonio. Courtesy
of San Antonio
Light Collection,
UTSA's Institute
of Texan Cultures,
image L-0351-B.

incident on August 2, 1929, Stevens led a raid on Tom Chandler's farm-house near Poteet, south of San Antonio in Atascosa County. Four agents stormed the shack where the small-scale distiller and his family lived. "As we approached, I called out that we were federal officers," Stevens recounted. Three of four men lounging on the porch bolted for the brush, but Chandler himself dashed inside the house, where officers saw him heading for a gun. As the lawmen tried to rush the house, Charlie Stevens stumbled, inadvertently discharging his rifle. The bullet struck the farmer in the heart, killing him instantly. Though a grand jury found the incident an accident, the agent gained a reputa-tion among lawbreakers as a man who shot first and asked questions later.

The nip-and-tuck activities of Charlie Stevens and Lynn Stephens continued. Finally the agent received the tip that he had been wait-ing for. From still unknown sources he learned where Lynn Stephens's largest distillery operated south of San Antonio in the Atascosa County brush country half a dozen miles north of Pleasanton. Federal agent James Pat Murphy described the plant as "a frame building about 100

The Broadway Garage at 1509 Broadway Street just north of downtown San Antonio. This business served as a front for Lynn Stephens's distribution of illegal alcohol to his customers. The site lies beneath the interchange where Broadway Street passes beneath Interstate 35 in the city. Courtesy of San Antonio Light Collection, UTSA's Institute of Texan Cultures, image L-1160-H.

by 40 feet, in a clearing, heavily barricaded by brush." A side road crossing a bridge led to the compound, but "an electric warning bell was fixed on the bridge, so that anyone who crossed would sound the signal in the still house." Early on the morning of Tuesday, September 24, 1929, several officers left their vehicles on the main road, approached the distillery on foot, and entered the compound through culverts beneath brush and barbed wire, surprising several youthful tenders.

What Charlie Stevens and his fellow officers did not know was that Lynn Stephens had learned what was happening and was on the way to the scene as well. Gang member McCullen "Red" Schenck had been at the facility that morning but was headed back to San Antonio. On the way he saw a caravan of automobiles filled with law officers headed south on the Pleasanton Road. Recognizing agents Stevens and James Pat Murphy, Schenck drove to the nearest telephone at Pleasanton and

McCullen "Red" Schenck, the rum runner who alerted Lynn Stephens that his distillery in Atascosa County was about to be raided and who participated in the retaliatory ambush. Courtesy of San Antonio Light Collection, UTSA's Institute of Texan Cultures, image L-1159-S.

warned Lynn Stephens, "I think we are going to get raided." Stephens and other gang members quickly joined Schenck at the site, hiding in the thick brush. There for forty-five minutes they listened and watched the wholesale destruction of their entire plant. They saw two of their teenaged boiler stokers, John Edward Pike and Frank Reyna, being arrested. Leaving the officers to spend the rest of the day and evening destroying the facility and collecting evidence, the moonshiner and his henchmen avoided detection and retreated to San Antonio to plan their response.

The greatest threat in the day's events had been the capture of Pike and Reyna, whom Lynn Stephens feared might talk. He desperately decided to try to liberate the two teenagers without delay, telling "Red" Schenck, "We're going back and get those boys." Schenck knew the officers' reputations and later reported, "I said Charley [sic] Stevens would never let him take nobody without a fight." That afternoon gang members began gathering, some of them at the Broadway Garage. Lynn Stephens ordered Joe Hobrecht to fill his car with gas and oil and to meet him and others at George Keene's drugstore, across from the city hall in downtown. From there the party then drove in five automobiles to the area of a low culvertlike bridge where the unpaved Pleasanton Road crossed a neck of Mitchell Lake, the sewage lagoon for San Antonio. There Lynn Stephens set his trap, positioning Joe Hobrecht; "Red" Schenck; "Little Joe" Rohmer; Lee Cottle; Thurman Petty; Jimmy Larson; Pete Guajardo; his wife, Luisa Guajardo; and his own sister, Altha Stephens, like figures on a chess board.

View northward from the point where Altha Stephens first stopped the lawmen on the night of Tuesday, September 24, 1929. This photograph, made the morning after the shooting, shows vehicles parked at the Mitchell Lake bridge in the same area where the murderers had positioned theirs during the ambush the night before. Courtesy of San Antonio Light Collection, UTSA's Institute of Texan Cultures, image L-1160-C.

The master criminal arranged three automobiles and a truck on the side of the road at the Mitchell Lake culverts so that any vehicle coming or going would have to slow down to squeeze past. Darkness was setting in, but a full moon provided gloomy light. As part of his plan, Stephens had Pete and Luisa Guajardo buy several baskets full of cabbages, which they scattered around the roadway near the cars. Then he stationed his sister in a new Ford coupe partially blocking the road at a slight curve on an elevated point about 150 yards to the south. From there she could see the other gang members, and they could see her. About the same time all of his men loaded firearms. They waited, expecting that the officers and prisoners would return to the city the same way they had gone, on the Pleasanton Road.

After a strenuous day and evening of destroying the Atascosa County distillery, the three fatigued lawmen headed back to San Antonio with their two teenaged prisoners about 11:00 PM. Agent James Pat Murphy reported that about six miles outside the city they ran into what they deduced might be some kind of trap. "A white woman had a car parked across the road, and stood beside it, waving a flash light," he reported. As the officers stopped their vehicles, attractive Altha Stephens

Officers searching the murder scene for clues at the culvertlike Mitchell Lake bridge on the morning of Wednesday, September 25, 1929. Courtesy of San Antonio Light *Collection, UTSA's Institute of Texan Cultures, image L-1160-D.*

approached, shining her light in their faces and exclaiming, "My husband is down there. He had a wreck with a vegetable wagon." She then stepped back and started waving the flashlight back and forth over her head. Suspecting some type of deception, Officer R. L. Hirzel took the woman into custody and drove ahead in the direction of the Mitchell Lake bridge.

Gang member Joe Rohmer remembered that he could see lights flashing on the rise from his place at the Mitchell Lake crossing. The gunmen saw the lawmen's cars pause on the slight elevation and then watched as Hirzel's vehicle approached with Altha Stephens inside. "This is not the car," Lynn Stephens advised, staying back in the shadows as the auto slowly made its way between the closely parked vehicles.

Next came a two-door sedan with James Pat Murphy at the wheel, Charlie Stevens in the front passenger seat, and the two teenaged prisoners in the back. Down at the culverts, Joe Rohmer, Lee Cottle, and Jimmy Larson, all armed, were positioned in tall reeds next to a fence about ten feet from the road, while Pete Guajardo crouched across the road with a .30–30 rifle. Lynn Stephens waited with a .45-caliber pistol behind the parked cars. In the open stood Luisa Guajardo, surrounded by cabbages on the roadway and with one of the vegetables in each hand.

Luisa Guajardo, who rolled cabbages onto the roadway to make the ambush location appear to be the scene of a vehicle crash involving a vegetable truck. Courtesy of San Antonio Light Collection, UTSA's Institute of Texan Cultures, image L-1160-G.

As Murphy started to thread his way through the closely parked vehicles, Lynn Stephens darted from the east side of the road. In a single desperate move he jumped onto the car's running board and broke out the passenger-side rear window, thrusting the pistol inside. What proceeded was reported by prisoner John Pike: "He [officer Stevens] grabbed his own gun with his left hand and grabbed at Stephens's gun with his right hand," struggling with him over the seat. The Rum King fired five times wildly in the interior. The other gang members began shooting, whereupon agent Murphy returned fire. He emptied his weapon, with at least one of the shots hitting Pete Guajardo. Murphy picked up the latter's .30–30 and cleared it. Then seeing a pistol dropped by another attacker, he fired all of its shells at the shadowy figures as well. Murphy put up such a stout defense of his friend, Stevens, and the prisoners that the assailants withdrew into the darkness, leaving Pete and Luisa Guajardo behind.

Charlie Stevens, gravely wounded, released the catch on his door and fell onto the ground. Murphy directed Frank Reyna, one of the prisoners, to lift him into the back seat of a big sedan one of the shooters had parked beside the road. By this time Officer R. L. Hirzel, who had heard the gunshots, had turned around and returned to the scene of the ambush. After placing injured Pete Guajardo in Hirzel's car, the entire party sped in two vehicles to San Antonio. At the Santa Rosa Hospital Dr. James W. Nixon attended to agent Charlie Stevens's injuries, which he described as a large wound on the left side of the body with a number of fractured ribs and exposed internal organs. San Antonio police chief Owen M. Kilday provided his own blood in a futile effort to save his friend's life. The agent died just after noon the next day. Pete Guajardo followed him in death a day later.

The attackers who escaped the murder scene went into hiding. City, county, state, and federal officers staged an impressive series of raids on multiple illegal liquor operations throughout the Alamo City. The day after the ambush, they struck Lynn Stephens's handsome two-story stone home at 214 Claremont Avenue, in a quiet neighborhood just east of Brackenridge Park. Hastily vacated by the moonshiner, the structure served not only as his home but also as a warehouse and "fin-

Lee Cottle, a twenty-year-old member of Lynn Stephens's gang who was one of the shooters in the ambush at Mitchell Lake. Courtesy of San Antonio Light Collection, UTSA's Institute of Texan Cultures, image L-1161-B.

ishing plant" for huge volumes of illegal whiskey. With the exception of an "elegantly furnished" bedroom, the house was stacked from floor to ceiling with whiskey kegs, jars, bottles, and cases. Built-in racks for ten-gallon kegs ensured that there was no wasted space. Upstairs officers found a laboratorylike work area with test tubes, flavoring extracts, and labels used to give illicit booze the appearance of pre-prohibition bottled-in-bond liquor. While officers set about destroying a large volume of alcohol that evening, an accidental fire started about eight-thirty. Much of the evidence was lost as the roof burned.

Eventually forty-five individuals were arrested for conspiracy to sell illegal alcohol as part of Lynn Stephens's ring, but not one was

Charlie Stevens's bullet-riddled automobile the day after his murder. Courtesy of San Antonio Light Collection, UTSA's Institute of Texan Cultures, image L-1160-E.

Lynn Stephens's home at 214 Claremont Avenue in San Antonio the morning after it caught fire during a raid by lawmen on Wednesday, September 25, 1929. Courtesy of San Antonio Light Collection, UTSA's Institute of Texan Cultures, image L-1160-F.

On trial for
murder in
Floresville, Texas,
in 1950, Lynn
Stephens shows
the jury a scar
from a gunshot
wound he received
in his foot on the
night of Septem-
ber 24, 1929, when
liquor agent
Charlie Stevens
was killed.
Courtesy of San
Antonio Light
Collection, UTSA's
Institute of Texan
Cultures, image
L-3953-A.

ever convicted. Authorities prosecuted Joe Rohmer for the murder of Charlie Stevens and secured a conviction, but then the state court of civil appeals reversed the case and Rohmer went free. Despite a massive manhunt, Lynn Stephens, the mastermind and true murderer, escaped completely. He disappeared from the scene, and in time most people forgot about him.

After the passage of twenty years, in the fall of 1949, Lynn Stephens reappeared. Ill from a serious stomach ailment and out of money, the former moonshiner of prohibition days turned himself in to the Bexar County sheriff. The legal establishment creaked into action to prosecute the old murder case, transferring it from San Antonio to nearby Floresville for trial. After the jury selection, proceedings began in earnest on April 18, 1950. The state presented a vigorous case, securing multiple surprise witnesses. The district attorney located not only former assailants "Little Joe" Rohmer and McCullen "Red" Schenk but also John Edward Pike, one of the prisoners in the back seat during the shoot-out. Their testimony devastated Stephens's defense, and the jury five days later found him guilty, sentencing him to thirty-eight years in the state penitentiary. Claiming innocence and arrogant to the end, Stephens told a newspaper reporter, "The boys just got together and told the same lie."

CHARLIE STEVENS LIQUOR RAID, 236 RIDGEWOOD COURT, SAN ANTONIO, NOVEMBER 3, 1927

Most of the places Charlie Stevens raided in his efforts against liquor runner Lynn Stephens are so changed today that they are unrecognizable. An exception is the bungalow residence located at 236 Ridgewood Court, a short distance west of Trinity University off West Hildebrand Avenue in San Antonio. The raid on this house, which Stephens had purchased under the alias S. C. Norris, netted the prohibition forces forty gallons of alcohol, which they destroyed on the spot. Today it remains a private residence in a quiet neighborhood.

Bungalow residence used by Lynn Stephens for illegal liquor storage at 236 Ridgewood Court in San Antonio, which agent Charlie Stevens raided on November 3, 1927. Photograph by the author, 2007.

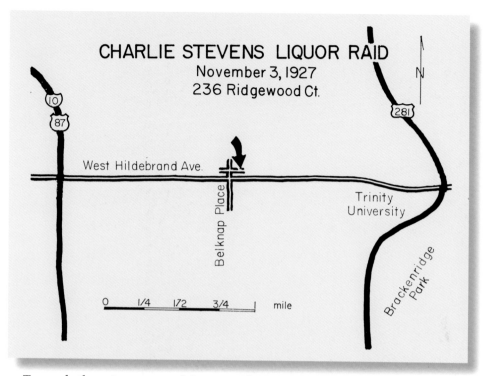

CHARLIE STEVENS LIQUOR RAID
November 3, 1927
236 Ridgewood Ct.

West Hildebrand Ave.

Belknap Place

Trinity University

Brackenridge Park

0   1/4   1/2   3/4   1   mile

To reach the crime scene, drive 1.4 miles west on West Hildebrand Avenue from its intersection with U.S. Highway 281 or alternatively drive 1.0 mile east on West Hildebrand from its intersection with Interstate 10/U.S. Highway 87. At Belknap Place turn north and drive one short block to Ridgewood Court. Then turn east (right) on Ridgewood Court and drive to the second house on the south side of the street. The entire neighborhood has free curbside parking.

KEENE'S DRUGSTORE, RENDEZVOUS FOR THE KILLERS, 101 SOUTH FLORES STREET, SAN ANTONIO, SEPTEMBER 24, 1929

Lynn Stephens made hasty plans to ambush agent Charlie Stevens in response to the raid on Stephens's large distillery in Atascosa County. He chose the popular Keene's Drugstore on the south side of the old Military Plaza in San Antonio as a rendezvous point for his gang members. Joe Hobrecht remembered that Stephens directed him to fill his car with fuel and "meet . . . at George Keene's. . . . When I got there Pete Guajardo and his wife were there." Within a few minutes Lynn and his sister Altha, as well as four more gang members, joined them. Once they all had gathered, Hobrecht related, "Lynn . . . told us to follow him." They all headed south from the city by the Pleasanton Road.

George Keene's drugstore, just across from San Antonio City Hall, was a popular meeting place in downtown. It occupied the prime busi-

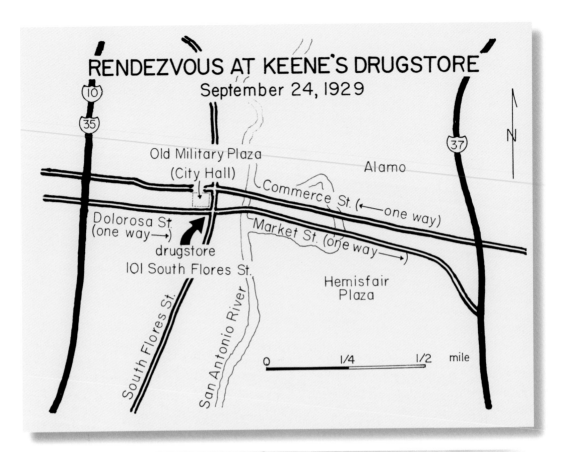

RENDEZVOUS AT KEENE'S DRUGSTORE
September 24, 1929

10

35

Old Military Plaza
(City Hall)

Alamo

37

N

Commerce St. (←——one way)

Dolorosa St.
(one way→)

Market St. (one way——→)

drugstore

101 South Flores St.

Hemisfair
Plaza

South Flores St.

San Antonio River

0   1/4   1/2   mile

Keene's Drugstore (presently Globe Pawn) in the Kallison Building, 101 South Flores Street, San Antonio. Lynn Stephens's gang gathered at this location before driving south of the city to set up their ambush for Charlie Stevens on September 24, 1929. Photograph by the author, 2007.

GLOBE PAWN
222-0303
101 S. Flores St.

ness location at the intersection of Dolorosa and South Flores streets on the ground floor of the 1920s two-story Kallison Building, which also housed several stores and a hotel. Constructed of variegated ocher and tan bricks with cream-colored limestone trim, it remains a handsome and distinctive commercial building to this day.

To reach the store, drive east on Dolorosa Street 0.4 mile from Interstate 10/35 to its intersection with South Flores. From Interstate 37, drive west on Commerce Street 0.9 mile to Flores Street; turn south on Flores and drive one block. The area offers curbside metered parking and nearby commercial parking lots.

AMBUSH SITE, OLD PLEASANTON ROAD
SOUTH OF SAN ANTONIO, SEPTEMBER 24, 1929

After leaving Keene's Drugstore, Lynn Stephens and his gang members drove south out of San Antonio in several vehicles to the place where the Pleasanton Road crossed a neck of Mitchell Lake. This reservoir was actually the sewage lagoon for the city, so it was not an especially popular area. Stephens set up a two-stage ambush, positioning his sister, Altha, in a car beside the road at a low rise just south of the culvertlike bridge and arranging his other people around a cluster of vehicles pulled up so closely at the bridge that they almost blocked the roadway.

The first of the two ambush sites set up by Lynn Stephens on the night of September 24, 1929. It was on this somewhat elevated point at a slight bend in Pleasanton Road that he positioned his sister, Altha, as a lookout. Photograph by the author, 2007.

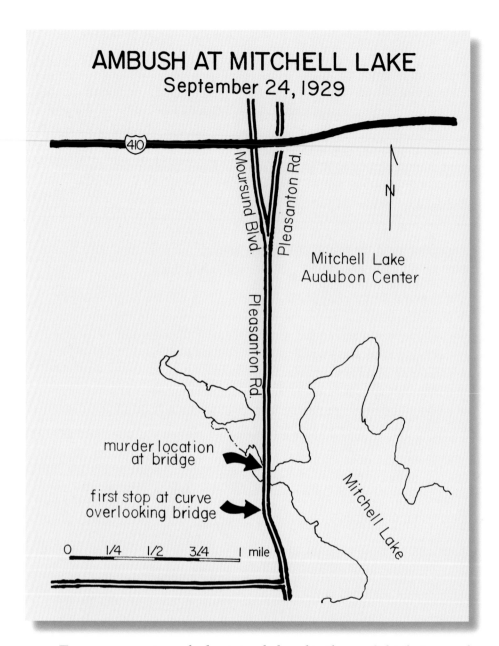

AMBUSH AT MITCHELL LAKE
September 24, 1929

410

Moursund Blvd.

Pleasanton Rd.

Pleasanton Rd.

N

Mitchell Lake
Audubon Center

Mitchell Lake

murder location
at bridge

first stop at curve
overlooking bridge

0   1/4   1/2   3/4   1 mile

The arrangements worked as intended, and in the gunfight that ensued Lynn Stephens himself killed his longtime enemy.

The murder scene today is little changed from 1929. The old two-lane Pleasanton Road has been paved with asphalt and the bridge across Mitchell Lake has been renovated, but otherwise the landscape appears as it did in press photos made the morning after the murder.

To reach the crime scene, take exit 46 for Moursund Boulevard from Interstate 410 on the south side of San Antonio just west of U.S. Highway 281. Drive 1.9 miles south on Moursund, which quickly merges with the old Pleasanton Road, to the bridge that crosses the upper end

View south from the murder scene at the Mitchell Lake bridge on the old Pleasanton Road toward the location where Altha Stephens identified liquor agent Charlie Stevens. Photograph by the author, 2007.

of Mitchell Lake, the murder location. To reach the spot where Altha Stephens identified Charlie Stevens and signaled to the killers with her flashlight, proceed another 150 yards southward on Pleasanton Road to a slight curve at a modest rise on the south side of the valley.

LYNN STEPHENS'S HOME, POST-AMBUSH LIQUOR RAID, 214 CLAREMONT AVENUE, SAN ANTONIO, SEPTEMBER 25, 1929

In the aftermath of Charlie Stevens's murder on the night of September 24, 1929, local, state, and federal prohibition agents raided every location in the San Antonio area associated with Lynn Stephens's liquor empire in the hope of nabbing the mastermind. The dwelling they knew as his two-story home at 214 Claremont Avenue was an obvious target. Going to the house during the day, lawmen found no one around but discovered the house served as a distribution facility for illicit liquor. While officers were pouring out illegal alcohol that evening, a spark, possibly from a cigarette, ignited fumes about eight-thirty, and an ensuing fire gutted the upper floor of the house and burned holes in the roof.

The fire damage to Lynn Stephens's house was soon repaired, and the structure returned to being an ordinary private residence. It stands in a quiet neighborhood just east of Brackenridge Park on the near north side of San Antonio. To reach the two-story, cream-colored limestone

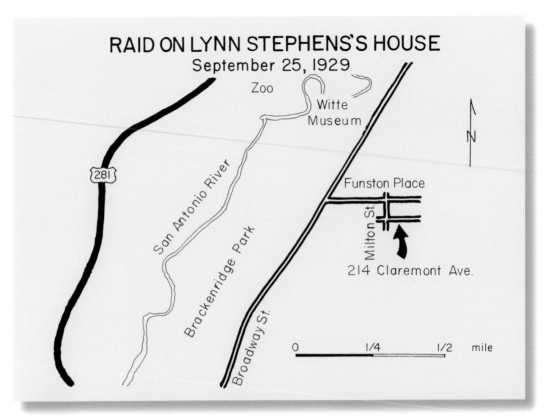

RAID ON LYNN STEPHENS'S HOUSE
September 25, 1929

Zoo

Witte Museum

N

281

San Antonio River

Funston Place

Brackenridge Park

Milton St.

214 Claremont Ave.

Broadway St.

0   1/4   1/2   mile

Lynn Stephens's residence located at 214 Claremont Avenue in San Antonio. On September 25, 1929, the day after the ambush and murder of "dry" agent Charlie Stevens, law officers raided this home and found it filled with kegs and bottles containing an estimated five thousand gallons of illegal alcohol. Photograph by the author, 2007.

house with a gray roof, turn east from the 3400 block of Broadway Street onto Funston Place. Drive a long block east on Funston, parallel with Mahncke Park, to its intersection with Milton Street. Turn south (right) on Milton and drive one block to Claremont Avenue. Then turn east (left) on Claremont and drive to the fourth house on the south side. Curbside free parking is readily available in the residential neighborhood. Take care to set hand brakes when parking in this hilly neighborhood.

JUDGE THE EVIDENCE FOR YOURSELF

Cude, Elton R. *The Wild and Free Dukedom of Bexar.* San Antonio, Tex.: Monguia Printers, 1978.

Floresville Chronicle-Journal (Floresville, Tex.), April 14, 1950, p. 1; April 21, 1950, p. 1; April 28, 1950, p. 1.

San Antonio Evening News, September 25, 1929, pp. 1, 2; September 26, 1929, pp. 1, 12; September 27, 1929, pp. 1, 5; September 28, 1929, p. 1; September 30, 1929, pp. 1, 5.

San Antonio Express, October 2, 1922, p. 6; September 25, 1929, p. 1; September 26, 1929, pp. 1, 2; September 27, 1929, pp. 1, 5; September 28, 1929, p. 2; September 29, 1929, sec. A, pp. 1, 2; September 30, 1929, pp. 1, 2.

San Antonio Light, October 12, 1925, p. 1; August 3, 1929, sec. A, pp. 1, 2; August 4, 1929, sec. A, pp. 1, 2; August 5, 1929, sec. A, pp. 1, 7; September 25, 1929, sec. A, pp. 1, 8; September 26, 1929, sec. A, pp. 1, 12; September 27, 1929, sec. A, pp. 1, 17; sec. B, p. 2; September 28, 1929, sec. A, pp. 1, 2; September 29, 1929, sec. A, pp. 1, 14; September 30, 1929, sec. A, pp. 1, 4; October 1, 1929, sec. A, pp. 1, 9; October 29, 1929, sec. A, p. 1; May 15, 1930, sec. A, pp. 1, 2; February 15, 1932, sec. A, p. 1; February 16, 1932, sec. B, p. 10; February 20, 1932, sec. B, p. 1; April 14, 1950, sec. A, p. 12; April 17, 1950, sec. A, pp. 1, 3; April 18, 1950, sec. A, pp. 1, 2; April 19, 1950, sec. A, pp. 1, 6; April 20, 1950, sec. A, pp. 1, 10; April 21, 1950, sec. A, pp. 1, 12; April 22, 1950, sec. A, p. 1; April 24, 1950, sec. A, p. 2.

8 THE URSCHEL KIDNAPPING
MACHINE GUN KELLY'S FORAY INTO TEXAS

Charles F. Urschel and his wife, Berenice, played bridge with friends Walter R. Jarrett and his wife on the screened porch of the Urschel home in Oklahoma City on the warm evening of July 22, 1933. Out of darkness appeared two armed men. "Stick 'em up—we want Urschel . . . Which man is Urschel?" they snapped. Since neither man answered, one of the gunmen said, "We'll take you both."

Urschel was no ordinary businessman. He had served for years as financial manager for Tom B. Slick, "King of the Wildcatters," the richest man in Oklahoma. After Slick's death in 1930, Urschel continued running his financial empire and married Slick's widow, Berenice. The two hoodlums were no ordinary thugs either. One was bank robber Albert L. Bates, and the other was no less than George Kelly Barnes (alias George Kelly) but better known to criminals and lawmen alike as Machine Gun Kelly.

Determining which abductee on that summer night was indeed Urschel, the kidnappers ejected Jarrett from their car nine miles east of Oklahoma City and took a circuitous route southward, crossing the Red River into Texas. Their destination was a farm outside Paradise, southwest of Decatur, owned by the stepfather of George Kelly's wife, Kathryn. There they held Urschel captive for nine days.

The motive behind the abduction was ransom money from Berenice Urschel—lots of money. The kidnappers demanded two hundred thousand dollars in used twenty-dollar bills and stipulated a very quick pick-up of the cash to prevent lawmen from recording all the serial numbers on the bank notes. Urschel's friend E. E. Kirkpatrick made the money delivery in Kansas City on Sunday, July 30, 1933, eight days after the abduction. The next evening a disheveled man approached the back door of the Urschel mansion. It was the missing Charles F. Urschel, who had been carried to the outskirts of Norman, just south of Oklahoma City, and left at the side of the road.

Kelly, Bates, and their accomplices congratulated themselves on what they believed had been a perfect crime. Kathryn Kelly had planned the kidnapping, while her husband and Bates had engineered the abduction, collected the ransom money, and returned victim. Kathryn's

Charles F. Urschel, the victim of Machine Gun Kelly's kidnapping plot in 1933.
Courtesy of Research Division of the Oklahoma Historical Society, image #14438.

*The Shannon farmhouse, headquarters for the kidnappers who held Charles F. Urschel for ransom,
as it appeared in August 1933. Courtesy of Fort Worth Star-Telegram Collection, Special Collections,
the University of Texas at Arlington Libraries, image 217-1, glass negative.*

The farmhouse where the kidnappers held Charles Urschel during his nine-day confinement. Courtesy of Fort Worth Star-Telegram Collection, Special Collections, Special Collections, the University of Texas at Arlington Libraries, image 217-7, glass negative.

mother, stepfather, and stepbrother had helped them hold the oil financier on their Texas farm. While captive, Urschel's eyes were covered with adhesive tape except for the few minutes he needed to write a letter and then to shave before his release. George and Kathryn Kelly spent part of this time in a Fort Worth safe house, miles away from the farm. Although Urschel had had only brief moments to see his captors, what Kelly and the others did not realize was that Charles F. Urschel was not just a financial genius. He had what today might be called a photographic memory—the uncanny ability to remember vividly the tiniest details of his ordeal.

On the fourteen-hour trip to Texas, the blindfolded Urschel made mental notes of sounds he heard. Once delivered to the farm of Robert G. "Boss" Shannon outside Paradise, Texas, Urschel remembered every sound: a bull, four milk cows, chickens, a flock of guinea fowl, and even snippets of conversations about a local teenaged prostitute. He noted rainfall and wind. Even though he was kept in chains, the captive consciously left clear fingerprints on smooth surfaces like windowpanes and a bedstead. Perhaps most importantly, he noted hearing the regular drone of an airplane. He surreptitiously queried his captors about the time of day, noting that the plane passed overhead at 9:15 AM and 5:45 PM. Finally he roughly calculated the travel time from the hideout back to Oklahoma, and it was six hours shorter than the trip on the night of his abduction.

The bedstead to which the kidnappers chained Charles Urschel for most of his captivity at the Shannon farm and where he intentionally left his fingerprints. *Courtesy of* Fort Worth Star-Telegram Collection, Special Collections, the University of Texas at Arlington Libraries, image 217-6, glass negative.

From the outset of the kidnapping, the Urschel family placed itself in the hands of the local sheriff and agents of the newly formed Federal Bureau of Investigation. Officers "fed" the press only the information they wanted the abductors to know. The very evening that the fatigued and careworn Charles Urschel stumbled to his own back door, Monday, July 31, 1933, Special Agent Gus Jones peppered him with questions when he discovered the remarkable recall the oilman possessed. Urschel's observation that he had heard the kidnappers' car rattle across the bumpy Canadian River bridge between Lexington and Purcell, Oklahoma, going and coming from his captivity, plus his estimate of the eight-hour driving time leading up to his release, pointed southward toward Texas. Jones assigned investigators to find out what localities to the south experienced the same sequence of rain and wind that Urschel remembered and to check commercial airline schedules. They quickly concluded that the airplane sounds at the crime scene likely came from a daily American Airlines flight between Fort Worth and Amarillo.

Agents in a light plane flew over the American Airlines route, looking for a farm that fit Urschel's description. When they located such a farm in southwestern Wise County, Texas, in an area that had experienced the distinctive sequence of weather Urschel had described, Jones dispatched Edward Dowd to the neighborhood. The investigator arrived there only three days after Urschel's release, visiting in the guise of a mortgage salesman. Dowd confirmed what the oilman remembered. The house had a broken windowpane patched with cardboard; the floor boards ran the right directions; and he saw the correct number of cattle, mules, and even guineas. When the agent asked for a drink of water on the hot summer day, the pulley at the well made the right squeak and the water had the same mineralized taste that Urschel had described. In the vicinity Dowd learned about the same teenaged prostitute that the Oklahoman had heard of. There was no question in the lawman's mind—he had found the crime scene.

Meanwhile George Kelly and Albert Bates absconded with the ransom money, splitting it between them. George and wife Kathryn initially went to Cleveland, Chicago, and Des Moines but then returned to Texas. They headed to Coleman County, where Kathryn had lived as a teenager and where her uncle, Cass E. Coleman, lived on a farm thir-

Interior of a room in the farmhouse where the kidnappers held Charles Urschel.
Courtesy of Fort Worth Star-Telegram Collection, Special Collections, the University
of Texas at Arlington Libraries, image 2046 #2 Aug. 1947.

teen miles south of the town of Coleman. In mid-August Cass and Kelly buried $73,250 near a tree in a cotton field. Cass then found a tenant shack for Kelly to rent as a hideout on the farm of Will Casey, fifteen miles east of Coleman. George and Kathryn then departed, hiding out in Biloxi and elsewhere but spending part of the time in a bungalow at 160 Mahncke Court in San Antonio. Eventually, in the third week of September 1933, the couple headed to Memphis, Tennessee.

Having identified the farm where Urschel was held, federal agents joined Texas officers to raid the site. They reached Decatur, the seat of Wise County, at four o'clock on the afternoon of Friday, August 11, 1933. Fearing they might lose some of their quarry if darkness fell, they decided to postpone the incursion until the next morning. Officers gathered at the Blackstone Hotel in Fort Worth at four o'clock the next morning and headed in several cars toward Paradise and thence via a sandy county road to the Shannon farm. To maintain secrecy, some of the junior officers had not even been informed where they were going. Fort Worth police officer Charlie G. Carmichael remarked in the car, "I wish they'd tell us what to expect when we get where we're going." The stranger next to him spoke up, saying, "I thought you knew. I'm Charles Urschel, the man . . . kidnapped. We're going after them." The Oklahoman was included in the group in order to identify the kidnappers by the sounds of their voices.

Unknown to the officers, the overnight delay would enable them to arrest one of the most notable American criminals of their day. Harvey

S. A. HIDEOUT OF HUNTED DESPERADO

Above is the cottage at 160 Mahncke Court where George ("Machine Gun") Kelly, arrested in Memphis Tuesday in connection with Urschel kidnaping, stayed for several days. Federal and state officers had machine guns trained on house for week or more in hope Kelly would return, but were too late.

A press photograph of the safe house that George and Kathryn Kelly occupied in San Antonio in September 1933 following the lawmen's raid on the kidnappers at the Shannon farm. Courtesy of the San Antonio Express-News *and UTSA's Institute of Texan Cultures, image 107-0523.*

Bailey arguably had been the most successful bank robber in the history of the United States. By a quirk of coincidence, he chose the night before the raid on the Shannon farm to return a borrowed Thompson submachine gun to George Kelly. Having been awake two days and nights before he got to Paradise, Bailey remembered, "I was dead to the world." "Boss" Shannon gave Bailey some money that George Kelly owed him and encouraged him to get some sleep on a cot outside the house. The next morning, as lawmen surrounded the farmhouse, agent Gus Jones spotted Bailey asleep in the open air and awakened him with

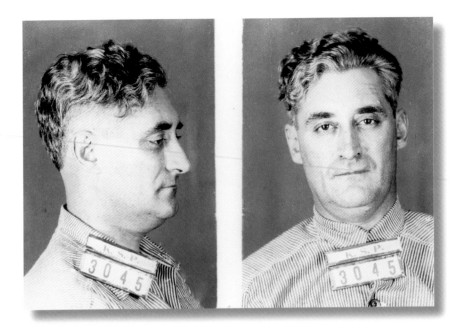

the muzzle of a machine gun. The officers found in his pockets $540 reimbursed to Bailey by Shannon on behalf of Kelly the night before. It was in $20 bills, and they all bore recorded serial numbers from the Urschel ransom money.

The raid was successful. Officers arrested R. G. "Boss" Shannon; his wife, Ora Shannon, the mother of Kathryn Kelly; and Shannon's twenty-two-year-old son and young wife, not to mention the unexpected Harvey Bailey. The search went on for George and Kathryn Kelly, as well as for Albert Bates and others who had aided and abetted the kidnappers. Officers in time moved the arrestees to Dallas, where the federal government contracted for cell space in the calaboose atop the multistory Dallas County Criminal Courts Building. Despite the momentary distraction of Harvey Bailey temporarily escaping from the so-called "escape-proof" building, authorities proceeded to transfer the prisoners to Oklahoma City, where they were joined by Bates, for trial in U.S. court. The case was the first major crime prosecuted under the newly passed federal statute against transporting people across state lines against their will. Congress had passed the law in 1932 in response to the Charles A. Lindbergh baby kidnapping.

George and Kathryn Kelly were caught in Memphis on the morning of Tuesday, September 28, 1933. They were flown to Oklahoma City, where all the principals in the Urschel kidnapping were convicted. Twenty-two-year-old Armon Shannon received a suspended sentence of ten years for his truthful testimony in court despite the fact that he had guarded the abductee. Even though Harvey Bailey had nothing whatever to do with the kidnapping, he was sentenced to life in prison

Dallas County sheriff Richard A. "Smoot" Schmidt, standing in a white shirt and necktie between the two columns, looks on as authorities question (left to right) R. G. Shannon, Ora Shannon, Armon Shannon, and Oleta Shannon seated on a bench at the Dallas jail after their arrest in Wise County on August 12, 1933. Courtesy of the Texas/Dallas History and Archives Division, Dallas Public Library, image PA76-1/37341.4.

as part of the conspiracy, proved by his possession of some of the ransom money. George Kelly, R. G. Shannon, Albert Bates, and Harvey Bailey all went to the federal penitentiary at Leavenworth, Kansas, while Kathryn Kelly and her mother, Ora Shannon, went to penal institutions for women. All of them received life sentences. When the U.S. Department of Justice opened a new maximum security prison on Alcatraz Island in California, it transferred Kelly, Bates, and Bailey there.

While the trials in Oklahoma City grabbed headlines, postscripts followed in Texas. Once court testimony revealed that Cass Coleman and Will Casey had aided the kidnappers, attention shifted to the retrieval of the ransom money. Officers descended on the Cass Coleman farm the night of September 26–27, 1933. With flashlights, Coleman led local and federal officers to two spots in his cotton field where he and George Kelly had hidden a Thermos bottle and a syrup can filled with $73,250

Armon Shannon (left) with his father R. G. Shannon (right) in the Dallas jail after their arrest on August 12, 1933, for participating in the kidnapping of Charles F. Urschel. Courtesy of the Texas/Dallas History and Archives Division, Dallas Public Library, image PA76-1/37340.

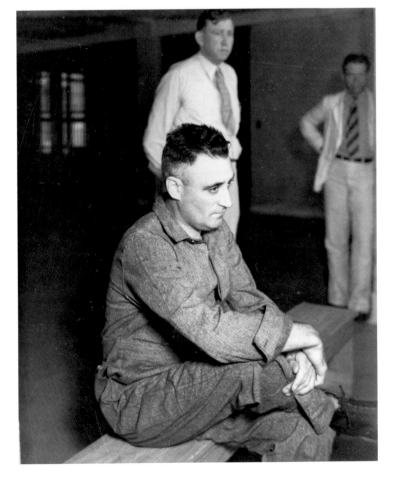

Bank robber Harvey Bailey in the Dallas County Jail following his arrest along with the kidnappers at the Shannon farm on August 12, 1933, with Sheriff R. A. "Smoot" Schmidt in a white shirt and necktie in the background. Courtesy of the Texas/Dallas History and Archives Division, Dallas Public Library, image PA76-1/37342.1.

The Dallas County Criminal Courts Building as it appeared at the time of Harvey Bailey's jail break on September 4, 1933. Author's collection.

Ardmore, Oklahoma, lawmen who captured Harvey Bailey after his escape from the Dallas jail. Courtesy of the Fort Worth Star-Telegram Collection, *Special Collections, the University of Texas at Arlington Libraries, image 295-8, glass negative.*

Machine Gun Kelly in handcuffs after being apprehended by law officers, 1933. Courtesy of San Antonio Light Collection, UTSA's Institute of Texan Cultures, image L-6654-B.

Ora Shannon and R. G. "Boss" Shannon shackled to each other as they enter the federal building in Fort Worth for arraignment on August 25, 1933. Courtesy of the Fort Worth Star-Telegram Collection, Special Collections, the University of Texas at Arlington Libraries, image 289-3, glass negative.

The federal penitentiary on Alcatraz Island in San Francisco Bay, California, where Machine Gun Kelly, Albert Bates, and Harvey Bailey eventually were imprisoned. Author's collection.

ALCATRAZ ISLAND - SAN FRANCISCO BAY

Machine Gun Kelly as a prison inmate. Courtesy of San Antonio Light Collection, UTSA's Institute of Texan Cultures, image L-6654-A.

The coffin containing the remains of Machine Gun Kelly being transferred from the express car of a passenger train to a hearse in Decatur, Texas, on July 19, 1954, prior to his burial at the Cottondale Cemetery near Paradise. Courtesy of the Fort Worth Star-Telegram Collection, Special Collections, the University of Texas at Arlington Libraries, image 3273 7/19/1954.

R. G. "Boss" Shannon viewing the mortal remains of Machine Gun Kelly at graveside services for the latter on July 25, 1954, in the Cottondale Cemetery in Wise County. Courtesy of the Fort Worth Star-Telegram Collection, Special Collections, the University of Texas at Arlington Libraries, image 3274 7/25/1954.

in $20 bills. Coleman was prosecuted for helping the kidnappers secret the loot, and Casey was tried for providing Kelly with a hiding place. In the San Angelo trial, Coleman received a one-year sentence and Casey, two years. Weeks later the dragnet netted another Texan, Louise Magness of San Angelo. This girlhood friend of Kathryn Kelly had provided an automobile while they were on the lam. In April 1934 the court sentenced her to one year and a day in prison for this transgression.

In 1954 George Kelly died in federal prison. His body went unclaimed, so a released R. G. "Boss" Shannon agreed to bury him in a plot at the Cottondale Cemetery south of Paradise. There lie the remains of the man who coined the term still used for the FBI when he declared at his Memphis arrest, "I knew you G-men would get me."

VISIT
THE
CRIME
SCENES

SHANNON FARM HEADQUARTERS FOR KIDNAPPERS, 355 WISE COUNTY ROAD 3470, SOUTH OF PARADISE, JULY, AUGUST, AND SEPTEMBER 1933

During the summer of 1933, the farm home of Robert G. "Boss" Shannon served as the base of operations for George Kelly's gang of kidnappers before, during, and after the abduction of Charles F. Urschel. The shack where they actually held the victim no longer exists. Modernized over the years, the recognizable Shannon house remains a comfortable rural home to this day.

To reach the crime scene, from Farm to Market Road 51 between Paradise and Springtown, Texas, turn west on Farm to Market Road 2123 and drive 3.4 miles to its intersection with Wise County Road 3355 north and Wise County Road 3585 south at a crossroads store. Turn north (right) and drive 2.5 miles in a northerly direction on paved Wise County Road 3355 (Schoolhouse Road), taking several curves, to a juncture with paved Wise County Road 3470 in an area of scattered suburban dwellings. Turn west (left) and drive 0.6 mile on Wise County Road 3470 to the house on the south (left) side of the road at the crest of a slight natural rise behind a row of seven mature ornamental pine trees. The private residence has a modern veneer of brown variegated bricks and an added detached carport on the west side, but the structure itself has an unchanged general shape, a similar hipped roof, and the same

The historic Shannon farmhouse, headquarters for Charles F. Urschel's kidnappers near Paradise, Texas, in its current remodeled appearance. Photograph by the author, 2010.

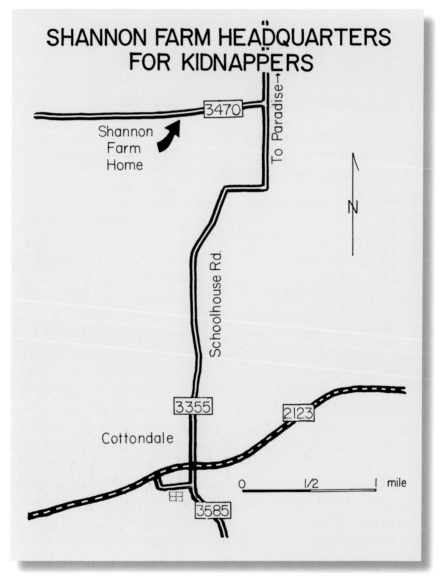

SHANNON FARM HEADQUARTERS
FOR KIDNAPPERS

design of inset front porch supported by four posts as shown in 1933 crime scene photographs.

FORT WORTH SAFE HOUSE OF GEORGE AND KATHRYN KELLY, 857 EAST MULKEY STREET, FORT WORTH, 1933

During the first half of 1933, George and Kathryn Kelly came and went from a handsome brick home at 857 East Mulkey in the Morningside district of Fort Worth. According to property titles it belonged to Kathryn's mother, Ora Shannon. Described as lavishly furnished and served by a maid, the house became their residence in Texas through the planning and execution of the Urschel kidnapping. Neighbors later reported that they were impressed with a 16-cylinder Cadillac the couple drove. After the gang members were convicted, ownership of the home passed to Kathryn's fifteen-year-old daughter, Pauline Frye. It remains a private residence today.

To reach the Fort Worth safe house of George and Kathryn Kelly, exit Interstate 35W at Berry Drive and drive one block east on Berry. At the intersection with Evans Avenue, turn north (left) and drive 0.7 mile, passing Morningside Elementary School. A dull tan, painted brick bungalow with white woodwork and a curved front porch, the dwelling stands at 857 on the northwest side of Evans where it intersects with East Mulkey Street in a well-preserved 1920s and 1930s residential neighborhood.

The Fort Worth "safe house" used by George and Kathryn Kelly during part of their time in Texas in 1933. It served as a secure place to stay as they partied in Fort Worth and visited with Kathryn's family just to the northwest in Wise County. Photograph by the author, 2006.

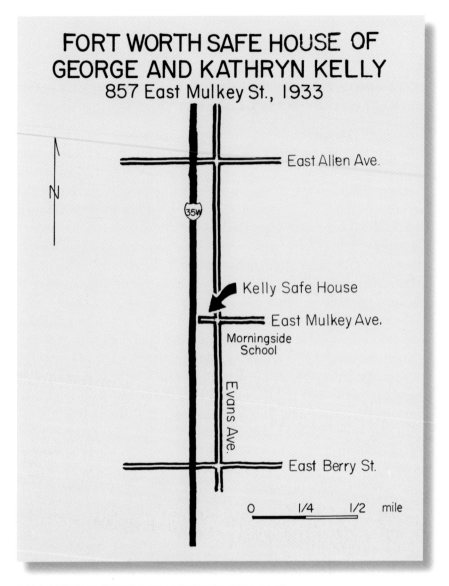

FORT WORTH SAFE HOUSE OF
GEORGE AND KATHRYN KELLY
857 East Mulkey St., 1933

N

East Allen Ave.

Kelly Safe House

East Mulkey Ave.

Morningside
School

Evans Ave.

East Berry St.

0   1/4   1/2   mile

SAN ANTONIO HIDEOUT OF GEORGE AND
KATHRYN KELLY, 1058 STEVES AVENUE
(FORMERLY 160 MAHNCKE COURT), SAN ANTONIO,
SEPTEMBER 7–12, 1933

While on the run following the arrests of their gang members at the Shannon farm, George and Kathryn Kelly, together with a teenaged girl used as a front to obscure their identities, occupied a bungalow on a quiet street southeast of downtown San Antonio, Texas. Kathryn paid one month's rent in advance on September 7, 1933, and she and the girl moved in. Neighbors saw a man fitting George Kelly's description. When police raided the residence on September 13, 1933, they discovered the couple had vacated the house. Although the residence remains

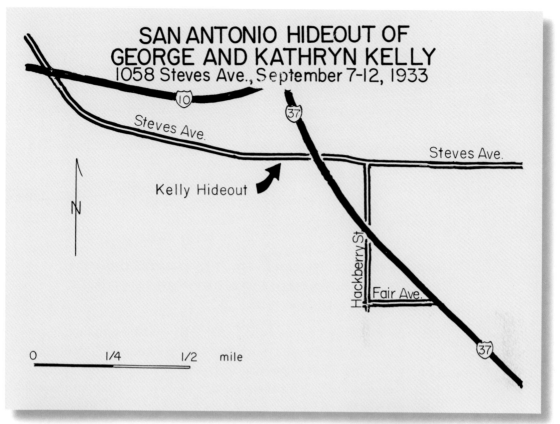

SAN ANTONIO HIDEOUT OF GEORGE AND KATHRYN KELLY
1058 Steves Ave., September 7-12, 1933

Steves Ave.

10

37

Steves Ave.

Kelly Hideout

N

Hackberry St.

Fair Ave.

Steves Ave.

37

0   1/4   1/2   mile

The bungalow home in San Antonio that served George and Kathryn Kelly as a hideout during part of their time on the run from law officers after August 12, 1933. Photograph by the author, 2007.

well preserved, its setting has changed dramatically from the quiet cul-de-sac that Mahncke Court once was. Nearby Steves Avenue, an east-west arterial thoroughfare, was rerouted down Mahncke Court and its dead end was opened to provide access to the other side of a new free-way after World War II. With these major changes, the address for the house went from being 160 Mahncke Court to 1058 Steves Avenue.

To reach the San Antonio hideout for George and Kathryn Kelly, leave Interstate 37 southeast of downtown San Antonio at exit 138C. Turn west on Fair Avenue, and drive one long block, passing under Interstate 37, to an intersection with Hackberry Street at a stoplight. At Hackberry turn north (right) and drive eight short blocks, passing under Interstate 37 again, to a stoplight intersection with Steves Avenue. Turn west (left) onto Steves and drive two blocks, pass under Interstate 37 a third time, and proceed to the 1000 block of Steves. The wooden bungalow, still a private residence, sits on the south (left) side of the street, the fourth house on the left after passing Cherry Street. Parking is unsafe on the very busy Steves Avenue but may be found conveniently at the side of Cherry Street.

ESCAPE OF HARVEY BAILEY, DALLAS COUNTY CRIMINAL COURTS BUILDING, MAIN STREET AT HOUSTON STREET, DALLAS, SEPTEMBER 4, 1933

After their arrests at the Shannon farm, Harvey Bailey and members of the Shannon family were transported for safekeeping to the Dallas County Criminal Courts Building in Dallas. The U.S. Justice Department had leased cell space there for detention of suspects in federal crimes. It was here on September 4, 1933, that Bailey used smuggled-in hacksaw blades to cut through the steel bars in his cell door and an

The Dallas County Criminal Courts Building in downtown Dallas, from which Harvey Bailey, armed with a pistol, made a daring escape to short-lived freedom on September 4, 1933. Photograph by the author, 2009.

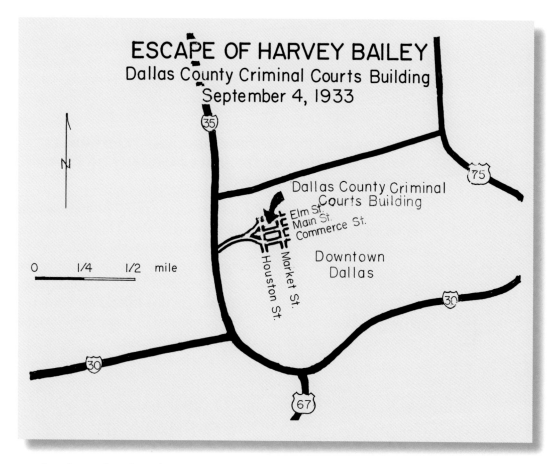

ESCAPE OF HARVEY BAILEY
Dallas County Criminal Courts Building
September 4, 1933

Dallas County Criminal
Courts Building

Elm St.
Main St.
Commerce St.

Downtown
Dallas

Houston St.

Market St.

0   1/4   1/2   mile

N

outdated pistol to force his way past several guards to escape for a few hours before being recaptured by lawmen in Ardmore, Oklahoma.

To reach the crime scene from Interstate 35E northbound in Dallas, take exit 428C marked for Reunion Boulevard and Commerce Street. Proceed in a northerly direction on the access road 0.5 mile, passing through the intersection at Reunion Boulevard, to Commerce Street. Bear to the right on Commerce, pass beneath a railway underpass, and emerge onto the Dealey Plaza green space. To reach this point from Interstate 35E southbound, take exit 428E marked for Commerce Street, which loops around to merge onto Commerce. Proceed beneath the railway underpass to enter Dealey Plaza. From the green space proceed east on one-way Commerce Street through a stoplight at Houston Street, where one sees the restored 1890s red stone Dallas County Courthouse on the left. Continue one block east to Market Street. Turn north (left) on this one-way street and drive one block to an intersection with Main Street, which has two-way traffic. On Main Street turn west (left) and drive one block to the Criminal Courts Building, which stands on the north (right) side of Main Street at its intersection with Houston Street, with one side fronting on Dealey Plaza. Metered street-side parking is available in the immediate vicinity, as is commercial parking space. This historic structure is only about one block away from the former Texas School Book Depository, where the Sixth Floor Museum and its exhibits recount President John F. Kennedy's assassination in Dealey Plaza on November 22, 1963.

GRAVES OF GEORGE "MACHINE GUN" KELLY AND ROBERT G. "BOSS" SHANNON, COTTONDALE CEMETERY, SOUTH OF PARADISE, WISE COUNTY, 1950S

When George Kelly died at the Leavenworth federal penitentiary on July 18, 1954, no immediate family members claimed his remains. His former stepfather-in-law, R. G. "Boss" Shannon, who had been released from prison, agreed to bury his body in a plot that he owned in the cemetery at the Cottondale community about two and a half miles south of his Wise County farm. It was here that the old man interred the gangster beneath a homemade concrete marker bearing the garbled inscription, "George B Kelley 1954."

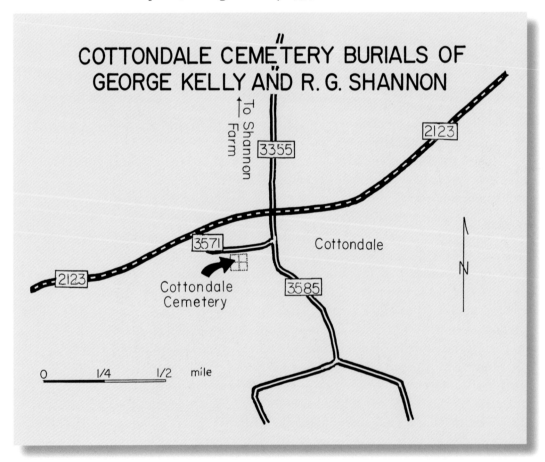

The modest concrete marker at the grave of George "Machine Gun" Kelly,
with his name misspelled, in the country cemetery at Cottondale, Texas. Photograph
by the author, 2010.

To reach the cemetery from Farm to Market Road 51 between Paradise and Springtown, Texas, turn west on Farm to Market Road 2123 and drive 3.4 miles to its intersection with Wise County Road 3355 north and Wise County Road 3585 south, where there is a crossroads store. Instead of taking Wise County Road 3355 north toward the Shannon farm, turn south (left) onto Wise County Road 3585 and drive only about the length of one city block, just beyond the white Church of Christ building, to a juncture with paved Wise County Road 3571, which at first looks like a gently curving private driveway. Turn west (right) onto the county road and drive 0.1 mile to the Cottondale Cemetery, which lies just behind the white-painted wooden Cottondale Community Building, the former community school.

The cemetery has no general vehicular access, so visitors should park in the areas provided at the community building. Enter on foot by the main gate of the cemetery, noting that it is laid out in four quadrants that are separated by broad concrete walkways. The Kelly and Shannon burials lie in the northwest section. From the gate walk west, slightly downhill, on the central path. After reaching the intercepting perpendicular pavement at the center, proceed a further distance of approximately sixty feet to the modest cement tombstone for Kelly, set flush with the ground adjacent to the north (right) side of the walkway. The marker is so nondescript that it is easy to miss. Once at the Kelly burial, it is easy to find the tombstone for R. G. "Boss" Shannon just a few markers north in the same row of burials.

JUDGE THE EVIDENCE FOR YOURSELF

Baker, T. Lindsay. "The Escape of Harvey Bailey from the 'Escape-proof' Dallas County Jail in 1933." *Legacies: A History Journal for Dallas and North Central Texas* 18, no. 1 (spring 2006): 4–11.

Coleman County Chronicle (Coleman, Tex.), September 28, 1933, pp. 1, 7, 8; October 5, 1933, pp. 1, 2, 6; October 12, 1933, p. 1; October 19, 1933, pp. 1, 2, 6; October 26, 1933, p. 2.

Coleman Democrat-Voice (Coleman, Tex.), September 28, 1933, sec. 1, pp. 1, 3, 4; October 5, 1933, sec. 1, pp. 1, 3, 6; October 12, 1933, sec. 1, p. 1; October 19, 1933, sec. 1, p. 1; sec. 2, p. 1; October 26, 1933, sec. 1, p. 1.

Dallas Morning News (Dallas, Tex.), August 2, 1933, sec. I, pp. 1, 3; August 15, 1933, sec. I, pp. 1, 12; August 16, 1933, sec. I, pp. 1, 4; sec.

II, p. 4; August 17, 1933, sec. I, pp. 1, 5; August 18, 1933, sec. II, pp. 1, 15; August 24, 1933, sec. I, p. 1; sec. II, pp. 1, 12; September 5, 1933, sec. I, pp. 1, 2; September 26, 1933, sec. I, pp. 1, 4; September 26, 1933, sec. I, pp. 1, 12; September 28, 1933, sec. I, pp. 1, 10; September 29, 1933, sec. I, pp. 1, 2; September 30, 1933, sec. I, pp. 1, 10; October 1, 1933, sec. I, pp. 1, 4, 12; October 2, 1933, sec. I, pp. 1, 8; October 3, 1933, sec. I, pp. 1, 12; October 9, 1933, sec. I, pp. 1, 8; October 16, 1933, sec. I, pp. 1, 12; October 18, 1933, sec. I, p. 1.

Fort Worth Star-Telegram (Fort Worth, Tex.), August 14, 1933, evening ed., pp. 1, 4; August 15, 1933, evening ed., pp. 1, 4; August 16, 1933, evening ed., pp. 1, 8; August 18, 1933, evening ed., pp. 1, 2; August 20, 1933, sec. I, p. 1; August 24, 1933, evening ed., pp. 1, 4; September 26, 1933, evening ed., pp. 1, 4; October 3, 1933, evening ed., pp. 1, 2; October 9, 1933, evening ed., pp. 1, 4; October 10, 1933, evening ed., pp. 1, 4; October 11, 1933, evening ed., pp. 1, 4; October 12, 1933, evening ed., pp. 1, 4; October 16, 1933, evening ed., pp. 1, 4; October 17, 1933, evening ed., pp. 1, 4, 18; April 3, 1934, evening ed., p. 1; May 1, 1934, evening ed., p. 15; October 31, 1944, evening ed., pp. 1, 6; July 26, 1954, morning ed., pp. 1, 3; June 17, 1958, evening ed., pp. 1, 2.

Haley, J. Evetts. *Robbing Banks Was My Business: The Story of J. Harvey Bailey, America's Most Successful Bank Robber*. Canyon, Tex.: Palo Duro Press, 1973.

Hamilton, Stanley. *Machine Gun Kelly's Last Stand*. Lawrence: University Press of Kansas, 2003.

Kirkpatrick, E. E. *Crime's Paradise: The Authentic Inside Story of the Urschel Kidnapping*. San Antonio: Naylor Company, 1934.

———. *Voices from Alcatraz: The Authentic Inside Story of the Urschel Kidnapping*. San Antonio: Naylor Company, 1947.

San Antonio Evening News (San Antonio, Tex.), September 29, 1933, p. 1.

San Antonio Express (San Antonio, Tex.), September 28, 1933, pp. 1, 2.

San Antonio Light (San Antonio, Tex.), September 28, 1933, sec. A, p. 3.

Wise County Messenger (Decatur, Tex.), August 17, 1933, pp. 1, 2; August 24, 1933, p. 1; September 7, 1933, pp. 1, 3; September 14, 1933, p. 1; October 12, 1933, pp. 1, 3.

THE TEXAS AND PACIFIC MAIL ROBBERY IN FORT WORTH
ROBBERY, COLD-BLOODED MURDER, AND INCARCERATION ON ALCATRAZ

Tarrant County deputy sheriff H. W. "Dusty" Rhodes had not had a good day. Having spent all of the hot, sweaty hours of July 12, 1933, hunting for three missing men in the Trinity bottoms east of Fort Worth, he decided to take a shortcut home over the river at the East First Street Bridge. Even after spending the day in and around stagnant water, he smelled something that was even worse: "As I was rounding a gravel curve that turns into East First Street, a sudden odor assailed my senses." He wondered to himself how anyone living in the area could stand it.

"It was a hunch . . . that caused me to stop the car on the bridge. I got out and looked over the south side." The lawman observed nothing unusual, so he crossed to the other side. "An oily scum covered the slow-moving water," he remembered. "There seemed to be a kind of eddy in the stream. I climbed higher on the concrete parapet to get a better look . . . and I saw . . . three faces, cold and white . . . looking straight up at me." How did "Dusty" Rhodes find himself looking squarely into the faces of three decomposing dead men?

The story went back four decades to the area along the state line between Louisiana and Arkansas where Olin DeWitt Stevens came into the world on February 17, 1894. Growing up in a large family on a hardscrabble farm near Magnolia, Arkansas, he later found work at a restaurant and in buying and selling things. By the 1920s he had married, had three children, and relocated to Fort Worth, Texas, where he earned his livelihood by dealing in illegal alcohol and narcotics. Burglary and auto theft soon followed. The law caught up with Stevens, and he spent part of 1928 and 1929 in the federal penitentiary at Leavenworth. By 1930 he was back in Fort Worth living at 4921 Avenue E, publicly calling himself a salesman for a novelty company.

O. D. Stevens had greater ambitions. He knew that his counterparts in crime, like George "Machine Gun" Kelly, Harvey Bailey, and Raymond Hamilton, were bringing in huge "hauls" through robbery, theft, and kidnapping, and he greedily aspired to join their ranks. Based

Tarrant County deputy sheriff H. W. "Dusty" Rhodes with two of the weapons associated with the deaths of Jack Sturdivant, Harry Rutherford, and Jewel B. Rutherford in July 1933. Courtesy of Fort Worth Star-Telegram Collection, Special Collections, the University of Texas at Arlington Libraries, image FWST 261-2, glass negative.

on his criminal experience, Stevens first planned in fall or winter 1932 for William D. "Bill" May, Johnny Carson, and Joe L. Martin, members of his narcotics network, to rob Leonard Brothers Department Store in Fort Worth, where he hoped to steal twenty-five thousand dollars. Complications prevented the heist. Then a retired mail guard living in Handley told him when and where the mail was vulnerable to theft in Fort Worth. He explained that postal employees trundled it on baggage carts drawn by a tractor from cars on passenger trains at the Texas and Pacific Railway depot in the open air to the nearby downtown Fort Worth post office. The insider said he could advise Stevens when the Dallas Federal Reserve Bank would be using registered mail to send money to banks in the region. Quickly O. D. Stevens hatched a plan.

Gang members May, Carson, and Martin were to surprise the tractor driver and accompanying armed guard on their way to the post office just as they rolled across the upper level of the underpass that carried the railroad tracks over Main Street. Planning to steal from a delivery arriving on board a train from Dallas at 9:45 PM, the stick-up men could hide in the dark behind a small wooden billboard on the north side

Fort Worth law enforcement mug shots of Olin DeWitt Stevens. Courtesy of Fort Worth Star-Telegram Collection, Special Collections, the University of Texas at Arlington Libraries, image FWST 2318 10/24/1949 #10.

of the roadway at the east end of the underpass until just the right moment. Stevens's informant advised him that crews loaded the registered mail in white bags on the very front of the trucks. After grabbing their prize, the robbers could haul the sacks to a car waiting at the side of East Lancaster Avenue and escape into the darkness. It looked like an ideal set-up.

As early as December 1932, Bill May, Johnny Carson, and Joe Martin were attempting unsuccessfully to stage a robbery. Problems impeded them three times. Once they argued so long over who would drive the Reo getaway car that the mail rolled by undisturbed. Another time they saw a man walking along the route of the mail trucks, and they took him to be a railway mail agent. The third time, on December 23, 1932, the getaway driver drank so much at a Christmas party that he wrecked the stolen car intended as the escape vehicle. Johnny Carson remembered O. D. Stevens's anger: "'You boys will hang around until that mail man gets tired of waiting and gets someone else to pull the job.'" According to Carson, Stevens added that he had already "put out $200 or $300" for his informer and that he was going to have to "get someone else" to do the job. Stevens dumped Carson and Martin but kept gang member Bill May, whom he had met in the late 1920s at the Leavenworth prison.

At this stage M. T. Howard, alias M. T. Pettijohn, became actively involved in planning the robbery. An accomplice in O. D. Stevens's dealings, Howard had collaborated in liquor deals with and even been in the homes of two young West Texans who wanted to get ahead financially: Ferman "Jack" Sturdivant of Eula and Harry Rutherford of Abilene. With no local criminal records, they were ideal prospects as stick-up men.

Mug shots of Jack Sturdivant (left) and Harry Rutherford (right) *provided by Abilene authorities to Tarrant County lawmen in July 1933. Courtesy of Fort Worth Star-Telegram Collection, Special Collections, the University of Texas at Arlington Libraries, image FWST 2318 10/24/1949 #10.*

In the meantime events were taking place that forced the criminals' hands. A new Fort Worth post office under construction for months just west of the 1931 art deco Texas and Pacific Railway station would open on February 22, 1933. This meant that employees would begin transferring registered mail directly into the new trackside postal facility beneath a canopy in a secure location. No longer would workers haul the mail bags on tractor-drawn trucks through the open air from the trains across to the old post office. Time was running out for the thieves, and they knew it.

The very night that the old post office was scheduled to close, the robbers struck. Bill May, Jack Sturdivant, and Harry Rutherford, with women's stockings pulled over their heads to disguise their appearance, emerged in the dark from behind the signboard at the east end of the Main Street underpass as a tractor drove up pulling a string of baggage carts loaded with about fifty mail bags. "As we were approaching the platform near the South Main street crossing, we were held up," reported Conrad T. Black, a substitute railway mail clerk. "They took my gun and knocked me down. Then they led us down an incline." Each of the robbers took two white bags of registered mail, forcing one of the guards to carry a seventh. Harry Rutherford started out with an especially heavy pouch containing coins, but he quickly gave it to a guard to carry. The latter complained about the weight, to which Rutherford barked, "Take it on and rush" or he would blow his head off. Once the thieves approached East Lancaster Avenue, they ordered the two postal employees to lie down and "hug the earth" for thirty minutes. The three then manhandled the bags into a waiting 1929 brown Ford sedan and departed. All this time O. D. Stevens sat in a nearby South Main Street domino parlor, as planned, so that he would have an alibi should the thieves be apprehended.

Joe Martin drove the car down East Lancaster to Chicago Street, where he met another vehicle. There the men hastily transferred the mail sacks into the second car, which transported the booty to O. D. Stevens's old residence at 4921 Avenue E. There for the first time the mastermind and his trusted partners viewed the loot. Although they did not take the time to count it, the prize consisted of a shipment of coins and bank notes from the Federal Reserve Bank in Dallas, including sixty thousand dollars destined for the First National Bank in Fort Worth plus another ten thousand dollars for smaller banks scattered from Killeen and Moody to Rowena and Ozona. The thieves also found other valuables in the registered mail, including two diamond rings sent by Mrs. F. M. Quisenberry from Dallas to her husband in Menard. "The morning after the robbery," remembered one of Stevens's minor hoods, Weldon "Soapy" Routt, "I went to Stevens'[s] house near Handley and asked him how much he got out of it," with the master crook responding, "Oh, $60,000 or $70,000—we haven't counted it yet."

The haul consisted of an estimated seventy-one thousand dollars in cash or valuables, the largest armed robbery in Fort Worth up to 1933—but they couldn't do very much with it. Even though the Federal Reserve Bank did not record the individual serial numbers of all of the bank notes, Stevens and his confederates knew that the stolen money was "hot" and that immediately spending it could lead to their apprehension. Using aliases such as R. H. Doyle, W. J. Krantz, and R. H. Strong, Stevens flew to New York and Chicago with the stolen money, reportedly paying a 25 percent commission to money launderer Max Kassoff to get "cool" money that could safely be spent.

In the meantime Jack Sturdivant and Harry Rutherford began asking for their share of the proceeds, which were to be divided among Stevens, May, Howard, and the two young men from West Texas. Through M. T. Howard, Stevens gave the young men modest installments of their take, but they were impatient. Harry Rutherford responded, "I told Howard that I was tired of this $15 and $20 business and wanted all that was coming to me." When gang member Soapy Routt asked Stevens about trouble he was having, "Stevens said they wanted money. He said he had given them $3,000 or $4,000, and they spent it like water. If he gave them any more, he said, we would all wind up in the pen." The erstwhile stick-up men began frequenting the private drive leading to the Stevens farm and generally became nuisances. This situation irritated O. D. Stevens's wife, Mrs. Orley Stevens, who once ordered them to leave, saying that she "didn't associate with the same kind of people Stevens did." O. D. told Soapy Routt that "he was expecting trouble from them because they hadn't got their money."

Events came to a head on Saturday, July 8, 1933. Jack Sturdivant, his wife, Melva, and Harry Rutherford had spent Friday evening at the home of Harry's brother and sister-in-law, Jewel B. "J. B." Rutherford and Hazel Rutherford, at 128½ Sunset in Dallas. This was a family gathering, as Melva was Harry and J. B.'s sister. After they got up the next morning, all three men headed out about ten-thirty in Jack's black Chrysler coupe for Handley to collect Jack and Harry's full share of the loot. J. B. went along "to protect" his younger brother. As they got into the car, Jack called out, "If I don't return by 4 o'clock. . . ." Melva Sturdivant and Hazel Rutherford, both young brides from West Texas, became worried and then frantic as night fell on a hot Saturday in Dallas and the men failed to come back.

The young women were frightened because they knew that their husbands had been up to no good. When they did not come home, Melva and Hazel started looking for them. Leaving Dallas about 9:00 PM, they first went to the side-by-side farms of O. D. Stevens and Bill May north of Handley. They had learned from their husbands that Stevens and May had been associated with the mail robbery, but neither of them had ever met the men before. No one was at either farm, so they drove to an address in Fort Worth where they thought M. T. Howard lived. Again they found no one. The wives returned to the Stevens farm between 11:00 and 11:30 PM, but only his wife and children were there. During the drive from Fort Worth to the farm, they met a truck with a broken windshield going the opposite direction, but they could not recognize the driver. After going back into Handley, where Stevens operated a drugstore, they returned to the farmhouses one last time just past midnight. There were still no signs of the missing men. With no better ideas of where to look, they returned to Dallas and tried to sleep for a few hours.

The next morning, Sunday, July 9, 1933, the two young women got up and drove back to the Stevens and May farms north of Handley. Finding neither man home, they headed to Fort Worth to try again to locate Howard, still to no avail. Returning to Handley, they found Stevens sitting in a car in the town. "What do you mean? I hardly know the boys," he replied to their questions about their husbands. Rather than taking the women to meet Howard, Stevens advised, "No, I'd rather you wouldn't. You'd better go to the Broadway Inn," a tourist camp on East Lancaster Avenue between Handley and Fort Worth, "and wait for us there." About half an hour later Stevens and Howard drove up to the rendezvous point, blocked the women's car, and got out to see them. "We discussed the possibility of our husbands being in jail,"

Hazel Rutherford recalled, with Stevens suggesting that they wait a while before contacting the police. The women returned home to Dallas only to find law officers waiting for them.

Unbeknown to the women, Jack Sturdivant and the two Rutherford brothers had indeed spent most of Saturday, July 8, with O. D. Stevens, Bill May, and M. T. Howard. Gang member Soapy Routt remembered their coming to Handley about ten or eleven o'clock in the morning. They spent time in Stevens's drugstore, where they played dominoes and talked and where Stevens chased away a couple of neighborhood boys, saying, "Run along. I've got some business to take up with these men." The local telephone operator, Essie H. Joiner, saw the young men together with Stevens several times, until they left in separate cars about five-thirty in the evening, everyone heading in the direction of the Stevens and May farms. It was about this time that Soapy Routt brought Harry Rutherford a pint of whiskey and found everyone having a good time.

The gaiety seemingly continued at Bill May's farm, where he and his family had been occupying a large tent while constructing a home from the same native sandstone that O. D. Stevens had used in building his. The party of young men had apparently been through a case of beer; several empties were on the dining table, and two unopened cases of beer sat nearby. Then about 11:00 PM arch criminals Stevens and May killed all three young men—Sturdivant and the Rutherford brothers—with pistol and shotgun fire. Several people attending a party at a nearby farm reported hearing the series of gunshots and the sounds of vehicles coming and going at the May and Stevens places around eleven o'clock. The murderers stripped the men of their clothing and identification, cut wire from a nearby V-mesh hog wire fence, and used the wire mesh to wrap the garments and personal effects together with chunks of native sandstone. Then, while standing on the open flatbed of a farm truck, they rolled the three bodies, with two hundred-pound bags of cement inside more of the same net wire, to make an awkward bundle. The killers drove to the East First Street Bridge over the Trinity River, got as close to the railing as they could, and awkwardly pushed the wrapped bodies and weights into the water. Either that night or the next morning, they dropped the wire-wrapped bundle of clothes into the Trinity at another nearby location, the Ray Crossing.

Both Stevens and May were up early the next morning, July 9, 1933. Speaking to no one about their activities, the two men began erasing the evidence of the previous night's acts. After breakfast both men left and then returned to the barn, with May coming back drenched with water to the neck. After May changed clothes, they left and then returned again, making two inspections of the yard. "Steve [Stevens] walked in front, pointing to spots on the ground," Mrs. May reported, "and my husband followed with a rake, raking the sand around each place." Once he picked up a piece of hog wire and asked, "What about the wire?" to which Stevens replied, "They won't pay any attention to that." Mrs. May observed that the farm truck in her husband's barn looked different than it had the evening before. "The windshield was broken," she noted, adding, "It looked like it had been struck by a bullet. There were no cushions and . . . the bed looked like it had been scrubbed with lime." The events played out this way in the deaths of Jack Sturdivant and Harry and J. B. Rutherford, but soon Bill May and O. D. Stevens would be paying the penalty.

When Melva Sturdivant and Hazel Rutherford met police officers at the Rutherford home in Dallas on Sunday, July 9, 1933, the lawmen informed them that torn and blood-stained clothing with items identifying the missing men had been found in a "cage" or contraption of wire fencing in the Trinity River. A seven-year-old boy had been the first to spot the gruesome evidence. Young E. M. Bilger Jr., his father, E. M. Bilger Sr., and T. W. Mumford had spent that Sunday on a fishing excursion along the Trinity in the area of the Ray Crossing between the Handley and Ederville communities. With still plenty of daylight to see, young "Junior" Bilger called out, "Papa, there's a fish trap." Wading out to examine the wire container, the elder Bilger found boots, trousers, shirts, and underclothing. Suspecting foul play, the fishermen called the authorities, who retrieved the belongings. With the blood-stained clothing were wallets and papers that identified the owners as Jack Sturdivant, Harry Rutherford, and J. B. Rutherford.

Realizing that they had little choice, Melva Sturdivant and Hazel Rutherford began telling law officers what they knew about the slain men's illegal involvement with Stevens, May, and Howard, all of whom were known by the authorities. That very day lawmen arrested the three criminals for mail robbery and as suspects in a triple murder. Along with many volunteers the Tarrant County sheriff's department began combing the bottoms of the Trinity River for the three missing men above and below where the bloody clothing had been found. The search now extended to the nearby adjacent hilltop farms of O. D. Stevens and Bill May. There authorities dragged a pond and even secured the services of an Arlington fire truck to pump empty a hand-dug well just outside Stevens's imposing newly built two-story stone residence. At the same time they searched the home three times, discovering that its cupboards and drawers had hidden compartments. They also found a hidden basement chamber accessible only by lifting part of a staircase. Then they realized that an upstairs room had no door. It had access only through exterior windows. Soon the press started

Fort Worth lawmen W. T. Evans (left) and W. A. Pulliam (right) inspect the wire mesh basket in which E. M. Bilger Jr. discovered the clothing of three slain men near the Ray Crossing of the Trinity River on July 9, 1933. Courtesy of Fort Worth Star-Telegram Collection, Special Collections, the University of Texas at Arlington Libraries, image FWST 261-1, glass negative.

Law officers W. T. Evans (left) and W. A. Pulliam (right) with victims' boots removed from the hog wire container found in the Trinity River by young E. M. Bilger Jr. on July 9, 1933. Courtesy of Fort Worth Star-Telegram Collection, Special Collections, the University of Texas at Arlington Libraries, image FWST 261-2, glass negative.

calling the place the "Mystery House." In hiding places officers found heroin and other drugs with an estimated value of twenty thousand dollars. Some of them were narcotics that had been burgled from the Southwestern Drug Company in Waco earlier that year. This discovery led to more charges against mastermind Stevens. Clearly he had created his handsome new hilltop residence as a headquarters for illicit drug dealing.

The searches on the east side of Fort Worth inadvertently led to Deputy H. W. "Dusty" Rhodes's discovery of the three men's bodies on July 12. Three days in the warm water of the Trinity had not improved their condition. The killers had wrapped the nude bodies in the same V-mesh hog wire they had used in disposing of the clothing, adding to the bundle two hundred-pound sacks of Lone Star cement that they hoped would make the remains sink to the bottom. The swelling of the bodies, however, had caused the whole grisly bundle to float half out of the water at the north side of the East First Street Bridge. The wire package weighed so much that officers had to call in a winch truck to lift it up to the roadway. Then the first ambulance driver on the scene refused to transport such badly decomposed bodies in his vehicle, so the officers had to summon a second ambulance to carry the remains into Fort Worth for examination. There authorities found all three men had

(top left) *A crew from the Arlington Fire Department pumps water out of a well in front of O. D. Stevens's house in an effort to find the bodies of the missing Jack Sturdivant, Harry Rutherford, and Jewel B. Rutherford on July 12, 1933. Courtesy of* Fort Worth Star-Telegram *Collection, Special Collections, the University of Texas at Arlington Libraries, image FWST 261-5, glass negative.*

(top right) *Firefighters and law officers grin as a man goes down into the pumped-out well at the O. D. Stevens house in search of the bodies of Jack Sturdivant, Harry Rutherford, and Jewel B. Rutherford on July 12, 1933. Courtesy of* Fort Worth Star-Telegram *Collection, Special Collections, the University of Texas at Arlington Libraries, image FWST 261-6, glass negative.*

(left) *The hand-dug well in front of the O. D. Stevens house as it appeared in 1976. Courtesy of* Fort Worth Star-Telegram *Collection, Special Collections, the University of Texas at Arlington Libraries, image FWST 6871 11/28/1976.*

Federal narcotics officer Buck Nance (left) and U.S. Commissioner Louis Newam (right) inspecting narcotics discovered in a hidden compartment inside O. D. Stevens's house during a raid in July 1933. Courtesy of Fort Worth Star-Telegram Collection, Special Collections, the University of Texas at Arlington Libraries, image FWST 261 7/15/1933.

been killed by gunshots. The killers had even cut a "Jack" tattoo from the arm of Sturdivant to make his body more difficult to identify.

Investigations continued at the May and Stevens farms. There detectives matched the two pieces of wire fencing found in the river with a gaping hole in a fence made of identical material. Then they located May's farm truck, its front windshield broken out. Despite the fact that someone had cleaned the bed with lime water, between the planks in the bed officers collected specimens of a solidified brown material, similar to dried blood. They found the same substance on the railing at the East First Street Bridge, and later a chemist determined it to be human blood. Lawmen also came across the wire remains of the truck seat cushion in ashes from a trash fire. Finally they found thirty-seven hundred-pound sacks of Lone Star cement identical to the two bags re-

View into a hidden windowless chamber located behind a hinged basement stairway in the O. D. Stevens house. Courtesy of Fort Worth Star-Telegram Collection, Special Collections, the University of Texas at Arlington Libraries, image FWST 6871 11/28/1976.

covered with the three bodies. All the circumstantial evidence pointed to O. D. Stevens and Bill May as the killers.

After the apprehension of O. D. Stevens, Bill May, and M. T. Howard, the police dragnet widened to bring in other members of the gang and even some of their wives. A federal court tried members of the criminal gang for mail robbery, while state courts tried May and Stevens for murder. The trial of Bill May for the murder of Jack Sturdivant came first, with a jury pronouncing a guilty verdict on February 24, 1934. Despite legal maneuvering, May went to the electric chair at the Huntsville penitentiary on September 6, 1935.

Next came the federal mail robbery case, in which a total of thirteen people eventually stood trial. Testimony began in Fort Worth on March 26, 1934, with the jury on April 3 finding O. D. Stevens, Bill May, and

(top left) *Federal narcotics investigator Buck Nance (left), U.S. District Court commissioner Louis Newam (center), and U.S. attorney Clyde Eastus (right) examining narcotics taken during raids on the O. D. Stevens house in July 1933.* Courtesy of Fort Worth Star-Telegram Collection, Special Collections, the University of Texas at Arlington Libraries, image FWST 261-8, glass negative.

(top right) *The farm truck used to transport the corpses in the Handley triple murder to the East First Street Bridge on the night of July 8–9, 1933.* Courtesy of Fort Worth Star-Telegram Collection, Special Collections, the University of Texas at Arlington Libraries, image FWST 261-4, glass negative.

The fire-blackened metal remains of the backrest and springs from Bill May's farm truck after the seats were burned to destroy traces of blood in the wake of events on the night of July 8–9, 1933. Courtesy of Fort Worth Star-Telegram Collection, Special Collections, the University of Texas at Arlington Libraries, image FWST 261-3, glass negative.

O. D. Stevens in handcuffs and shielding his face from a newspaper photographer's camera as he walked between the courthouse and the criminal courts building in Fort Worth on July 12, 1933. Courtesy of Fort Worth Star-Telegram Collection, Special Collections, the University of Texas at Arlington Libraries, image FWST 261-9, glass negative.

Mrs. Orley Stevens and her attorney, Clyde Mayes, walking between the courthouse and the criminal courts building in Fort Worth on July 12, 1933. Courtesy of Fort Worth Star-Telegram Collection, Special Collections, the University of Texas at Arlington Libraries, image FWST 261-11, glass negative.

M. T. Howard guilty of the robbery and handing out prison sentences of twenty-seven years. The jury found gang members Joe L. Martin and Johnny Carson guilty of conspiracy and gave them much shorter prison terms. Officers transported four of the criminals to federal prisons, but state authorities held Stevens in Fort Worth to stand trial for murder.

Six weeks later O. D. Stevens's trial for the murder of Harry Rutherford began. He had not been an ideal prisoner. In fact, officers foiled three attempts by Stevens to break jail. The first time they found teenaged gang members waiting outside the Fort Worth jail with ropes and a pistol,

Gang member M. T. Howard in handcuffs and chains on the sidewalk outside the courthouse in Fort Worth on July 12, 1933. Courtesy of Fort Worth Star-Telegram Collection, Special Collections, the University of Texas at Arlington Libraries, image FWST 261-10, glass negative.

O. D. Stevens, in a gray suit and leaning on a desk, faces the camera while conferring with his attorney on March 28, 1934. Other defendants sit in a row behind him in the Fort Worth federal court trial for mail theft. Courtesy of Fort Worth Star-Telegram Collection, Special Collections, the University of Texas at Arlington Libraries, image FWST 280-4, glass negative.

the second time they located secreted hacksaw blades in his cell, and the third time he successfully sawed his cell door from its hinges and was using it to try to pry open the steel bars of an exterior window. Despite his escape attempts, Stevens's murder trial began on May 13, 1934, in district court at Fort Worth. Before a jammed courtroom, witnesses detailed the events of July 8, 1933, with the jury finding the defendant guilty of murder and sentencing him to death in the electric chair.

Expecting O. D. Stevens to seek a retrial, state authorities turned him over to federal officers, who transported him to join M. T. Howard in the federal penitentiary at Leavenworth, Kansas. They soon shipped Stevens to the new maximum security federal prison on Alcatraz Island in San Francisco Bay, where he became inmate number 127. To the surprise of both federal and state officers, the court of criminal appeals in December 1935 reversed Stevens's murder conviction because of errors in the charge by the trial judge. This meant that Texas officials had to bring him back for a second murder trial, in which witness testimony began on September 18, 1936. Mrs. W. D. May, whose husband had been electrocuted for one of the Handley murders, became the star witness for the prosecution. The jury, however, could not agree to convict Stevens and eventually acquitted him.

No more trials followed, and O. D. Stevens spent a total of sixteen years back at Alcatraz, eventually completing his last years of imprisonment at Leavenworth. Authorities released the mastermind of the Texas and Pacific Mail Robbery in July 1950. He quietly traveled to Hot Springs, Arkansas, near which place he resided with his son until his death in April 1972.

Reflecting on the 1933 Texas and Pacific Mail Robbery and the subsequent triple murder at Handley, A. C. Howerton, a junior detective at the time he participated in the investigations, reflected thirty years later, "This . . . convinced me that there's no honor among thieves."

VISIT THE CRIME SCENES

TEXAS AND PACIFIC MAIL ROBBERY, MAIN STREET UNDERPASS, FORT WORTH, FEBRUARY 21, 1933

On the night of February 21, 1933, Bill May, Jack Sturdivant, and Harry Rutherford robbed guards of the registered mail that had just arrived in Fort Worth from Dallas on a passenger train outside the Texas and Pacific Railway depot. The heist took place atop the 1931 underpass that carried (and still carries) Main Street traffic beneath the Texas and Pacific tracks adjacent to the station.

To reach the crime scene on the south side of the Fort Worth business district, leave Interstate 30 at its intersection with Texas Highway 199 (South Henderson Street). After reaching the point where the freeway ramp meets South Henderson Street, turn north and proceed to

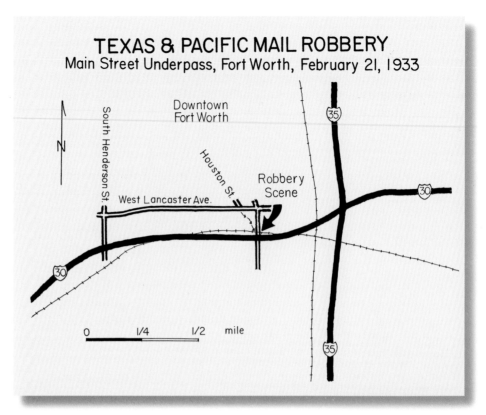

TEXAS & PACIFIC MAIL ROBBERY
Main Street Underpass, Fort Worth, February 21, 1933

Downtown
Fort Worth

South Henderson St.

Houston St.

West Lancaster Ave.

Robbery
Scene

N

0   1/4   1/2   mile

View west across the top of the Main Street underpass in Fort Worth, showing the base of a present-day billboard pedestal near the site where members of O. D. Stevens's gang stole bags of registered mail just unloaded from a Texas and Pacific passenger train on February 21, 1933. Photograph by the author, 2006.

the intersection with West Lancaster Avenue. (This juncture is located about one block from the outlet of the westbound ramp but a much longer 0.3 mile from the outlet of the eastbound ramp.) At West Lancaster Avenue, turn east (right) and drive 0.7 mile past the old main Fort Worth Post Office to the stoplight intersection at Houston Street. At this juncture turn south (right) into the parking area serving the Texas & Pacific Lofts apartment complex and the adjacent multistory art deco 1931 Texas and Pacific station and office building. After entering the parking area, bear to the left and drive up an inclined concrete ramp to a parking area on the upper level of the old underpass. The 1933 heist took place atop the underpass just beyond the east end of its north side, east of a small modern billboard. At the time of writing, short-term free parking was available in this area.

O. D. STEVENS'S DRUGSTORE, 6523 EAST LANCASTER AVENUE (TEXAS HIGHWAY 180), FORT WORTH, JULY 8, 1933

In 1933 O. D. Stevens erected a single-story masonry commercial building in Handley, a community on the east side of Fort Worth near his rural home. It is believed that he funded the project with proceeds from the February 1933 mail robbery. Placing a legitimate drugstore inside, he used the business as a front for his illegal narcotics dealings. The building, with a stone and petrified wood veneer, was the setting for his extended visit and domino games with Jack Sturdivant and the two

Commercial drugstore building erected by O. D. Stevens in 1933 in Handley, now part of Fort Worth, as a front for his illegal narcotics dealings. It is believed that he funded the construction project with proceeds from the February 21, 1933, Texas and Pacific Mail Robbery. Photograph by the author, 2006.

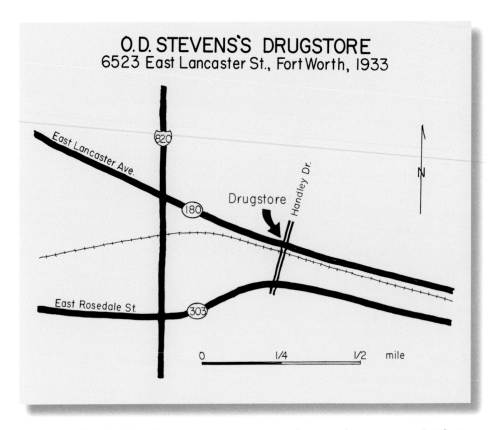

O.D. STEVENS'S DRUGSTORE
6523 East Lancaster St., Fort Worth, 1933

East Lancaster Ave.

820

180

Drugstore

Handley Dr.

N

East Rosedale St.

303

0   1/4   1/2   mile

Rutherford brothers prior to their murders on the evening of July 8, 1933.

To reach the crime scene, from Interstate 30 on the east side of Fort Worth drive south on East Loop 820 South a distance of 1.7 miles to its juncture with Texas Highway 180 (East Lancaster Avenue). Turn east (left) on Texas Highway 180 and drive six blocks to its stoplight intersection with South Handley Drive, where the distinctive building stands at the northwest corner of the crossroads.

O. D. STEVENS'S RESIDENCE, 1408 MORRISON DRIVE, FORT WORTH, JULY 8, 1933

On the night of July 8, 1933, Bill May and O. D. Stevens murdered Jack Sturdivant, Harry Rutherford, and Jewel B. Rutherford somewhere in or around Stevens's home or the adjacent site where May was building a house. At the time, the setting was a partially wooded rural area with only scattered farms. Once they began their investigations, law officers discovered that Stevens had built his two-story, solid stone masonry home with hidden rooms and compartments for illicit narcotics activities. The still handsome and well preserved building serves as a commercial day-care center for children.

O. D. Stevens's stone house at 1408 Morrison Drive in Fort Worth, erected in 1933 with hidden rooms and compartments as a base of operations for his illicit narcotics network. Photograph by the author, 2006.

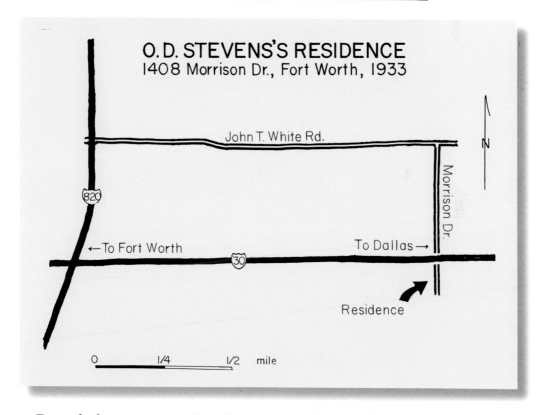

O. D. STEVENS'S RESIDENCE
1408 Morrison Dr., Fort Worth, 1933

John T. White Rd.

820

←To Fort Worth   To Dallas →

30

Morrison Dr.

Residence

0   1/4   1/2   mile

N

To reach the crime scene from Interstate 30, drive north on East Loop 820 North a distance of 0.5 mile to its intersection with Bridge Street/John T. White Road. Turn east (right) on John T. White Road and drive 1.3 miles through a neighborhood filled with modern apartments and residences to the 7600 block and the intersection with Morrison Road. Turn south (right) onto Morrison and drive 0.5 mile, crossing

Interstate 30 on a narrow, two-lane overpass. The former Stevens house stands set back about half a block to the west (right) from Morrison Road just south of the I-30 bridge. A parking lot occupies the area in front of the building, which as a private child-care facility is not open to casual visitors.

EAST FIRST STREET BRIDGE, 4500 BLOCK OF EAST FIRST STREET ALONGSIDE GATEWAY PARK, FORT WORTH, JULY 8–9, 1933

Sometime on the night of July 8–9, 1933, Bill May and O. D. Stevens pushed a hog wire–wrapped bundle of three human corpses and two hundred-pound sacks of cement over the railing of the East First Street Bridge into the Trinity River. They expected the weight of the material would hold the bodies underwater until they fully decomposed, but they misjudged the buoyancy of the corpses. Four evenings later Fort Worth detective Dusty Rhodes gazed down from the bridge and discovered the remains. The setting has changed little since that hot summer night.

To reach the crime scene from Interstate 30 on the southeast side of downtown Fort Worth, take the exit for Beach Street and drive north on Beach Street 1.1 miles, passing an entrance into Gateway Park. At

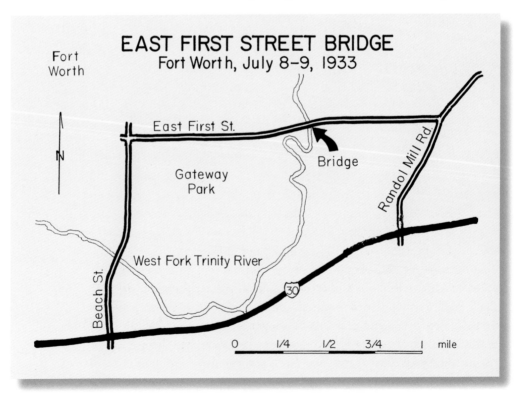

EAST FIRST STREET BRIDGE
Fort Worth, July 8–9, 1933

Fort Worth

N

East First St.

Bridge

Gateway Park

Randol Mill Rd

West Fork Trinity River

Beach St.

30

0   1/4   1/2   3/4   1   mile

The East First Street Bridge across the Trinity River on the east side of Fort Worth, over the railing of which O. D. Stevens and Bill May shoved a hog-wire-wrapped bundle containing the bodies of Jack Sturdivant, Harry Rutherford, and J. B. Rutherford during the night of July 8–9, 1933. Photograph by the author, 2006.

the stoplight intersection with East First Street, turn east (right) and drive 1.0 mile, bypassing another entrance into Gateway Park, to reach the historic two-lane bridge. The railings where detectives found a brown substance that later proved to be human blood are in the sixth section from the west end on the south side of the structure. Street-side parking may be found east of the bridge, but the area becomes muddy after rains. Visitors must take great care in walking on this very narrow bridge. At the time of research, plans were being made to construct a new vehicular bridge parallel to and just north of the East First Street Bridge, with the 1931 structure to be reserved for pedestrians and bicyclists, but it will remain very dangerous for visitors on foot until this occurs. (A historical plaque observed during field work at the west abutment inaccurately noted the bridge as having been built in 1936, three years after the events described here.)

☛ JUDGE THE EVIDENCE FOR YOURSELF

Abilene Daily Reporter (Abilene, Tex.), July 10, 1933, pp. 1, 8; July 11, 1933, pp. 1, 11; July 13, 1933, pp. 1, 9.

Dallas Morning News (Dallas, Tex.), February 23, 1933, sec. I, p. 1; February 24, 1933, sec. II, p. 1; May 31, 1933, sec. I, p. 9; July 11, 1933, sec. I, pp. 1, 2; July 12, 1933, sec. I, pp. 1, 3; February 23, 1934, sec. I, pp. 1, 16; March 27, 1934, sec. I, pp. 1, 12; March 28, 1934, sec. I, pp. 1, 12; March 29, 1934, sec. I, pp. 1, 14; March 30, 1934, sec. I, pp. 1, 10; March 31, 1934, sec. I, pp. 1, 3; April 4, 1934, sec. I, p. 1; June 14, 1934, sec. I, p. 2; December 19, 1935, sec. I, pp. 1, 4.

Fort Worth Press (Fort Worth, Tex.), February 22, 1933, p. 1; February 23, 1933, p. 1; February 24, 1933, p. 1; July 10, 1933, pp. 1, 5; July 11, 1933, pp. 1, 3; July 12, 1933, pp. 1, 7; July 14, 1933, pp. 1, 10; July 15, 1933, pp. 1, 7; July 17, 1933, pp. 1, 5; February 22, 1934, pp. 1, 5; February 24, 1934, p. 1; March 26, 1934, pp. 1, 7; March 27, 1934, pp. 1, 3; March 28, 1934, pp. 1, 11; March 29, 1934, pp. 1, 8; March 30, 1934, pp. 1, 3; March 31, 1934, pp. 1, 2; April 3, 1934, pp. 1, 7; June 13, 1934, pp. 1, 3; June 14, 1934, pp. 1, 13; June 16, 1934, p. 1; September 14, 1936, p. 14; September 18, 1936, pp. 1, 2; September 19, 1936, pp. 1, 2; September 21, 1936, p. 12; September 23, 1936, pp. 1, 2.

Fort Worth Star-Telegram (Fort Worth, Tex.), February 22, 1933, evening ed., pp. 1, 4; February 24, 1933, evening ed., p. 1; March 2, 1933, evening ed., p. 1; July 10, 1933, evening ed., pp. 1, 5; July 11, 1933, evening ed., pp. 1, 4; July 12, 1933, evening ed., pp. 1, 4; July 13, 1933, evening ed., pp. 1, 4, 10; July 14, 1933, morning ed., sec. 2, p. 1; evening ed., pp. 1, 4; July 15, 1933, evening ed., pp. 1, 2; August 3, 1933, evening ed., pp. 1, 4; January 13, 1934, evening ed., p. 1; February 22, 1934, evening ed., pp. 1, 4; February 24, 1934, evening ed., p. 1; March 21, 1934, evening ed., pp. 1, 4; March 26, 1934, evening ed., pp. 1, 4; March 27, 1934, evening ed., pp. 1, 4; March 28, 1934, evening ed., pp. 1, 4; March 29, 1934, evening ed., pp. 1, 8; March 30, 1934, evening ed., pp. 1, 6; March 31, 1934, evening ed., pp. 1, 2; April 3, 1934, evening ed., pp. 1, 4; April 6, 1934, evening ed., pp. 1, 6; April 7, 1934, evening ed., pp. 1, 2; April 26, 1934, evening ed., p. 7; June 13, 1934, evening ed., pp. 1, 4; June 14, 1934, evening ed., pp. 1, 8; September 7, 1934, evening ed., p. 1; June 12, 1935, evening ed., p. 1; July 20, 1935, evening ed., pp. 1, 2; September 6, 1935, evening ed., pp. 1, 8; January 3, 1936, evening ed., p. 1; September 19, 1936, evening ed., pp. 1, 2; September 23, 1936, evening ed., pp. 1, 4; September 22, 1948, evening ed., pp. 1, 4; September 23, 1948, evening ed., pp. 1, 8; July 18, 1950, evening ed., p. 1; February 21, 1963, evening ed., sec. 1, pp. 1, 14; August 1, 2009, sec. A, p. 1; sec. B, pp. 1, 10.

10 THE UNSOLVED MURDER OF FRANK NAND SINGH: IMMIGRANT SMUGGLING ON THE MEXICAN BORDER IN THE 1930S

Raoul Gandara, better known in the Juarez, Mexico, underworld of the 1930s as "El Wrengo" and "Metcho," was a smuggler with a reputation as a hired gun. He would do just about anything for money, including hiding fugitives. This was just what he did in 1931 at the behest of Asa Singh, a transplanted South Asian ethnic community leader who cultivated fields outside San Elizario on the American side of the Rio Grande below El Paso.

Asa Singh was not an ordinary dirt farmer. By no means. Born the son of Uttam Singh in the town of Kharaudi in the Hoshiarpur district of British India, he immigrated to the United States in 1905. He then became a member of a California-based nationalistic organization called the Hindustani Gadar Party, the goal of which was independence for India from British colonial rule. Now seen as freedom fighters, Gadar Party members employed bombings, assassination, and even collaboration with Germans during World War I to achieve their ambition of Indian self-government. After returning to India in 1913 Asa Singh himself was involved in an attack committed by Ghaniya Singh in Patiala State. To escape British authorities he came back to the United States in 1916, first settling in the Imperial Valley of California and then in 1924 relocating to the fertile Rio Grande valley near El Paso. He remained an active member of the Hindustani Gadar Party, though the strength of the organization waned after several unsuccessful attempts at fomenting uprisings in India.

The Hindustani Gadar Party maintained itself financially through donations from immigrant Indians, and it was to its advantage as an organization for their numbers to grow. The Immigration Act of 1917, however, excluded most Asian Indians from entry to the United States. Gadar Party members consequently aided their compatriots in crossing the international boundary illegally, as each new immigrant in America potentially could support the revolutionary aims of the group in India. In smuggling aliens into the United States, party members became targets for immigration control officers, so each played a cat-and-mouse game with the other. In such a situation Asian-born U.S. government

interpreter Nagina Ram Dhami met his death at the hands of Indian hit-man Narain Singh in Sacramento on February 9, 1931. The party facilitated Narain's escape from California to Texas, where another group member, Asa Singh, hid the killer while making arrangements with Raoul Gandara and another Mexican, Pat Guerra, to transport the fugitive across the border and into the interior. One of the two Mexicans later reported, "A Hindu came here from Calif[ornia] and Asa came to me and said, 'I will give you about a hundred and fifty dollars to take this man to Chihuahua.'" For the next two years Narain Singh remained in Mexico, most of the time around Culiacan on the west coast of the country. "Hindu" was a term that frequently was used at the time along the border to refer to Asian Indians.

Two government agents searching for smuggled immigrants aboard cars of a freight train newly arrived in El Paso from Mexico in the 1930s. Courtesy of Farm Security Administration/Office of War Information Photograph Collection, Library of Congress, Washington, D.C., image LC-USF34-018222-E.

Asa Singh did more than just farm. He himself became active in helping Asian Indians cross the international boundary from Mexico into the United States. Geography simplified this for him. The river valley just below El Paso blossomed like a green oasis anywhere that irrigation water from the river could reach its cotton fields, though most of the time the Rio Grande itself was shallow enough for people to wade from one side to the other. Asa Singh's irrigated farm was only about a mile as the crow flies from the home of his parents-in-law across the river in San Ysidro, Mexico. El Paso County sheriff Chris P. Fox wrote in 1933, "The people to be smuggled put up at the mother-in-law's house and then when the time is right they slip across with the help of Asa's brother-in-law." Once on the American side, the sheriff added, "They have friends up and down the valley for a good many miles in each direction," and they went undetected as illegal aliens. Even if they were caught, most of the newcomers shared the common Indian surname of Singh, and they merely said who they were and claimed to have entered the country legally prior to the 1917 act.

Illegal movement of people from India into the United States after passage of the 1917 legislation became highly organized, but to succeed the operations required accomplices on the border like Asa Singh. Indians typically departed India by steamship, going first to Japan and then from Japanese ports to Panama. They next crossed the isthmus and then sailed the much shorter distance to Guatemala

California mug shot of Narain Singh about 1930. Courtesy of Investigation File on Murder of Frank Nand Singh, El Paso County Sheriff's Office.

on the Gulf of Mexico. There the Indians crossed the lightly guarded boundary into Mexico and made their way northward to border areas where Gadar Party members or Mexicans connected with them facilitated the illegal crossings into the United States. The movement was substantial, with an estimated one thousand Asian Indians being observed in Kobe, Japan, at one point in time, all of them awaiting passage to Latin American ports. U.S. immigration inspector P. J. Farrelly at San Francisco in spring 1933 declared, "It can be safely assumed that 90% of the Indians who traveled to Mexico and South American countries from Japan and India within the past fifteen years have all succeeded in effecting their entry into the United States." Only a minority of these Indians made their way to the El Paso Valley, but enough of them settled there to form a very distinctive enclave in the mostly Hispanic agricultural communities like Ysleta, San Elizario, and Socorro. There outsiders knew Asa Singh as the head man or "kingfish" of the Asians.

There probably never was any community where all persons got along with everyone else, and Asa Singh had his own nemesis among the Indians in the El Paso Valley. This individual was Nand Singh, known as "Frank" to outsiders. He had come to the Ysleta area in the 1920s, married a Mexican woman, had three children, and by 1933 leased and operated an irrigated cotton farm belonging to Bernie Berg. Located just west of the Ysleta/Socorro Road, the property lay mostly between the Southside Ditch and the Franklin Drain close to the Rio Grande. The site today is almost adjacent to the modern Zaragoza Bridge international border crossing. Frank Nand Singh not only had trouble getting along with community leader Asa Singh but also seemingly had problems with all of his neighbors, both Indian and Mexican. He had a reputation for cheating his Latino field hands, sometimes driving them off with a hoe or shovel with no pay at the end of a work day. Sheriff Fox in 1933 noted, "Every single . . . Hindu and Mexican in this valley that had business or social relations with Nand, hated him with all their heart." If this were not enough, Nand openly served as an interpreter and informer for federal immigration agents, his reports leading to the deportation of several of his fellow countrymen. He became so despised that Asa Singh and other Gadar Party members knowingly circulated false rumors that he was a secret agent for the British government. The immigrant farmer had virtually no friends.

The local Indians decided that they had taken all of Nand Singh that they could stand. As Asa Singh later admitted, "We all agreed to get rid of Frank." They pooled about three hundred dollars and approached a Mexican criminal named Pedro to assassinate Nand. Then the Indian farmers had second thoughts. Asa later wrote, "We were a little afraid of him that he may expose us."

Asa Singh next contacted Nidham Singh, at the time president of the Gadar Party in San Francisco, to seek help. He undoubtedly complained about Nand's informing against party members in their efforts to bring East Indians into the United States illegally. Of equal interest to Nidham as party president, always with his eye on the purse, was the assertion that Nand never "let us collect money down there." All the conspirators knew that Asa had helped the party in 1931 to arrange the escape of informer-killer Narain Singh to Mexico, and they thought that President Nidham Singh might be able to bring the professional killer back to Texas for another "job." In time this is just what happened.

Nidham Singh wrote to fugitive Narain Singh in Culiacan, asking him to come to Juarez at once. There the gunman stayed with Pat Guerra, one of the people who had conducted him to safety two years earlier. Guerra later reported, "He came to my house and stayed there for four days" before moving to another dwelling in Juarez, where he stayed until about September 19, 1933. Then he disappeared across the river. The Indian triggerman next showed up in the hut of Manuel Vasquez adjacent to the Rio Grande not far from Asa Singh's farmhouse. Thirteen-year-old Refugio Duarte lived in Asa's household because his sister, Trinidad, had married Asa. On several occasions Singh had young Refugio carry food across the fields to the hut where Narain was camping. "One day when I took the lunch over to the Hindu in the field, Asa was in the house and he told me not to tell anyone that I saw the Hindu, or that he was there. I waited while the Hindu ate and . . . it gave me a good chance to look at him," the young man reported. Importantly he added, "I do recognize the picture shown me as being the man that was always out in the cotton field; the name on the picture is Narain Singh."

Sometime in mid-September 1933, a few days before the killer appeared in the hut next to the river, a much higher profile guest had arrived. This was Gadar Party president Nidham Singh himself. Rather than hide in an adobe hovel, the dignitary became an honored guest in Asa Singh's home at Socorro, Texas. Nidham made a full circuit of the Indian households in the El Paso Valley, everywhere seeking contributions to support the political and educational efforts of the Gadar Party. The leader cut a striking figure, standing about five feet, nine inches, tall, weighing about 175 pounds, and having a full head of dark hair and a smooth-shaved round face with a sharp nose. He spoke quickly in fluent English as well as in Indian languages. Young Refugio Duarte remembered, "This Hindu I called Pie used to leave the house every day and many times at night." President Nidham regularly spoke with Narain, the mystery man from the hut. Refugio Duarte reported, "I saw him [Narain] two times in the cotton field and saw him talking to Asa Singh and also saw him talking to Pie," noting, "he never came to the house . . . Pie used to visit with him quite often" but always away from the house.

Nidham Singh and Narain Singh had not come to El Paso for a tea party. The widely hated Frank Nand Singh had drawn them there, and there was work to be done. Starting about Tuesday, September 19, Narain Singh and another man began lurking in the vicinity of Nand's house on the Bernie Berg farm. Nand told his neighbors, Delip and Concha Singh, that when he and an African American worker were irrigating a field that week, they had seen two men at the edge of a ditch about seven o'clock in the evening. In the last light, they could not recognize the strangers. The farmer went home to get his wife, Guadalupe, and together they returned to the field to look, unsuccessfully, for the unidentified men. Casculo Parra, who also lived in the neighborhood, related that he walked from his farm into Ysleta every evening for his supper. For several days starting in the third week of September, he passed two unidentified men lounging on a canal bank or beside the road. He told sheriff's deputy Anthony Apodaca, "They never would answer. One of the fellows was tall and slim and had a big black moustache." He described the other as about five and a half feet tall, light-complexioned, and weighing about 175 pounds. One evening on the way back, Parra was feeling a little tipsy. When the two men again ignored his greeting, he cursed them, but then he wished he hadn't. He had to run all the way home because he thought it looked like the two had started following him.

Nidham Singh, president of the Hindustani Gadar Party, as shown in a California mug shot made about 1930. Courtesy of Investigation File on Murder of Frank Nand Singh, El Paso County Sheriff's Office.

Triggerman Jesus Duarte, brother-in-law of Asa Singh, in a mug shot provided to El Paso County sheriff Chris Fox by the U.S. Immigration Service about 1933. Courtesy of Investigation File on Murder of Frank Nand Singh, El Paso County Sheriff's Office.

By Saturday, September 23, 1933, the plans had been drawn. After dark Narain Singh went in the direction of Nand Singh's three-room house with Jesus Duarte, Asa Singh's Mexican brother-in-law. Both carried .45-caliber automatic pistols. The sun had set at 6:02 PM, and because of cloudy skies, it was dark by 6:40. Even so, the two assailants waited more than an hour and a half before they approached the farmhouse. Guadalupe Singh remembered, "My husband called to me and said, 'Listen, I hear some noises outside. Go and see what it is.'" She went outdoors and returned to say, "The chickens were making a little noise." Once again from the bedroom he called to her, seeming to be agitated: "I hear noises again, but do not go out." Despite his warning, she went out to a corral, coming back to assure her husband that she had heard only the cows eating corn. "He did not want for me to go out because he was afraid I would get shot," she later reported. Nand obviously had been spooked by seeing the mysterious men in the field. That very night Casculo Parra again saw the same two strange men, later than usual, around eight o'clock. In the meantime Nand lay down with his infant son on a bed across the room from an open window and began drifting off to sleep.

Guadalupe Singh had just closed the kitchen door, locking it with a key, when she saw flashes, heard four rapid gunshots, and smelled acrid gunpowder smoke. Knowing that her husband had feared for his life, she dashed to the bedroom with a lamp in her hands. In alarm she dropped the lamp as she reached down to pick up her baby, who was lying on the bed in its father's blood. Nand Singh was dead, and the time was 8:35 PM. The other children in their beds, Guadalupe dashed outside and ran around the house with the infant in her arms. In the gloom she saw two men running toward the west in the direction of the river. Having been married to an Indian for eleven years, she could understand much of his native language, and she understood Narain as he called out, "Fuck the son-of-a-bitch. He is now dead." Then one of the murderers yelled to the widow to keep her mouth shut or she would suffer the same fate. "I did not run after them because I was afraid they would kill me," she reported. After hearing the gunshots, a neighbor boy named Manuel Cassillas came on foot to see what had happened. Guadalupe sent him in a truck to the home of other neighbors, Delip and Concha Singh, where there was a telephone, to call for help.

The call went to the sheriff's department in downtown El Paso, but the dispatcher there radioed the alarm to squad cars already in the lower valley. Sheriff Chris P. Fox happened to be in the area investigating an assault, heard the radio call, and drove to the crime scene just as another car arrived bearing two deputies. "We reached the place at exactly 8:51 PM," he noted. Fox began the investigation immediately, with inspection of the body, a search for clues, and interviews with the widow and neighbors. He found the victim still lying in his bed with multiple gunshot wounds: one in the left temple, the second in the heart, the third just above the heart, and the last in the left shoulder. "The killers were expert gunners," he observed, "because if they had not been the child would have been hit." Any of the first three wounds in themselves would have been fatal. Although local people had flocked to the house after hearing the gunfire, they had not disturbed things too badly. With their flashlights the investigating officers found emptied cases from four .45-caliber automatic pistol cartridges outside the bedroom window, while inside they recovered three bullets in the mattress. Later they retrieved the fourth, the one fired into the temple, at the morgue. The location of holes in the window screen also showed four shots, two by a taller shooter and two from a shorter one.

The assailants successfully vanished into the darkness. Asa Singh and Nidham Singh had already made arrangements a second time with Pat Guerra and Raoul Gandara to transport both Narain Singh and Jesus Duarte in Gandara's automobile to Chihuahua. From there the killers could take a train to Culiacan. While the actual shooters escaped, the law officers arrested four local Indians, including Asa Singh, but then released them within days for lack of evidence. Gadar Party president Nidham Singh remained in the El Paso area until he learned that the two killers had securely reached the west coast of Mexico, and then he boarded a bus back to California.

Sheriff Fox began an extensive investigation into the crime. He started by taking statements from the South Asian residents of the lower El Paso Valley, quickly learning that no one seemed to like Frank Nand Singh. Early he learned about the visit by President Nidham Singh that coincided with the murder, so he contacted criminal investigators in San Francisco, Sacramento, and El Centro, California, making a quick study of the information they provided on the Hindustani Gadar Party and its leaders. While pursuing these leads, Fox concurrently sent criminal investigators to learn what informers on both sides of the Rio Grande could reveal.

One of the significant pieces of information that came to Fox from California was that after President Nidham Singh returned to the West Coast, he had begun telling people about the recent events in El Paso. Kishan Singh reported that in a meeting attended by thirty-five Indians at Calipatria, California, Nidham had reported, "Everyone [in El Paso] is okay down there except one man and the person we do not like down there we fixed him up." In a private conversation with one Bishan Singh at Brawley, California, the president gave a somewhat garbled account of the killing, taking credit himself for being one of the gunmen. While this was going on, another group of Gadar Party officials, including a vice president named Jagat Singh, came to El Paso, but Sheriff Fox interpreted this visit as an effort to divert attention from President Nidham Singh.

The sheriff pursued leads doggedly. Becoming convinced that answers to his questions lay in California, he and Assistant District Attorney John Penn traveled to El Centro in January 1934 to seek more evidence. The next month Asa Singh willingly gave Fox a signed confession of his complicity in the murder. The sheriff and his staff worked hard to gather sufficient evidence for a grand jury to indict participants. Even as early as October 22 he wrote, "I have talked to the D.A. today and he is about ready to shoot the works when we get a few more holes plugged up." The Indians in the El Paso Valley, however, were hesitant to say anything against members of the Gadar Party. Fox complained, "We are having one hell of a time to get anyone to talk." Through careful detective work the lawmen clearly identified the killers as Narain Singh and Jesus Duarte, but both of them remained in Mexico and Fox could not get enough hard evidence for a grand jury to indict them. An indictment was necessary in order for the U.S. government to request extradition.

In frustration after almost five years of investigation, Chris Fox on June 5, 1940, wrote a letter of complaint to the sheriff in El Centro. "We are stymied in this matter because the two men that did the killing are still in Mexico and perhaps will never return," he penned. The case has remained stalled at that point to this very day, and Fox's 1940 letter remains the last piece of paper in a thick file of evidence he compiled on the killing of Frank Nand Singh. The original records still lie in a file cabinet of the Criminal Investigations Division in the El Paso County sheriff's department. There is no statute of limitations on murder, and Frank Nand Singh's death remains an unsolved "live murder case."

MURDER OF FRANK NAND SINGH, BERNIE BERG FARM, 400 BLOCK OF TEXAS LOOP 375 (SOUTH AMERICAS AVENUE) NEAR YSLETA AND THE PRESENT-DAY ZARAGOZA INTERNATIONAL BRIDGE, EL PASO, SEPTEMBER 23, 1933

Frank Nand Singh raised irrigated cotton on the sixty-four-acre Bernie Berg farm on the south side of Ysleta in the Rio Grande valley downstream from El Paso. Today the area is incorporated into the city of El Paso. The roughly trapezoid-shaped tract of farmland measured about 870 feet wide and 3,300 feet long and stretched roughly east to west between two still-existing ditches, the Franklin Drain and the South Side Feeder. Much of the area today is covered by Texas Loop 375 (Americas Avenue) and by modern warehouses that serve the export-import commerce at the nearby Zaragoza International Bridge.

To reach the crime scene from Interstate 10, take the exit for Texas Loop 375 (Americas Avenue) on the extreme south side of El Paso. Drive 2.0 miles southwest on Loop 375 to the exit for Texas Highway 20 and Farm to Market Road 258. From the exit proceed southwestward 0.7 mile on the north-side access road (crossing straight through junctions with Texas Highway 20 and Farm to Market Road 258). Where the access road intersects Carl Longuemare Road and crosses over the Franklin Drain, one enters what historically was the Bernie Berg farm property. On the right one sees modern warehouses built on top of soil that Frank Singh once cultivated. His farmhouse stood on the former farmland that extended about thirty-three hundred feet westward to the South Side Feeder ditch, alongside present-day Southside Road. To this day there are nearby irrigated cotton fields that have changed little since the 1930s, when the Asian immigrant farmer raised crops on Bernie Berg's property.

View northeastward along the north-side access road of Texas Loop 375 from Southside Road into the warehouse area that occupies part of the former Bernie Berg farm, where assailants murdered Frank Nand Singh on September 23, 1933. At the time this photograph was made, crews were burying drainpipe beneath Southside Road. Photograph by the author, 2006.

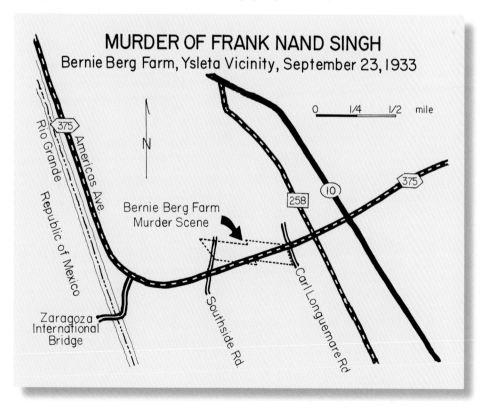

☛ JUDGE THE EVIDENCE FOR YOURSELF

El Paso County, Tex. Sheriff's Department. Investigation File on Murder of Frank Nand Singh, September 23, 1933. Criminal Records, Evidence and Forensics Section, Criminal Investigations Division, El Paso County Sheriff's Department, El Paso, Tex.

El Paso County Survey Maps (Accession Number 090–2000–028–001). El Paso County Historical Society, El Paso, Tex.

El Paso Herald-Post (El Paso, Tex.), September 25, 1933, p. 2; September 26, 1933, p. 1; September 28, 1933, p. 9.

El Paso Times (El Paso, Tex.), September 24, 1933, p. 1; September 25, 1933, pp. 1, 3; September 26, 1933, p. 2; September 29, 1933, p. 2.

Government of India. Home Department. Intelligence Bureau. Director. *The Ghadar Directory: Containing the Names of Persons Who Have Taken Part in the Ghadar Movement in America, Europe, Africa and Afghanistan as Well as in India.* New Delhi: Government of India Press, 1934; rpt. ed., Patiala, India: Punjabi University, 1997.

Leibson, Art. "The Killing of Frank Singh." *Password* (El Paso, Tex.), 34, no. 2 (summer 1989): 98–99.

Sood, Malini. "Expatriate Nationalism and Ethnic Radicalism: The Ghadar Party in North America, 1910–1920." PhD dissertation, State University of New York at Stony Brook, 1995.

11 THE POST MORPHINE RING DOPE DEALING AT THE EDGE OF THE CAPROCK

It would be an understatement to say that William F. Cato was trigger happy. He loved guns and the sense of authority they gave him.

Even before the citizens of Garza County elected the former blacksmith their sheriff in 1926, he surrounded himself with firearms. Cato lined the walls of his office at the jail at Post with guns of all types. He installed special holsters in his patrol car, even one above the sun visor so that, if a lawbreaker ordered him to "stick 'em up," in complying he could reach his pistol.

He purchased the first Thompson submachine gun known on the Texas South Plains and complained when county commissioners balked at reimbursing him for the expense. When the raw-boned sheriff responded to emergency calls, he frequently raced down roadways with siren wailing and lights flashing. While practicing a quick draw, Cato accidentally shot himself in the neck but didn't seem to learn anything from the mishap. Always the first officer to set up a roadblock for suspected criminals, he once frightened two friends by aiming his Tommy gun at them until he realized who they were. One resident declared, "I didn't like him. Hell, I was afraid of him. He wanted to shoot someone, and I was afraid he'd decide to shoot me."

After W. F. Cato moved from the Southland community to the county seat as sheriff in the mid-1920s, he became intimately acquainted with physician Verner A. Hartman and veterinarian Lewis W. Kitchen. The latter had resided in the community at least since World War I and in 1922 had purchased the half city block where he practiced veterinary medicine. Kitchen housed the clinic in a south-facing wooden building two blocks south of the main commercial district. It fronted on what today is Seventh Street between avenues H and I. Behind the building he erected a corral to contain large animals he was treating. Doctors Hartman and Kitchen did more than practice legitimate medicine— they also illegally sold morphine to addicts from a wide territory.

Morphine was the drug of choice for most Texas addicts during the 1920s and 1930s. Derived from the immature seeds of opium poppies, morphine first was isolated by a German pharmacist in 1803. Commonly employed by military surgeons to reduce soldiers' pain from battle

William F. Cato, sheriff of Garza County, Texas, 1926–1936. Courtesy of Garza County Historical Museum, Post, Texas.

Concrete footings for a floodlamp that stood behind Dr. Lewis W. Kitchen's veterinary clinic to illuminate corrals where he penned livestock brought for treatment. Photograph by the author, 2006.

wounds, morphine found widespread use in the American Civil War and afterward. Many doughboys came home from World War I hooked on the narcotic. It remained the most popular drug among American addicts until the introduction of heroin, an opiate both stronger in effect and faster acting. The U.S. Congress on December 17, 1914, passed the Harrison Narcotics Act, which for the first time restricted the dispensing of morphine and similar substances to such professionals as doctors, veterinarians, and pharmacists. Then, to regulate narcotic use, in 1923 the Narcotics Division of the U.S. Treasury Department (the first federal drug agency) banned sales of addictive drugs by all except licensed providers.

These events led doctors Hartman and Kitchen in quiet Post, Texas, into the world of illegal narcotics dealing. Paying hush money to Sheriff Cato to turn a blind eye to their activities, the two medical men received a wide range of stolen goods that morphine-addicted thieves bartered for drugs. They legally purchased morphine from a drug wholesaler in Lubbock for nine cents a grain (64.79 milligrams). The dealers then bartered and sold the same narcotic at one dollar a grain, a massive markup. The key to their success as early as 1929 was to manipulate purchase and sales records to hide the illicit trade from the occasional U.S. Treasury Department inspectors.

O. W. "Curly" Wood of Choctaw County, Oklahoma, was a regular customer of veterinarian Lewis Kitchen. Wood made it a regular practice to hitchhike through the South Plains region, stealing wearing apparel, firearms, silverware, nice fountain pens, and other articles to exchange for morphine. When asked how many times he had fenced stolen goods to the veterinarian, he replied, "so many times and so often it'd be hard to answer." Bricklayer Elzie Clay once worked on the foundation and chimneys of the vet's house in trade for drugs. On one occasion he and Kitchen went to a local lumberyard, and while "Doctor Kitchen . . . called the man to the car," Clay at his boss's direction went inside the now unguarded sales room and helped himself to two gallons of paint. Charlie Fowler of Fort Worth was another junkie who depended on the Post veterinarian. In November 1934 he delivered thirty-four pairs of hose, five negligees, eighteen pairs of step-ins (panties), and one black dress to Kitchen's veterinary clinic but discovered the animal doctor was away. Sheriff Cato drove up. Fowler reported, "He said Kitchen was not in town, and I couldn't get dope from him, and why didn't I take it [the stolen goods] to Doctor Hartman." The addict added, "I said Doctor Hartman didn't like me. The sheriff said he'd fix that up." Fowler and the officer then drove to the physician's office, where Cato kept the loot but advised nurse Lena Roberts, "This boy here is okay." Fowler got his morphine.

Not all the Post drug deals were made for stolen property. Twenty-one-year-old Alta Mae Hodge of Odessa in 1935 reported that she had gone to Dr. Lewis Kitchen for morphine a year and a half before. When asked how much she had paid for three grains of the drug, she replied, "I didn't pay him. . . . I had a date with him." Vera Gentry, another twenty-one-year-old customer from Odessa, stated that she "made dates" with Kitchen "six or seven times," on each occasion receiving four grains of morphine. "You mean sexual intercourse?" an attorney later asked, to which she nodded her head in assent. "Where?" he asked. "In his office," she responded. He then questioned, "Was he drunk or sober?" She answered, "Drunk sometimes."

For at least half a dozen years the doctor, the veterinarian, and the sheriff prospered in clandestine partnership. If anyone in Post realized what they were doing, the word seemingly did not escape the town. Finally in 1935 two federal narcotics agents based in Fort Worth and Dallas became curious about Kitchen's dealings. His drug sales did not seem to tally with his written records. U.S. Treasury officers Spencer Stafford and V. C. McCullough met with Kitchen in Post on Tuesday, February 5, 1935. The veterinarian chanced to see documents that incriminated both him and Hartman for irregularities in morphine handling. Kitchen alerted the physician and perhaps also Sheriff Cato, because he expected further investigation. The inquiry came sooner than later.

On the morning of Thursday, February 7, 1935, the two agents returned to Post looking for Kitchen. This time they were not alone; with them rode Eva Michelle and Dewey L. Lowery, morphine-addict stool pigeons. As government "plants," both of them had purchased morphine from unsuspecting Kitchen and Hartman as part of the investigation. Discovering the animal clinic closed, the government party drove to a nearby gasoline station operated by Kitchen's brother, where they found the man they wanted. When the veterinarian saw the two informers inside the vehicle he agreed to return to his office to meet with the lawmen. Lewis Kitchen realized that a day of crisis had come.

About this time someone, perhaps from the filling station, telephoned Sheriff Cato to report "strangers" in town and to give him the license number on their car. Once parked in front of the animal clinic, the officers and Kitchen went inside to reexamine his drug purchase and sale records. Eva Michelle and Dewey Lowery remained in the car, one of three parked diagonally in front of the office.

Dewey Lowery, gray-haired though only thirty-seven, remembered the events this way. While agents Stafford and McCullough conferred with Dr. Kitchen in the office, Sheriff W. F. Cato and an unidentified man walked up to the sedan where Lowery was seated in the back and Michelle in the front. "What're you hauling in there?" asked the sheriff, who was holding his Thompson submachine gun in one hand. Cato probably looked a little stouter than he really was, for he had put on a bullet-proof vest beneath his outer coat. "I told him nothing but a brief case and a typewriter," Lowery remembered responding. Thereupon the sheriff, pointing the automatic weapon directly at the informer, ordered him out of the car and searched him for any weapons with his free hand. "Don't you move or I'll let you have it now," he threatened. Alarmed by Cato's behavior, Lowery feared the sheriff might "accidentally" shoot him on the spot.

From her position in the front seat, Eva Michelle remembered the morning about the same way. Speaking about the sheriff, she said, "He poked the machine gun in the . . . door at Lowery." After the sheriff questioned him about what was inside the car, the woman interjected, "This is a government car and there're two government agents in there," gesturing toward the clinic. It was at this point that Lowery excitedly began calling to officer McCullough for protection.

Inside the office, heavy-set and graying V. C. McCullough and fellow agent Spencer Stafford were still inspecting drug ledgers. "Doctor Kitchen asked what records we wanted to see," McCullough recalled. "He got the duplicate order forms and we sat down to make a check of requisitions." Things remained quiet until they heard Lowery cry out for assistance. Officer Stafford got up from the table and went outside. No more than thirty seconds elapsed before McCullough and

Dr. Kitchen heard sounds of a scuffle. From the door McCullough saw his partner dodging behind one of the parked cars, with the sheriff standing in full view holding a Tommy gun. "My God, don't shoot that man, he's a federal officer," McCullough yelled out. He later remembered Sheriff Cato facing him for a moment before he turned to take a step or two. McCullough heard rapid-fire machine-gun shots "like a trip-hammer—four or five real quick, then a slight pause and one more. . . . I heard Stafford scream." Seeing his colleague fall, McCullough froze as the sheriff called out, "Stand away, or I'll let you have it." Dr. Kitchen advised agent McCullough, "Don't fool with him, he's dangerous, he'll kill every one of you."

Even though Sheriff Cato later claimed that no one alerted him that federal agents were in Dr. Kitchen's office, witness after witness disagreed. Eva Michelle from the car informed him that federal officers were inside the office, while officer McCullough asserted "we were shouting we were officers." As he emerged from the clinic door, Spencer Stafford held his treasury agent's identification badge in his hand and tossed it and his service pistol at Cato's feet as proof of his status. Eva Michelle remembered his words, "Here's my gun and here's my badge."

When he drove to the Kitchen veterinary clinic on the fateful winter morning, the sheriff was not alone. On the way he stopped and deputized Tom Morgan, a livestock raiser who lived a mile east of town. Morgan's recollection was that he had just driven into Post when "I heard the brakes of a car, and I saw Mr. Cato. He motioned to me. He told me John Putman had told him there were some suspicious characters in south Post." As they rode off in the sheriff's vehicle, Cato "pulled out a six-shooter and laid it over in my lap and said, 'Take that.'" When they arrived at the animal clinic, each man approached an opposite side of the car bearing the two informers. Morgan remembered that Cato ordered Dewey Lowery to get out of the vehicle and queried him, "Do you mean to say you're not going to answer my question?" Frightened, the informer called out, "Oh, Mac, come here quick. It looks like this guy's going to shoot me." At this point the deputy looked up to see agent Spencer Stafford emerging from the clinic door.

According to Tom Morgan, "I looked up and saw a man running toward us." The deputized rancher stated that Sheriff Cato whirled around and grabbed for a pistol that Stafford had removed from his pocket, while the latter tried to take hold of the Tommy gun that was pointed at Lowery. "I had my gun just stuck down in my pants," remembered Morgan. "When Cato said, 'Shoot him, Tom,' I pulled my gun." The two informers then manhandled Morgan's arm to keep him from firing at the officer, but Cato's machine-gun bullets made their mark. Eva Michelle got out of the car and stooped down in an attempt to cradle Stafford's head in his last moments. "Get away from him, or I'll give you some of it," yelled Cato, while winking knowingly to Dr. Kitchen, who had just come out of the clinic with agent McCullough. About this time Cato walked over to Dewey Lowery, the chief informer, and spat out, "You're the blame for this." Later an attorney declared that by this time the sheriff had realized "his playhouse had been broken up and his gravy-train cut off."

Agent McCullough demanded medical help for Stafford. Cato assented, saying, "Take him to Doctor Hartman." Realizing the physician was also a member of the same narcotics gang, the federal agent argued, "No, don't do that, take him to any other doctor, but not to Doctor Hartman." It was too late. Spencer Stafford suffered multiple grievous gunshot wounds, four of them to the torso, and he expired in the dirt in front of the animal clinic. His death certificate, still on file in the Garza County Courthouse, notes his killing as a homicide that took place about 11:30 AM.

Before Spencer Stafford's mortal remains were transported home to New York State, federal authorities in Texas began legal proceedings against Sheriff Cato and other members of the Post morphine ring. The next evening a U.S. marshal and a deputy loaded Cato, Kitchen, and Hartman into a large maroon sedan and whisked them to Dallas, where they were jailed on charges of murder. The men were the second group of individuals prosecuted under a new law passed by Congress that made it a federal offense to kill any officer of the U.S. government engaged in official duties.

Later federal charges against the Post morphine ring included illegal sales of drugs under the 1914 Harrison Act and conspiracy to obstruct justice. Eventually other individuals, including deputized rancher Tom Morgan and Hartman's twenty-three-year-old nurse, Lena Roberts, found themselves in federal court. Legal proceedings for all the defendants were complicated by the actions of Sheriff Cato's attorney, N. C. Outlaw. The Post lawyer arranged for two people to give untruthful grand jury testimony under oath to support Cato's case. On the afternoon following the shooting, Outlaw went to the home of E. R. Braddock and coached the man to give specific testimony even though he had not witnessed the shooting. The attorney then offered C. M. Loe, a forty-year-old drayman, five hundred dollars to testify that he had seen Stafford leave the clinic building carrying what appeared to be a firearm. On March 11, 1935, a federal court in Dallas convicted Outlaw of suborning grand jury witnesses and sentenced him to fifteen months in federal prison. The attorney appealed the conviction to the Supreme Court of the United States, which affirmed the decision and the punishment.

Legal proceedings continued against members of the gang. Despite Outlaw's conviction for suborning witnesses, he and Cato were acquitted on charges of conspiracy to obstruct justice. Both Kitchen and Hartman plead guilty to breaking federal narcotics statutes, but because of conflicting evidence a jury found them and Cato innocent of murder. Spencer Stafford's widow was vindicated, however, when a federal court awarded her fifteen thousand dollars in damages from the impetuous sheriff and his bondsmen over the shooting death of her husband. Doctors V. A. Hartman and Lewis Kitchen went to federal prison for their illegal drug dealings.

Eventually most of the residents in Post forgot this Depression-era brush with junkies, drug dealers, and a bribe-taking county official, but stories are still told in the West Texas town of the winter day when the sheriff shot and killed a federal narcotics officer. Although physician Hartman did not return to Post after imprisonment, Lewis Kitchen did. While he was locked up, his wife continued teaching in the local school. Losing his license to practice veterinary medicine, he still unofficially treated people's animals delivered to a corral behind his house via the alley. W. F. Cato failed in his bid for reelection as sheriff in 1936, and the next year he took his own life during a spell of unhappiness over the turn of events he had experienced.

Because they felt that federal authorities were punishing their community over the death of treasury agent Spencer Stafford, many Post residents united behind Sheriff Cato and the two doctors. These people may not have personally liked them or approved of what they did, but more than a dozen leading citizens traveled to Dallas and personally put up tens of thousands of dollars as surety to provide bail for Cato, Kitchen, Hartman, and Morgan. When the sheriff returned to Post from his initial incarceration in the Dallas jail, more than a hundred individuals welcomed him home at the train station. Despite this show of solidarity, the locals knew that their trigger-happy sheriff had indeed killed an officer of the national government and that a neighborhood physician and a local veterinarian for years had promoted drug addiction for personal gain. Other people were less understanding. From the perspective of Clyde O. Eastus, the U.S. attorney in Dallas who prosecuted the cases, the level of criminality uncovered in 1935 Garza County was "comparable to Chicago's gang-ridden South Side in Al Capone's heyday."

SHOOTING AT KITCHEN'S VETERINARY CLINIC, EAST SIDE OF ALLEY ON THE NORTH SIDE OF EAST SEVENTH STREET BETWEEN AVENUE H AND AVENUE I, POST, FEBRUARY 7, 1935

Little remains at the place once occupied by Dr. Lewis W. Kitchen's veterinary clinic and livestock corrals and where federal drug agent Spencer Stafford met his death. The lightly built wooden clinic was razed years ago, and a modern residence now stands just to the east. Even so, the concrete footings for a floodlight that illuminated the corrals behind the treatment center may be seen. Both street paving and concrete curbs have been added since the 1930s shooting.

To visit the crime scene, turn east from U.S. Highway 84 (Broadway Street) onto U.S. Highway 380 East (East Main Street) in downtown Post. Proceed two blocks east on Main Street to the intersection with South Avenue H. Turn south (right) on Avenue H and drive two blocks

View north from East Seventh Street in Post, Texas, to the greatly altered location where Sheriff William F. Cato shot federal drug agent Spencer Stafford in 1935. Photograph by the author, 2006.

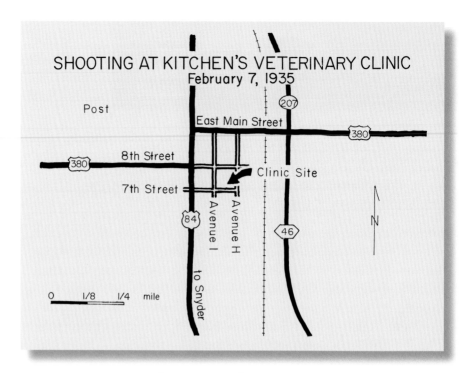

SHOOTING AT KITCHEN'S VETERINARY CLINIC
February 7, 1935

Post

207

East Main Street

380

8th Street

380

7th Street

Clinic Site

84

Avenue I

Avenue H

46

N

to Snyder

0   1/8   1/4   mile

to its intersection with East Seventh Street. At this juncture, turn west (right) and drive half a block to the alley in the middle of the block on the north (right) side. This area today comprises the side yard for a modern residence. The historic south-facing veterinary clinic with street-side parking fronted on East Seventh Street at the immediate east side of the alley, behind which the former corrals stood. Free parking is available alongside the curb.

JUDGE THE EVIDENCE FOR YOURSELF

Boren, Mildred. "A Garza County Murder." *West Texas Historical Association Yearbook* 67 (1991): 122–29.

Dallas Morning News (Dallas, Tex.), February 8, 1935, sec. I, pp. 1, 20; February 9, 1935, sec. I, pp. 1, 12; February 10, 1935, sec. II, pp. 1, 7; February 11, 1935, sec. II, p. 1; February 12, 1935, sec. I, pp. 1, 4; February 14, 1935, sec. II, p. 1; February 20, 1935, sec. II, pp. 1, 12; February 21, 1935, sec. II, pp. 1, 10; February 22, 1935, sec. II, pp. 1, 6; March 3, 1935, sec. II, p. 1; March 7, 1935, sec. II, p. 1; March 8, 1935, sec. I, p. 3; March 9, 1935, sec. II, pp. 1, 10; March 10, 1935, sec. I, p. 4; sec. II, pp. 1, 7; March 11, 1935, sec. I, p. 1; March 12, 1935, sec. I, pp. 1, 8; March 15, 1935, sec. II, pp. 1, 16; March 16, 1935, sec. II, pp. 1, 9; March 17, 1935, sec. II, p. 1; March 24, 1935, sec. II, p. 1; May 5, 1935, sec. II, pp. 1, 8; May 8, 1935, sec. I, pp. 1, 16; May 24, 1935, sec. I, p. 1; May 25, 1935, sec. I, pp. 1, 12; May 26, 1935, sec. I, pp. 1, 9; May 28, 1935, sec. I, pp. 1, 3; June 2, 1935, sec. I, pp. 1, 9; April 28, 1936, sec. I, p. 1.

Lubbock Evening Journal (Lubbock, Tex.), February 7, 1935, pp. 1, 9; February 8, 1935, pp. 1, 13; February 11, 1935, p. 1; February 12, 1935, pp. 1, 9; February 13, 1935, p. 1; February 14, 1935, pp. 1, 5; February 21, 1935, pp. 1, 9; February 22, 1935, pp. 1, 15; March 8, 1935, pp. 1, 13; May 8, 1935, pp. 1, 13; May 22, 1935, pp. 1, 9; May 23, 1935, pp. 1, 11; May 24, 1935, pp. 1, 13; May 27, 1935, pp. 1, 9; May 28, 1935, pp. 1, 9; May 29, 1935, pp. 1, 9; May 31, 1935, pp. 1, 13; June 21, 1935, pp. 1, 13; November 2, 1937, pp. 1, 9.

Lubbock Morning Avalanche (Lubbock, Tex.), February 8, 1935, pp. 1, 13; February 9, 1935, pp. 1, 9; February 12, 1935, p. 1; February 14, 1935, pp. 1, 11; February 20, 1935, pp. 1, 9; February 21, 1935, pp. 1, 11; February 22, 1935, pp. 1, 15; February 23, 1935, pp. 1, 9; March 9, 1935, pp. 1, 7; March 12, 1935, p. 1; March 15, 1935, pp. 1, 15; May 8, 1935, pp. 1, 11; May 21, 1935, pp. 1, 9; May 22, 1935, pp. 1, 9; May 24, 1935, pp. 1, 15; May 25, 1935, pp. 1, 7; May 28, 1935, pp. 1, 11; May 29, 1935, pp. 1, 11; May 30, 1935, pp. 1, 9; May 31, 1935, pp. 1, 15; June 21, 1935, pp. 1, 10; March 17, 1936, pp. 1, 11; April 28, 1936, p. 1; November 3, 1937, pp. 1, 9.

Sunday Avalanche-Journal (Lubbock, Tex.), February 10, 1935, [sec. 1], pp. 1, 6; March 3, 1935, [sec. 1], pp. 1, 10; May 5, 1935, [sec. 1], pp. 1, 10; May 26, 1935, [sec. 1], pp. 1, 11; June 2, 1935, [sec. 1], pp. 1, 8.

Texas. Department of Health. Bureau of Vital Statistics. Death Certificate for Spencer Stafford, February 7, 1935. Office of County and District Clerk, Garza County Courthouse, Post, Tex.

12 THE GREATEST MEDICAL CHARLATAN OF THEM ALL
DR. JOHN R. BRINKLEY AND HIS EMPIRE OF FRAUD IN DEL RIO

Long before today's TV ads for "male enhancement" products, radio audiences across North America could hear Dr. John Romulus Brinkley's programming announce that "we want to broadcast sunshine. Give Dr. Brinkley your medical problems. He will tell you the truth even if it makes you mad. . . . Before you have your prostate gland removed send 25¢ to the Brinkley Hospital for booklets." In 1931 Dr. Brinkley broadcast these words from radio station XER in Mexico, just across the Rio Grande from Del Rio, Texas, using the strongest radio transmitter in North America. Across the continent people heard the resonant voice of this bespectacled, goateed physician. He looked almost like the stereotypical picture of a German scientist. How did this country physician become a pioneer in broadcasting, build a medical empire based on rejuvenating aging men's sexual vitality, and become a millionaire based on fraud?

The story begins with John Brinkley coming into the world in North Carolina on July 8, 1885, the son of a "mountain girl" and a country doctor. Orphaned at an early age, he set out "to be a doctor like my daddy." First attending a legitimate medical school in Chicago in 1911, he dropped out and then went to classes in 1915 at the Eclectic Medical School of Kansas City, which let him "finish" his degree for a hundred dollars. Only eight states recognized the school's diplomas, among them Kansas. In 1917 Brinkley settled with his wife in the town of Milford in the Sunflower State, where he struggled to begin a practice. After a few months an unexpected event changed the young physician's career.

A local farmer came to Dr. Brinkley complaining, "I'm all in, no pep." He lamented that he had been unable to father another child, and the physician said that medicine had little to offer. Their conversation then drifted to farming, rams, and buck goats. According to a biographer, Brinkley joked to his patient that he "wouldn't have any trouble if you had a pair of those buck glands in you." The farmer unexpectedly responded, "Well, why don't you put 'em in?" Gland transplantation was

Dr. John R. Brinkley about the time that he relocated his radio broadcasting to Del Rio, Texas. Courtesy of Whitehead Memorial museum, Del Rio, Texas.

an experimental medical field in the 1910s, but Brinkley agreed to implant slivers of male goat testicles in his patient's scrotum. A year afterward the farmer and his forty-two-year-old wife became parents of a healthy son, whom they reportedly named Billy for the goat donor. The doctor declared the operation a success without asking any further questions, and soon other patients heard of the small-town physician. Brinkley went on the road, declaring in Chicago, "A man is as old as his glands, and his glands are as old as his sex glands."

Young Dr. Brinkley expanded his Milford family practice to include a hospital, behind which stood a corral filled with billy goats shipped weekly from Arkansas. He promoted his operation as curing not only male sexual dysfunction but also such afflictions as high blood pressure, epilepsy, diabetes, deafness, and senility. He even recommended gland transplantation for women to solve problems of infertility, obesity, and dementia. The doctor had so much business that he had to hire other surgeons to assist with the patients.

To promote his practice to more distant audiences, Brinkley secured a license for a new AM radio station. Given the call letters KFKB (for "Kansas Farmers Know Best" or "Kansas First, Kansas Best), he went on the air in September 1923. This was the third year of commercial radio broadcasting anywhere in America, and the fad for wireless receivers was rapidly growing. Between commercial announcements for his medical services and talks about health concerns, Brinkley broadcast live music, drama, or comedy entertainment. The format proved to be more than successful; in a 1930 poll by *Radio Digest* magazine KFKB received 256,827 votes, making it the most popular station in the country—a significant achievement for an erstwhile unknown country doctor on the Kansas prairie.

"Doctor," as he liked to be called, had a very pleasing radio voice. Combining the somewhat flat intonation of a Midwesterner with an Appalachian drawl, he found across rural America avid listeners for his monologues on child care, hygiene, and procreation. "All energy is sex energy," he proclaimed. Because so many people wrote to him for advice, Brinkley added in 1928 what he called his "Medical Question Box." On the air he read letters from listeners, diagnosed their ailments, and prescribed drugs from his own chain of pharmacies. In response to a writer whose daughter suffered from cramps, he advised, for example, "I think she is wormy. Ask for prescription 94 for worms." With each pharmaceutical sale, Brinkley received a one-dollar kickback. As soon as he received listeners' addresses, the doctor's clerks mailed a flurry of flyers, circulars, and other advertisements. The physician dictated individual letters, like one to a listener in Detroit who hesitated to travel to Milford for surgery: "If you go ahead to the doctors there (Detroit) and

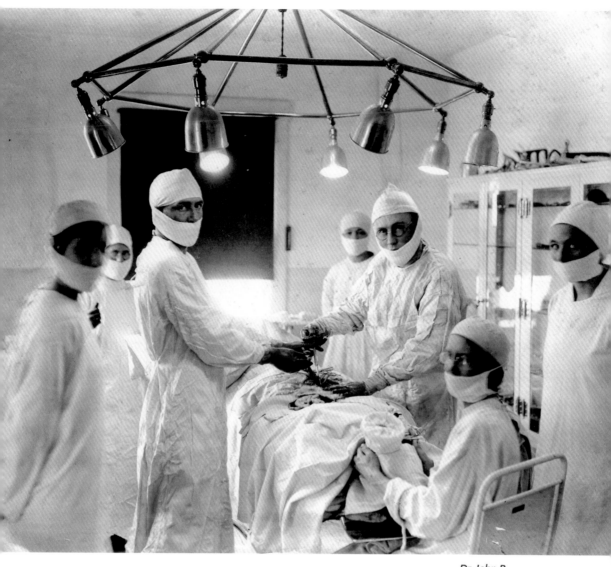

Dr. John R.
Brinkley, standing
to the right of a
patient and
wearing eyeglasses,
in the operating
room. Courtesy of
Kansas State
Historical Society.

have your prostate removed, you will be the same as a castrated man or an old steer and good for nothing."

As early as 1928 the American Medical Association began monitoring Brinkley's activities. Two years later the organization singled him out in its journal as "reeking with charlatanism of the crudest type." Over the airwaves from Milford, the doctor lashed back at the group that he derided as "the Amalgamated Meatcutters Association." His mostly rural listeners reveled in the doctor's folksy descriptions characterizing grasping physicians, crooked politicians, and scheming Jews.

The Federal Radio Commission chose in June 1930 not to renew Brinkley's broadcasting license because station KFKB had ceased serving public interests. Then the Kansas Medical Board in September of

The central business district of Del Rio, Texas, about the time that Dr. Brinkley first arrived in 1931. Author's collection.

the same year withdrew Brinkley's license (number 5845) to practice medicine within the state. In three short months he had lost both his broadcasting license and his personal medical practice, so he started looking for fresh, new fields. His first response was to run for public office—for the governorship of Kansas. Entering the campaign so late that voters had to write his name onto the ballots, he remarkably almost won. Two years later he ran again, but this time disappointingly came in third.

After the unsuccessful attempt at public office, John R. Brinkley took a new direction. He decided that if the U.S. government had taken away his radio license to prevent him from broadcasting what he wanted to say, he would move outside the country and beam his messages back. "Radio waves pay no attention to lines on a map," he quipped. Selling station KFKB for ninety thousand dollars to an insurance company, he traveled to Mexico in early 1931 to find out if he could build a broadcasting station somewhere near the international boundary. Timing could not have been better for Brinkley, because Mexican authorities were incensed over the United States and Canada having divided up long-range radio wavelengths in North America, leaving virtually no

The identification card that the Mexican government issued to Dr. Brinkley on May 16, 1931. Courtesy of Whitehead Memorial Museum, Del Rio, Texas

space for south-of-the-border broadcasters. The doctor was permitted to build a 50,000-watt station anywhere he wished along the border. About this time A. C. Easterling, manager of the chamber of commerce in Del Rio, Texas, heard of Brinkley's search for a new home and suggested that he inspect "the Queen City of the Rio Grande." He had no clue that the sleepy little border town was about to achieve notoriety.

Dr. Brinkley flew in his private plane to Del Rio to meet with local officials there and in its sister city, Villa Acuña, across the Rio Grande. Authorities in both places invited the flamboyant physician to relocate, with the Mexicans offering a ten-acre site for a broadcasting station at no cost.

Brinkley liked the oasislike location on the international boundary and made plans for a new radio operation. The station was unlike anything in America. When Brinkley explained what broadcasting power he wanted, his engineer replied that tubes like that would cost thirty-six thousand dollars. According to the *Saturday Evening Post*, "Doctor just reached in his pants pocket for a roll, peeled off thirty-six grand in irreproachable U.S. legal tender and directed that the tubes be sent to Mexico as soon as possible." With an authorized strength of 50,000 watts, the new station would have the same broadcasting power as the strongest American stations. So that he could continue personally supervising his hospital in Kansas, Brinkley leased a dedicated telephone line to transmit his programming from Milford to Villa Acuña, where broadcasting began on October 21, 1931. Then during fall 1933 the doctor decided to consolidate all his interests on the border. His employees packed up all of the usable furnishings and equipment from the facilities at Milford, loaded them onto trucks, and drove southward to Texas.

The broadcasting station and towers for XER and later XERA across the Rio Grande from Del Rio in Villa Acuña, Mexico, in the 1930s. Courtesy of Whitehead Memorial Museum, Del Rio, Texas.

The six-story Roswell Hotel, location of Dr. John R. Brinkley's hospital in Del Rio, Texas, starting in 1933. Author's collection.

Dr. Brinkley made the six-story, air-conditioned Roswell Hotel his Del Rio medical headquarters. His "hospital" occupied the entire mezzanine level, while the x-ray department operated in the basement. On the ground floor he opened his pharmacy. The remaining floors housed patients, who arrived in cars, buses, and Southern Pacific passenger trains. A whole staff of physicians and nurses assisted. Still using a dedicated telephone line across the border to the broadcast facility, Doctor opened studios in several different Del Rio locations over the years.

An aerial view of Del Rio, Texas, in the 1930s, showing Greenwood Park in the foreground, the six-story Roswell Hotel on the left, and the downtown business district in the center. Author's collection.

In addition to their primary function of attracting patients to the hospital, radio stations XER and later XERA made money on their own. Brinkley and his advertisers used the broadcasts to sell everything from tomato plants to Last Supper tablecloths, from mining stock to gasoline additives. He continued to bring a large number of musicians to Del Rio to perform on the air. With a target audience of rural people, he featured many of the pioneers in commercial country music. Among these now-famous performers were A. P. Carter and his wife, Sara, his sister-in-law Maybelle, and their daughters, known collectively as the Carter Family; Gene Autry; Hank Williams; Leonard Sly, later known as Roy Rogers; the Sons of the Pioneers; and Tennessee Ernie Ford. All of them relished performing in Villa Acuña, where they did not have to pay royalties to the American Association of Composers, Authors, and Publishers as they did in the United States.

Among Brinkley's on-air personalities were his "spooks"—astrologers, psychics, promoters of occult beliefs, and other fortune tellers. The most successful was Rose Dawn, remembered for looking "much like Mae West" and driving a rose-colored Chrysler trimmed in green with "orchid" (pale purple) wheels. For mailed-in payments, she sent listeners "individual fortunes." Brinkley measured the success of his personalities by their "pull," meaning how many daily letters they received from listeners. Rose Dawn did better than anyone other than Doctor himself, consistently drawing hundreds daily. Clifford J. Harle grew up in Del Rio and spent one summer working as a clerk in her business office, located in the local Odd Fellows building. The radio star had an assembly line of workers who opened hundreds of letters daily, removed cash and checks, and mailed out selected fortunes and other

ROSE DAWN, The Star Girl
Radio Station XERA, Del Rio

Rose Dawn, an astrologer and psychic reader who was one of the popular radio personalities on Dr. John R. Brinkley's XER and XERA stations during the 1930s. Courtesy of Whitehead Memorial Museum, Del Rio, Texas.

printed materials. "All eyes were on her when she made her daily appearance," Harle remembered. Generally her only comment to anyone was to the cashier, whom she asked, "What's the take?"

The broadcasting strength of Brinkley's station astounded many people and angered others. His on-air lectures on bloating, fistulae, and enlarged prostates could be heard all across the Great Plains to Canada and at times on both the Atlantic and Pacific coasts. The broadcasting power of the station grew in stages until late 1935, when XERA strength reached an incredible 1,000,000 watts. That wattage supposedly made it the most powerful radio transmitter in the world. The Mexican border super-station repeatedly drowned out legitimate American broadcasters near and far.

About the time that Dr. Brinkley came to Del Rio, he altered his medical treatments. No longer implanting slivers of goat glands in patients unless they insisted, he focused on radio-promoted "treatments" that purportedly reduced the size of enlarged prostate glands in men. Not bothering to determine cause—whether inflammation, natural growth with age, or cancer—he sent many patients home after useless procedures only to experience pain and death from undiagnosed medical problems. Even so, the radio station continued to attract eager customers to Del Rio, "where the summer months spend the winter." In fall 1932 he expanded his practice to include a second hospital at San Juan, Texas, near McAllen, to deal with ailments of the male and female rectum. "Remember, Del Rio for the prostate and San Juan for the colon," he advised radio listeners.

Tiring of competition from former employees who undercut his prices for treatments in Del Rio, the doctor in early 1938 relocated his entire medical operation to Arkansas while retaining the radio programming in Del Rio. He began weekly commutes by air between Little Rock and Del Rio in a luxuriously appointed blue-and-gold Lockheed Electra aircraft.

The flashy airplane was not the only way that Brinkley flaunted his financial success. In Del Rio he purchased a palatial eighteen-room home on sixteen acres and then decorated it lavishly. He maintained a menagerie of flamingos, penguins, and Galapagos tortoises as well as "dancing fountains" of water illuminated in color at night. He had

Dr. John R. Brinkley with wife and son together with their pilot and copilot standing in front of the doctor's blue-and-gold Lockheed Electra airplane used from 1938 onward to commute weekly between Del Rio and his hospital in Arkansas. Courtesy of Whitehead Memorial Museum, Del Rio, Texas.

a fleet of expensive automobiles, all with his name added on hubcaps, trunks, and elsewhere. The doctor himself loved diamonds, on a typical day wearing "dime-sized" diamond rings on both hands, large diamond cuff links, diamond lapel pins, a huge diamond stickpin in his necktie, and diamonds encrusting his watch chain. Interestingly, local residents seem not to have been offended by such outrageous conspicuous consumption. One later reminisced, "They looked upon Dr. Brinkley's display of vast wealth with awe and a certain amount of pride that it was happening in Del Rio."

Dr. John R. Brinkley's palatial home in Del Rio, depicted on a widely distributed real photo postcard that also shows two portraits of the doctor, his humble birthplace, and his oceangoing yacht. Author's collection.

Doctor knew that he needed the support of Del Rio residents in order to maintain his broadcasting and medical empires, so he went out of his way to cultivate people living in the community. Contemporary writers estimated that Brinkley paid twenty thousand dollars monthly in salaries, which was a substantial sum in a town of twelve thousand people during the Great Depression. He invested there, opening a lumberyard and even depositing fifty-four thousand dollars that he had formerly held in Kansas banks in the two Del Rio banks to help them weather the hard times. For years he maintained a charge account at the Guarantee Department Store that was open to any needy child who needed a coat and shoes for school in the fall, and every Christmas his employees distributed apples, bananas, and oranges with his compliments at the World War I pavilion in Greenwood Park. The strategy worked, so that even to this day, despite the pain and suffering that he caused, most Del Rioans speak in glowing terms of the good doctor.

When the end came for Dr. John Romulus Brinkley, it came quickly. His rapid fall began in 1938 when he sued Dr. Morris Fishbein of the American Medical Association for libel after he had declared in print that Brinkley deceived and abused his patients. In a trial that took place in the federal courthouse in Del Rio, a jury comprised mostly of local ranchers acquitted Fishbein in May 1939. Brinkley appealed, but the circuit court concluded that "there is no doubt that . . . the plaintiff should be considered a charlatan and a quack." Families of former patients began suing Brinkley and his staff of doctors for wrongful death. About the same time the Internal Revenue Service demanded $115,000 in back taxes. In an effort to control costs and save himself, Brinkley began moving his medical operations back to Del Rio from Arkansas, but then on February 1, 1941, he was forced to declare bankruptcy. In June of that year a newly elected Mexican president expropriated radio station XERA for having aired "news broadcasts unsuitable to the New World."

Following a heart attack during summer 1941, Brinkley developed a blood clot in his left leg. It became infected, gangrene set in, and the limb was removed. While he convalesced, federal marshals served Doctor with a warrant charging him with mail fraud. Referring to his amputation, he remarked to the officer, "I guess there isn't any danger of my running away." More seriously he wrote to his wife in February 1942 that they would "all go to the pen" unless his friends in high places could "get the indictment dismissed." This did not happen, but John R. Brinkley never went to trial. On May 26, 1942, the old goat gland doctor met his maker.

BRINKLEY MANSION, 512 QUALIA DRIVE, DEL RIO

Del Rio is filled with well-preserved locations associated with Dr. John R. Brinkley and his fraudulent medical empire, but the best known are his eighteen-room mansion and its grounds. Located on the edge of town, where he could see his radio transmitter towers across the river, the mansion enabled the doctor to display his wealth ostentatiously. Still a private residence, it remains an impressive home to this day. All the important Brinkley-related locations can be reached conveniently in a walking tour except for the mansion.

The former Brinkley mansion, still a private residence in Del Rio, Texas. Photograph by the author, 2006.

To reach the former Brinkley mansion, drive 0.9 mile south on Pecan Street from its intersection with Losoya Street alongside the Val Verde County Courthouse in downtown Del Rio. Pecan Street becomes Hudson Drive. At an intersection with Qualia Drive, marked by the historic Val Verde Winery, turn southwest (right) and drive 0.6 mile farther on

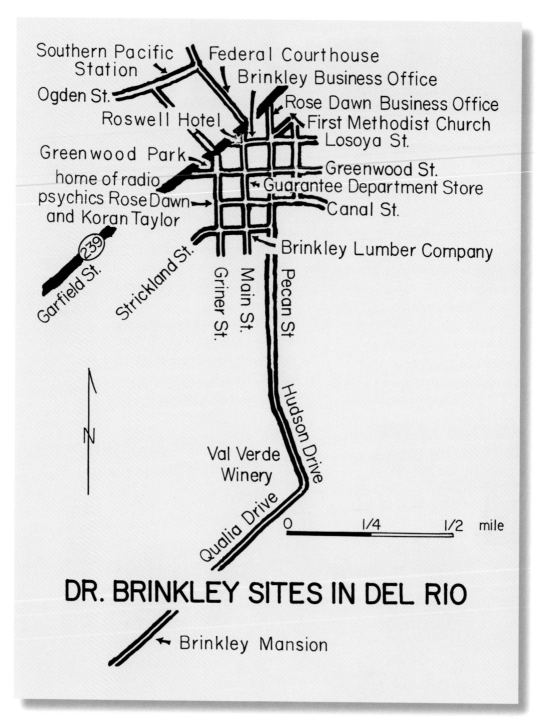

DR. BRINKLEY SITES IN DEL RIO

Southern Pacific Station
Ogden St.
Roswell Hotel
Greenwood Park
home of radio psychics Rose Dawn and Koran Taylor
239
Garfield St.
Strickland St.
Griner St.
Main St.
Pecan St.
Federal Courthouse
Brinkley Business Office
Rose Dawn Business Office
First Methodist Church
Losoya St.
Greenwood St.
Guarantee Department Store
Canal St.
Brinkley Lumber Company
Hudson Drive
Val Verde Winery
Qualia Drive
N
0   1/4   1/2 mile

← Brinkley Mansion

Qualia to the large pink stucco residence on the southeast (left) side of the street. The home is a private residence not open to tourists. The Val Verde Winery, founded in 1883, is the oldest bonded winery in the state. Visitors are welcomed.

SOUTHERN PACIFIC RAILROAD STATION,
100 NORTH MAIN STREET AT OGDEN STREET, DEL RIO

The Southern Pacific railroad station was the point of arrival in Del Rio for many patients seeking treatment at Dr. Brinkley's hospital. Erected in 1928, this handsome tan brick building with limestone trim and a red ceramic tile roof was a landmark in the town. Much to Brinkley's chagrin, hustlers hired by some of the doctor's former employees met trains at the station and on the platform and in the waiting room attempted to redirect potential patients to competing clinics that offered lower-priced treatments.

To reach the site from State Loop 239 (the east-west U.S. Highways 90/277 business route), turn south on North Main Street and drive one block, crossing the railway tracks, and turn west (right) to drive one-half block on West Ogden Street. From the downtown business district of Del Rio, drive north on South Main Street just a few blocks to the railway tracks at West Ogden Street and turn west (left). This handsome facility today houses the Del Rio Multi-Modal Transportation Center, serving three Amtrak passenger trains each direction weekly and multiple buses daily.

The 1928 Southern Pacific Railroad depot in Del Rio, Texas, where many of Dr. John R. Brinkley's patients arrived from across the nation. Photograph by the author, 2006.

ROSWELL HOTEL, SITE OF THE BRINKLEY HOSPITAL,
137 WEST GARFIELD STREET BETWEEN GRINER STREET
AND SOUTH MAIN STREET, DEL RIO

The six-story Roswell Hotel became the site for Dr. John R. Brinkley's hospital in Del Rio in October 1933. He occupied the mezzanine and basement levels, while patients rented rooms in the upper floors dur-

The handsome art deco entrance to the 1928 Roswell Hotel, which became Dr. John R. Brinkley's hospital in Del Rio, Texas, in 1933. Photograph by the author, 2006.

ing their treatment and recovery. Erected in 1928 and the first air-conditioned hotel in Del Rio, it offered first-class accommodations. Today the six-story beige brick building with handsome limestone trim houses the Roswell Housing Complex, a residence for seniors. The lobby retains much of its former appearance.

To reach the site from downtown Del Rio, drive north on South Main Street or north on Griner Street to West Garfield Street, where the imposing multistory structure is easily viewed on the northwest side of West Garfield.

JOHN R. BRINKLEY'S BUSINESS OFFICE, UPPER FLOOR OF THE WARNER BUILDING, 532 SOUTH MAIN STREET, NORTHEAST CORNER OF SOUTH MAIN STREET AND LOSOYA STREET, DEL RIO

The business offices of Dr. John R. Brinkley occupied the upper floor of the Warner Building in downtown Del Rio. Accessed by a side door and stairs, a series of work spaces upstairs housed managers, bookkeepers, and clerks who processed large amounts of money that passed through the suite of offices. The 1938 city directory lists the accounting and mailing department, under Miss Mabel Kirkpatrick, as being in rooms 3, 4, 5, and 9, while the business office, under the supervision of A. E. Johnson, occupied rooms 1 and 2. This two-story white limestone building was constructed by Italian stonemason John Taini in 1905, and that date can be seen carved in the stone above a side door.

To find the site, take South Main Street north or south from any

Looking west on Losoya Street in Del Rio, Texas, past the two-story stone Warner Building on the right where Dr. John R. Brinkley housed his business offices. It was on the upper floor of this structure that clerks, bookkeepers, and managers processed Brinkley's hundreds of thousands of dollars in mostly illicit income. Just over a block away, at the end of the street, stands the six-story Roswell Hotel. Photograph by the author, 2006.

point in downtown Del Rio to the building on the northeast corner of its intersection with East Losoya Street. If you are driving, note that traffic flows one way south on South Main Street.

BRINKLEY LUMBER COMPANY,
900 SOUTH MAIN STREET, DEL RIO

Once John R. Brinkley relocated to Del Rio, he attempted to diversify his business interests. One way that he accomplished this goal was by establishing a commercial lumberyard. He bought an existing building materials business at 900 South Main Street in 1935 and named it after himself. Eventually, after the physician's death, his son operated the enterprise. The original stucco office with red tile roof built in Spanish colonial revival style survives at the site and is notable for its handsome cream-colored exterior, ornamented with red and blue tiles at the entrance and side windows.

To reach the site, go north or south on South Main Street from anywhere in downtown Del Rio to the east side of its 900 block at the intersection with East Strickland Street. Take note of the one-way vehicular traffic southbound on South Main Street.

The office
building at the
former Brinkley
Lumber Company,
an enterprise
acquired by Dr.
John R. Brinkley in
1935 to diversify his
business interests
in Del Rio, Texas.
Photograph by the
author, 2006.

GUARANTEE DEPARTMENT STORE,
704 SOUTH MAIN STREET, DEL RIO

Max Stool, an immigrant from Russian Poland, came to Del Rio in 1904
and worked as a peddler. He later founded The Guarantee, a department
store at 704 South Main Street. An occasional patient of John Brinkley,
the Jewish merchant at the physician's request fitted any child in need
with a coat and/or footwear for school in the autumn and charged the
doctor for the cost. Through such means as this, Brinkley ensured that
he would have the support of many Del Rio residents.

To reach the site, walk north or south on South Main Street in the
main commercial district of Del Rio to the store on the east side of the
street at 704. If you are driving, note that the traffic flows southbound
only.

WORLD WAR I MEMORIAL PAVILION,
GREENWOOD PARK, DEL RIO

Every year John R. Brinkley dispatched employees to the World War I
Pavilion at Greenwood Park in a truck loaded with bananas, apples,
and oranges to distribute to local children. During the Great Depression, this holiday gesture earned the doctor loyalty from many local
residents. The concrete and wood pavilion had been erected in 1918
by the Del Rio Women's Club and dedicated to "the American Soldier."

As a means of securing the goodwill of local residents, Dr. John R. Brinkley every fall paid the Guarantee Department Store in downtown Del Rio to provide free coats and shoes for needy schoolchildren. Photograph by the author, 2006.

At Christmastime for years Dr. John R. Brinkley's employees would distribute fruit to Del Rio children at the World War I pavilion in Greenwood Park, just across the street from his medical facility in the Roswell Hotel. Photograph by the author, 2006.

Greenwood Park occupies a shaded triangle of land diagonally across the intersection of Griner Street and West Garfield Street from the Roswell Hotel, where the doctor operated his hospital.

To find the site, from South Main Street in downtown Del Rio, go one block west on either West Greenwood or West Garfield streets to the park, which is easily identified from its mature pecan, palm, juniper, and oak trees.

HOME OF RADIO PERSONALITIES ROSE DAWN AND KORAN TAYLOR, 613 GRINER STREET, DEL RIO

Among the most successful "mail pullers" from radio stations XER and XERA were psychic readers Rose Dawn and Koran Taylor. The couple resided in this Spanish-style home alongside one of the beautiful rock-lined spring-water-filled irrigation canals that course through Del Rio. The semitropical gardens behind the home were renowned far and wide as the setting for luxurious yard parties that the couple hosted during the 1930s.

To find the site, go west from South Main Street in downtown Del Rio one block on Canal Street to where it dead ends at 613 Griner Street, the location of the still-beautiful private residence.

The beautiful Spanish colonial revival home in Del Rio once occupied by XER and XERA radio psychic readers Rose Dawn and Koran Taylor. Photograph by the author, 2006.

ROSE DAWN'S BUSINESS OFFICE, ODD FELLOWS BUILDING, 312 SOUTH PECAN STREET, DEL RIO

It was in this striking five-sided masonry building that radio psychic reader Rose Dawn operated her business office. Here employees opened thousands of letters from listeners and filled their orders for fortunes and fortune-telling lessons. After the astrologer began accepting one-dollar contributions for her to pray for listeners and some of them actually came to Del Rio to see her "chapel," Rose Dawn was forced to construct a place of prayer in this building to satisfy her fans. The building also served as the meeting place for the local chapter of the International Order of Odd Fellows, a popular fraternal order.

To reach the site, go east on East Losoya Street one block from South Main Street in downtown Del Rio to the intersection with Pecan Street. Turn north (left) on Pecan and go one full block to its intersection on the right with narrow Cactus Street. The two-story masonry commercial building with a modern cream and tan exterior stands at 312 South Pecan at the southeast corner of the intersection with Cactus.

The Odd Fellows lodge building in Del Rio, which in addition to providing a meeting place for members also housed the business office for XER and XERA radio "spook" Rose Dawn. Photograph by the author, 2006.

FORMER FEDERAL COURTHOUSE AND POST OFFICE (SITE OF BRINKLEY LIBEL TRIAL), 320 SOUTH MAIN STREET, DEL RIO

Erected in 1912, the federal building in Del Rio housed a large U.S. Justice Department courtroom, with support areas on its upper floor and a post office beneath. It was in the second-floor room designated for law court that Judge Robert J. McMillan heard and the jury considered testimony in the spring 1939 case in which Dr. John R. Brinkley unsuccessfully sued Morris Fishbein and the American Medical Association for libel. At the time of the trial, participants typically accessed the courtroom by way of stairs adjacent to the south-side entrance facing East Broadway Street, and that stairway continues to serve the same purpose. Although the building has been remodeled over the years, the courtroom still retains historic furnishings that give it the feel of the past. Note the rails inside the jury box that permitted jurors, many of them ranchers wearing boots, to prop their feet up for comfort during long trials. The handsome two-story masonry building houses the actively used Val Verde County Judicial Center, so the courtroom sometimes has restricted visitor access.

To reach the site, drive north or south on South Main Street in downtown Del Rio to the two-story masonry building at northeast corner of the intersection with East Broadway Street. This section of Main Street has two-way vehicular traffic. To access the upstairs courtroom on the same steps that the participants in the 1939 trial used, enter by the exterior door on the south side and climb the stairs to the right.

The former federal courthouse and post office in downtown Del Rio, Texas, where the John R. Brinkley libel trial was held in 1939. Photograph by the author, 2006.

FIRST METHODIST CHURCH, SITE OF
DR. JOHN R. BRINKLEY'S FUNERAL,
100 SPRING STREET, DEL RIO

When the Brinkley family resided in Del Rio, they attended religious services at the First Methodist Church. The congregation had moved into this new Spanish Renaissance revival style sanctuary in 1930, and it remains in use today. The Reverend M. D. Council and two previous pastors in the church officiated at the well-attended memorial service held the day after John R. Brinkley's death, May 26, 1942.

To reach the site, from South Main Street in downtown Del Rio drive two full blocks east on East Losoya Street to its intersection with Mill Street, passing the Val Verde County Courthouse on the right. Turn north (left) on Mill Street and drive one block to its "T" intersection with Spring Street, the location of the church.

The First Methodist Church of Del Rio, Texas, location of the funeral for Dr. John R. Brinkley in May 1942. Photograph by the author, 2006.

Brinkley, John R. Papers. Kansas State Historical Society, Topeka, Kans.

———. Papers. Whitehead Memorial Museum, Del Rio, Tex.

Brock, Pope. *Charlatan: America's Most Dangerous Huckster, the Man Who Pursued Him, and the Age of Flimflam.* New York: Crown Publishers, 2008.

Del Rio News-Herald (Del Rio, Tex.), October 23, 1940, pp. 1, 6; June 16, 1976, sec. A, p. 14; February 19, 1978, sec. B, p. 11; February 14, 1979, sec. B, p. 5; July 27, 2003, sec. A, pp. 1, 13.

Fowler, Gene, and Bill Crawford. *Border Radio: Quacks, Yodelers, Pitchmen, Psychics, and Other Amazing Broadcasters of the American Airwaves.* Revised ed. Austin: University of Texas Press, 2002.

Harle, Clifford J. Interview by Rachel Maurer, n.d. Typescript in the Whitehead Memorial Museum, Del Rio, Tex.

Juhnke, Eric S. *Quacks and Crusaders: The Fabulous Careers of John Brinkley, Norman Baker, and Harry Hoxsey.* Lawrence: University Press of Kansas, 2002.

Lee, R. Alton. *The Bizarre Careers of John R. Brinkley.* Lexington: University Press of Kentucky, 2002.

Wood, Clement. *The Life of a Man: A Biography of John R. Brinkley.* Kansas City, Mo.: Goshorn Publishing Company, 1934.

13 HIGH STAKES GAMBLING UNDERGROUND AT TOP O'HILL TERRACE

It seemed like a lot of trouble to buy a ladies' tearoom in the country, move it from its foundation, dig a giant hole in the ground for a hidden basement, and then move the tearoom back on top. This is precisely what Fred Browning did in 1931 to camouflage the casino that became the swankiest illegal gaming retreat in North Texas. The strategy worked, for he operated his successful underground gambling house for more than a decade and a half. It became a legend.

The story of Top O'Hill Terrace began in 1921, when Mrs. Beulah Marshall opened the Top O'Hill Terrace Tea Room at the crest of a prominent hill just north of the main Dallas–Fort Worth highway about four miles west of the town of Arlington. In a rural setting, the knoll was, at more than seven hundred feet, one of the highest points in Tarrant County. It caught any cooling summer breezes in the days before air conditioning. It was there that Mrs. Marshall constructed a bungalow-style eating place that catered to ladies, who were starting to venture by automobile from Fort Worth and Dallas in search of genteel venues for sandwiches, pastries, tea, and coffee. The eating place prospered and became a popular setting for mostly daytime social gatherings like wedding showers, teas, and club meetings.

Beulah Marshall probably could not imagine what former plumber Fred Browning intended to do when, in his wife's name, he purchased the tearoom and surrounding acreage, paying off the note in late November 1931. He had very different plans for the popular retreat. Two years before, in 1929, rancher William T. Waggoner constructed an impressive racetrack, Arlington Downs, on a stock farm that he owned between the hilltop eating place and Arlington. Fred Browning knew that the wealthy cattleman was pushing the Texas Legislature to allow pari-mutuel betting on horse races. When the legislators agreed to this form of gambling in 1933, the racetrack began attracting well-heeled

275

Horse racing action at Arlington Downs during the 1930s. Courtesy of Fort Worth Star-Telegram Collection, Special Collections, the University of Texas at Arlington Libraries, image 1-2-23 negative C737.

Texans and others looking for ways to bet their money. Fred Browning was ready for them.

After Browning lifted the Top O'Hill Terrace Tea Room from its foundation, his crews excavated a huge depression. In it they poured cement in wooden forms to create a spacious underground casino measuring approximately fifty by sixty feet. After finishing the rough construction, he once again fitted the wooden tearoom structure on top of the concrete bunker to serve as his home and as kitchens and support areas for the gaming operation. He placed the main entrance in the rear, setting up secure access to the basement by requiring customers to pass through five individually guarded doors. Once in the lower level, guests enjoyed unlimited food and alcoholic beverages despite the fact that national prohibition continued until the summer of 1933. The gambler knew that he had certain legal protections if the gaming took place inside a "private residence," so he carefully avoided accepting any money for meals or drinks. Guests had their choice of playing roulette, blackjack, craps, slot machines, and other games. Former employee Jack Poe stated that it was not unusual for half a million dollars to change hands at Top O'Hill Terrace on a single good weekend during the horse racing season.

Outside the casino the landscaped forty-six-acre grounds were a wooded private park. Immediately behind the casino to the north was the old stone tea garden, with benches, handsome ironwork, a reflecting pool, and one of the most impressive views in all Tarrant County. Just east of the tea garden and casino was a ceramic tile–lined swimming pool, with stables for Fred Browning's racehorses also to the east. Back farther north on the hill stood a two-story wooden dwelling that housed a number of prostitutes, a further attraction for male customers on the hill. An ample parking lot comfortably accommodated dozens of automobiles.

When guests in their cars turned north onto the grounds from the Dallas–Fort Worth highway, personnel from a round stone guardhouse at the entry checked their identification and then admitted approved vehicles through a beautiful gate that had been custom fabricated by the Southern Ornamental Ironworks of Arlington. Should any unwanted guests, such as law officers, force their way in, the guards would alert other staff at the casino with an electric buzzer so they could remove the easily portable gambling paraphernalia into adjacent underground storage areas. Intruding officers would find guests sipping innocuous beverages and playing pool and gin rummy. Should it be necessary, a forty-foot-long concrete tunnel could allow customers to exit the subterranean chamber to the open air on the west side of the hill.

Despite all Fred Browning's precautions, Top O'Hill Terrace did experience several raids by law enforcement officers. His careful placing of money in the right hands, however, meant that for years he seldom had to close down for very long. One of the raids stemmed from Browning's nemesis, the Reverend J. Frank Norris, pastor of the First Baptist Church in Fort Worth. A leader in the fundamentalist wing of the Baptist denomination, the minister for years preached against the evils he saw being practiced at Top O'Hill Terrace. After the Fort Worth Ministerial Alliance made charges against Fred Browning and his wife, Mary, a county constable and two deputy sheriffs along with Norris forced their way into the casino on the afternoon of February 21, 1933, seizing two roulette wheels, two gaming tables, and an assortment of poker chips and dice. The next month a local grand jury concluded that there was insufficient evidence to indict Mr. or Mrs. Browning or any of their employees for illegal gaming activities. Regular gaming continued underground at Top O'Hill Terrace. This seeming immunity to prosecution galled the Baptist leader, who declared that one day he and his followers would convert the hilltop into a place for scriptural study. Very few people believed him.

The next two raids came within days of each other two and a half years later, in November 1935. Well-known Texas Ranger Tom Hickman led the first, which proved to be futile. When he and other officers forced their way through the guarded doors into the basement, they found a handful of patrons innocently playing pool. There were no gaming devices in sight. Shortly thereafter another ranger, Captain J. W. McCormick, and other law officers took advantage of rainy weather to sneak up to the casino entry. They, too, forced their way inside, this time to find customers at the tables putting money on their bets. The lawmen arrested a handful of employees, allowing the customers to leave, and again a

Texas Ranger Tom Hickman (seated on top of car), who headed an unsuccessful raid on Top O'Hill Terrace in 1935, seen after a deer hunt at one of the W. T. Waggoner ranches. Courtesy of Fort Worth Star-Telegram Collection, Special Collections, the University of Texas at Arlington Libraries, image FWST 292-3, glass negative.

friendly grand jury in Fort Worth found insufficient evidence on which to base prosecution. To the chagrin of J. Frank Norris and his fellow believers, the gaming again resumed. It seemed evident that certain powerful people in the county seat enjoyed having access to their "swank gambling resort" atop the hill.

After the Texas Legislature ended pari-mutuel horse race betting at the end of the 1937 season, many of the old Arlington Downs gamblers continued wagering their money at Top O'Hill Terrace. Although Fred Browning maintained his interest in horse racing, he found a new outlet for his energies and money in a boxer, Verlin E. "Lew" Jenkins. A native of Milburn in McCulloch County, Texas, he became known as the "Sweetwater Swatter" from his associations with that West Texas town. Browning "discovered" Jenkins, brought him to Top O'Hill Terrace, and hired New Yorker Hymie Caplin as his trainer. The terrific little puncher fought his way upward through the ranks of boxers to defeat Lou Ambers for the lightweight title in New York City on May 10, 1940. Fred Browning must have been riding high with the victory, which gave Jenkins the lightweight championship until his defeat a year and a half later by Sammy Angott.

FA smiling threesome of Fred Browning (left), Lew Jenkins (center), and trainer Hymie Caplin (right) about the time that Jenkins won the lightweight boxing title by defeating Lou Ambers in New York City on May 10, 1940. Courtesy of Fort Worth Star-Telegram Collection, Special Collections, the University of Texas at Arlington Libraries, image FWST 1161 #1 5/15/1940.

Boxer Lew Jenkins astride a horse outside one of Fred Browning's stables at Top O'Hill Terrace in 1940. Courtesy of Fort Worth Star-Telegram Collection, Special Collections, the University of Texas at Arlington Libraries, image FWST 1161 #2 5/15/1940.

All through the World War II years, Fred Browning maintained his gaming operations beneath the former tearoom on the scenic hilltop west of Arlington. The end came during the dog days of summer in 1947. Yet another Texas Ranger staged a raid on the subterranean casino. Captain M. T. "Lone Wolf" Gonzaullas, who had introduced scientific forensic investigation methods to state law enforcement in Texas, headed the party of lawmen. Avoiding the guarded vehicular entry, the officers crawled up the side of the hill to approach the old tearoom. From their vantage points they observed three lookout men outside and customers coming and going through the main entry at the rear. As a guest approached the door and it opened, the lawmen sprang forward and forced themselves inside and down the stairs. Several customers made their way to the escape tunnel, only to find another law officer waiting at its end. They arrested employees as well as guests and confiscated the gambling equipment, all of which had been designed to be whisked from sight at a moment's warning. Gonzaullas declared to the local press, "This raid is to serve notice on this place and any other in this area that they are going to be stopped if we have to call on them every night." Even so, the ranger filed only misdemeanor charges in order to avoid embarrassing "prominent Fort Worth and Dallas citizens" who were caught up in the operation.

The 1947 raid led to the end of gaming at Top O'Hill Terrace. Browning attempted to revive business, but potential customers seemed afraid that they too would be embarrassed by being caught in further raids. The scenic hilltop retreat fell quiet. Several real estate developers discussed dividing the parklike setting into lots for residences, but after the property passed through the hands of several of Fred Browning's creditors, no development occurred. In the mid-1950s the Bible Baptist Seminary, which pastor J. Frank Norris had helped organize twenty years earlier, learned that the Top O'Hill Terrace property was available. The school made several purchases and thus acquired the whole scenic hilltop and all the surviving buildings. Top O'Hill Terrace thus became the seminary's campus.

The school, which in 1972 became Arlington Baptist College, constructed its modern combined administration and student union building on the site of the old Top O'Hill Terrace casino. In so doing, the contractors left intact part of one of the subterranean rooms and the concrete escape tunnel. Although the centerpiece of the casino operation disappeared through this construction project, many of the auxiliary structures remained in place to serve the students. These areas included the beautiful stone-walled tea garden, two racehorse stables, a well house, and the round stone guard tower with the wrought-iron gate at the entry to the property. Inside a modern physical education building even the tile-lined swimming pool remains, although it is no longer used for water sports. A museum of college and casino history occupies the smaller of two historic stables.

On the drive up the hill to the campus buildings—the same drive that gamblers used to take—one passes an eight-foot bronze figure of the Reverend J. Frank Norris by the noted Texas sculptor, Pompeo Coppini. The pastor stands larger than life, with one hand on the Bible and the other gesturing upward. He seems as if he wants to remind everyone that, years before, he had declared, "One of these days we are going to own the place."

TOP O'HILL TERRACE, NOW ARLINGTON BAPTIST COLLEGE, 3001 WEST DIVISION STREET, ARLINGTON, ILLEGAL ACTIVITY 1931-1951

Top O'Hill Terrace consisted of a complex of buildings, a number of which survive wholly or partially intact. Entry to the landscaped grounds of Arlington Baptist College is by way of the historic gateway, which has a turret-shaped sandstone guardhouse and handsome iron gate. The underground casino, above-ground home of Fred Browning, and the restaurant kitchens were removed, and a combined modern administration and student union building for the college now occupies the site. The historic tile-lined swimming pool in time was enclosed by another college structure. The school still uses a beautiful rock-walled open-air tea garden, two of Fred Browning's sandstone racehorse stables (one now functioning as a museum), and a stone well house. From inside the lower level of the college administration/student union building, it is possible to look through a thick glass window into a subterranean chamber remaining from the former casino, while the exit to the concrete "escape tunnel" may be seen just west of the building on the side of the hill.

To reach the former casino site and present-day college campus, leave Interstate 30 at exit 23 on the east side of Fort Worth and turn south on Cooks Lane. Drive 2.0 miles south on Cooks Lane to its intersection with Texas Highway 180 (East Lancaster Avenue). Turn east (left) onto Texas Highway 180, which inside the Arlington city limits becomes West Division Street, and drive 1.5 miles to the entrance to

TOP O' HILL TERRACE CASINO
Arlington Baptist College, 3001 West Division St., Arlington

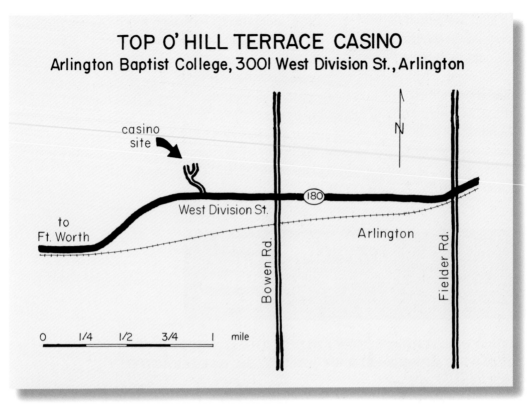

The entrance gate to the former Top O'Hill Terrace grounds at 3001 West Division Street in Arlington. In casino days the round stone structure on the right sheltered guards who opened the iron gate to admit only approved customers. Photograph by the author, 2006.

The tea garden located just south of the former casino site on the grounds of the present-day Arlington Baptist College. Photograph by the author, 2006.

One of casino operator Fred Browning's racehorse stables, currently used for academic purposes on the campus of Arlington Baptist College. Photograph by the author, 2006.

The concrete escape tunnel built to serve the Top O'Hill Terrace casino, now abandoned but still preserved at the side of the combined student union and administration building on the Arlington Baptist College campus. Photograph by the author, 2006.

Arlington Baptist College. Turn north (left) into the campus and take the meandering, tree-shaded roadway. Tours of the historic buildings on campus may be arranged through the college.

👉 JUDGE THE EVIDENCE FOR YOURSELF

Arnold, Ann. *Gamblers & Gangsters: Fort Worth's Jacksboro Highway in the 1940s and 1950s*. Austin: Eakin Press, 1998.

Bryant, Vickie. "Top O'Hill Terrace." Official Texas Historical Marker Application for Top O'Hill Terrace, Arlington, Tex. Library. Texas Historical Commission, Austin, Tex.

Dallas Morning News (Dallas, Tex.), February 25, 1933, sec. I, p. 5; March 31, 1933, sec. I, p. 11; November 7, 1935, sec. I, p. 11; November 12, 1935, sec. I, pp. 1, 12; November 13, 1935, sec. I, pp. 1, 3; November 20, 1935, sec. I, p. 2; November 21, 1935, sec. I, p. 2; December 4, 1935, sec. I, pp. 1, 6; February 5, 1936, sec. I, p. 6; May 26, 1938, sec. I, p. 6; July 21, 1943, sec. I, p. 9; August 11, 1947, sec. I, p. 1; August 15, 1947, sec. I, p. 5; February 15, 1952, sec. I, p. 1.

Fort Worth Star-Telegram (Fort Worth, Tex.), February 21, 1933, evening ed., pp. 1, 4; February 23, 1933, evening ed., p. 1; August 11, 1947, evening ed., p. 1; August 14, 1947, evening ed., pp. 1, 4; February 14, 1952, evening ed., pp. 1, 10.

14 BASCOM GILES
BRIBERY AT THE HIGHEST LEVELS IN THE TEXAS GENERAL LAND OFFICE

Ken Towery, the managing editor at the *Cuero Record* newspaper, knew that something was going on. For months unidentified people had been coming and going at the county clerk's office in the DeWitt County Courthouse. Then he heard about some unusual social gatherings of local whites and blacks, who in the 1950s customarily stayed quite separate. Several African American World War II veterans had been seen meeting with two local whites, and rumors circulated around Cuero that the former servicemen were signing papers to receive "free land." Wondering what was going on, Towery went to see Wiley Cheatham, the county attorney, and learned that the official had on his own initiative been investigating what seemed to be irregularities in the local operation of the Texas Veterans' Land Program. The plan had been set up by the Texas Legislature to provide low-interest loans to World War II veterans so that they could purchase land.

Towery was keenly interested in matters related to veterans because he was one himself. Born in 1923 and raised in South Texas, he had volunteered for the U.S. Army and was captured at the fall of Corregidor in the Philippines in early 1942. After spending three years as a prisoner of war, Towery returned home to Texas with tuberculosis and other ailments that plagued him for years. Wanting to study soil science, he got a part-time job at the *Cuero Record* to earn money to return to college. When as a journalist he discovered that fellow veterans were perhaps being swindled by promoters taking advantage of the land program, he decided to act.

Wiley Cheatham encouraged Ken Towery to confront Bascom Giles, the Texas land commissioner, with his findings—evidence of problems in the administration of the veterans' land program in DeWitt County. Getting up early on the morning of November 11, 1954, the journalist drove to Austin. He presented himself in the office of Bascom Giles in the 1918 Texas State Office Building, just across East Eleventh Street from the Capitol. He waited and waited but finally was ushered in. Towery began asking questions about the veterans' land program but was surprised when the commissioner seemed to start denying things that had not come up in the conversation. Giles apparently thought

For Commissioner General Land Office

BASCOM GILES

OF TRAVIS COUNTY

Born on a farm near Manor, September, 1900

Knows the Land Office—17 years experience under J. T. Robison and J. H. Walker, former Comms.

Chief Abstracter State-Wide Tax Survey for past year and a half. Knows Texas Lands and Titles

———

Restore Confidence in the Administration of the Land Office

 3 Subject to action Democratic Primary 1938

(Over)

Advertising card from Bascom Giles's first campaign to become commissioner of the Texas General Land Office, 1938. Author's collection.

that the journalist knew more about the "irregularities" than he actually did. The editor thought to himself that Wiley Cheatham was right: "It was so big . . . that we had a bear by the tail." The interview ended, and Ken Towery headed home to write what became the most important newspaper articles in his career.

We do not know what Bascom Giles did on the evening of November 11, 1954, but he must have felt uneasy. He had served as commissioner of the Texas Land Office since first being elected in 1938. Coming from an old Texas family, he had grown wealthy from real estate speculation and land development. Giles served for years as an able and honest administrator. At the end of World War II, he had proposed a program to the legislature to assist veterans with low-interest loans to purchase small tracts of land. By 1954 more than eleven thousand former service personnel had participated in this program, most of them legitimately. While it served these veterans well, flexibility in the program also permitted unscrupulous land dealers with "inside help" from within the agency to cheat the state and some veterans out of many thousands of dollars. Ken Towery and Wiley Cheatham had observed just the tip of an iceberg of theft, bribery, and conspiracy. Bascom Giles allowed greed to intrude into what up to that time had been a successful political career.

Not knowing such details, Towery on November 14, 1954, wrote the first of a series of front-page articles for the *Cuero Record* about what he and Cheatham had learned. The first article recounted his personal interview with Commissioner Giles, and following it came others that even included photographs of documents mailed from the Texas General Land Office to DeWitt County veterans about questionable land

deals. After Towery began the exposé, journalists from newspapers in Austin, Fort Worth, and elsewhere also began questioning what clearly were illegal transactions within the veterans' land program. Soon the state auditor, the Texas Department of Public Safety, and a legislative committee of inquiry began looking into the matter. Investigators eventually learned how criminals had been "working the system" to cheat the state and its veterans.

Bascom Giles (seated at left) watches as World War II veteran Sidney L. Eggleston signs papers to participate in the Texas Veterans' Land Program. Courtesy of Fort Worth Star-Telegram Collection, Special Collections, the University of Texas at Arlington Libraries, image FWST 2318 12/15/1949.

According to the land program rules established by the legislature, a veteran would first locate a tract of land that he wanted to buy, prepare an application form, sign it, get it notarized, and then submit the form with a copy of his military discharge to the board. The agency then would send one of its appraisers to examine the land to confirm that it was worth the proposed price. With the favorable nod of the appraiser, the board, consisting of the commissioner of the General Land Office, the governor, and the state attorney general, considered the application. (In reality the governor and the attorney general rarely attended these meetings and instead sent representatives, who nearly always agreed with Commissioner Bascom Giles's recommendations.) When the board approved, the state purchased the acreage and in turn sold it to the veteran for a 5 percent down payment, a fifty-dollar service charge, and installments at 3 percent interest over the next forty years. As described here, the plan operated legally for thousands of Texas veterans, but not for all of them.

When Ken Towery first wrote about "irregularities" in the Texas Veterans' Land Program, he could not have understood how effectively Bascom Giles and his fellow conspirators had manipulated a plan designed to benefit war veterans into a scheme to enrich themselves. The strategy was ingenious and originated from within the state agency. The printed forms issued by the land office included a paragraph stating that the applicant had agreed to buy the tract of land "described immediately below," followed by a blank space where a legal description of the property was to be written. (The process did not require the veteran to inspect the acreage before committing to purchase it.) Once

Cuero Record managing editor Ken Towery at his desk in 1955. Courtesy of Ken Towery.

the board approved the application, the document became a contract binding the former soldier or sailor to repay the state for the next forty years.

Using these standard application forms, agents of land companies preyed on illiterate or poorly educated veterans, using trickery or falsified "bonuses" to persuade them to sign blank applications. The unscrupulous agents then added whatever property descriptions they might choose and secured seals from unscrupulous notaries. In the meantime conspirators higher in the scheme purchased thousands of acres of cheap range land, divided it into smaller tracts, and had state appraisers declare that it was worth far more than it actually was. They then wrote descriptions of the overpriced tracts in the spaces left empty on the application forms. The Texas Veterans' Land Board processed the applications, with the state paying the criminals inflated prices for the land. Because the conspirators often made down payments, paid service charges, and sometimes even made second-year payments to conceal their activities, many of the veterans did not realize for months that they were liable for any payments at all. They made this discovery only after the perpetrators had stopped sending remittances. If the unfairly targeted veterans did not start making the payments, which few did, ownership of the land reverted to the state. In this way the criminals had money, Commissioner Giles received his share in bribes, and the state ended up with thousands of acres for which it had paid inflated prices.

The multiple investigations led eventually to twenty people being indicted for improper use of public monies and violating the rights of veterans. Bascom Giles himself was indicted in January 1955 on charges of conspiracy to take eighty-three thousand dollars in state funds. He resigned as head of the land office, only to be indicted again in March for accepting thirty thousand dollars in bribes. More charges followed. Eventually a jury convicted Giles, and he served six years in the Texas penitentiary. He became the first statewide elected official in Texas history to enter prison for a felony committed while in office. Also convicted were land promoters B. R. Sheffield of Brady and T. J. McLarty of Cuero. Civil lawsuits forced promoters to buy back the illegally sold land and to keep up the payments, so the state recovered most of the money it had lost. In the meantime the legislature revised the statute to close the loopholes that had enabled the criminals to take advantage of the otherwise beneficial veterans' land program.

Ken Towery, who had remained at the *Cuero Record*, came to be recognized as the hero of the story. His articles first brought to light the chicanery. While broadcast journalist Edward R. Murrow was filming Towery in Cuero in spring 1955 for his *See It Now* program on CBS television, the telephone rang. On the other end of the line was Houston newspaper reporter Jim Mathis. As the cameras rolled, he informed Towery that the selection committee had chosen him for the Pulitzer Prize in local reporting. The small-town journalist could only reply, "Oh, well, the world of wonders never ceases. I don't hardly believe it, feller," adding, "I think you're pulling my leg." Well, Mathis wasn't, and in time Towery did receive the prestigious national award.

OFFICE OF BASCOM GILES, FOURTH FLOOR,
1918 TEXAS STATE OFFICE BUILDING, 1019 BRAZOS STREET,
AUSTIN, 1938–1955

To reach the 1918 Texas State Office Building, known also as the James E. Rudder Building, where Bascom Giles had a fourth-floor office at the time of Ken Towery's interview in November 1954, take exit 234C from Interstate 35 adjacent to downtown Austin. Southbound from the upper level of the interstate, the exit is marked "12th–11th Streets/State Capitol" and northbound the exit is marked "6th–11th Streets." From either direction proceed on the access road to Eleventh Street, turn west, and drive 0.4 mile to the intersection with Brazos Street, where the building stands at the southeast corner diagonally across the street from the State Capitol grounds. There is limited street-side metered parking. Today this structure continues to house official state offices. The area that once was Giles's office now is occupied by mechanical systems and does not have public access.

The 1918 State Office Building, on the fourth floor of which Bascom Giles had his office, as seen from the grounds of the Texas State Capitol. Photograph by the author, 2009.

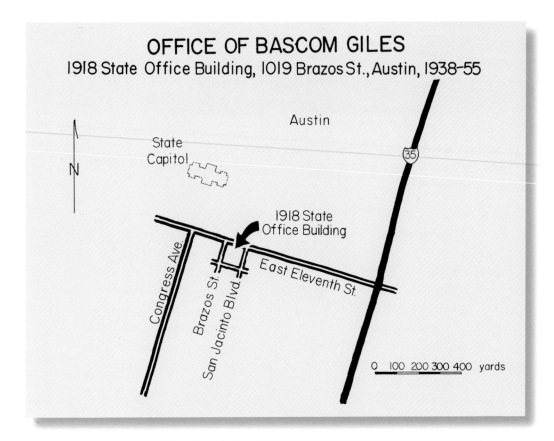

OFFICE OF BASCOM GILES
1918 State Office Building, 1019 Brazos St., Austin, 1938–55

Austin

State Capitol

1918 State Office Building

East Eleventh St.

Congress Ave

Brazos St.

San Jacinto Blvd.

N

35

0 100 200 300 400 yards

DELWOOD SHOPPING CENTER PROPERTY DEVELOPMENT, INTERSTATE 35 AT 38 ½ STREET, AUSTIN, 1951

During the early 1950s, Bascom Giles invested substantial amounts of money in developing the Delwood Shopping Center and adjacent residential subdivisions immediately east of Interstate 35. This was just at the time that he was receiving illegal payments through the subversion of the Texas Veterans' Land Program. He likely "laundered" some of these proceeds by investing them in this otherwise legitimate real estate venture. The shopping center opened to the public in October 1951 and operated for decades. Other owners renovated and greatly modified the commercial area in 1990 to accommodate a large supermarket, in the process removing many of the forty-year-old buildings, though they restored the original Delwood sign.

To reach the shopping center, leave the lower level of Interstate 35 southbound at exit 236B, which is marked "38½ Street," or leave the lower level of Interstate 35 northbound at exit 236, which is marked "Dean Keeton/32nd–38½ Streets." Proceed on the access roads to the intersection and overpass at 38½ Street. The shopping area fronts on the east side of the interstate highway immediately north of 38½ Street.

The original sign at the entry to the Delwood Shopping Center in Austin, where Bascom Giles invested much of his money. Photograph by the author, 2009.

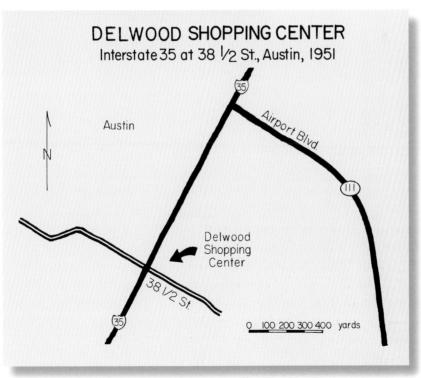

DELWOOD SHOPPING CENTER
Interstate 35 at 38 1/2 St., Austin, 1951

Austin

N

Airport Blvd.

35

111

Delwood
Shopping
Center

38 1/2 St.

35

0   100 200 300 400 yards

EDITORIAL OFFICES AND PRINTING SHOP OF THE
CUERO RECORD, 119 EAST MAIN STREET, CUERO, 1954

To reach the facilities of the *Cuero Record*, where Ken Towery wrote his articles exposing bribery and fraud in the Texas Veterans' Land Program, take U.S. Highway 77, 87, or 183 to downtown Cuero. Turn east on East Main Street and drive to the location on the south (right) side of the street near the middle of the block. The handsome two-story Victorian brick building to this day still houses the newspaper operations as it did during the 1950s. You can buy a copy of the latest issue inside.

The offices of the Cuero Record, *where Ken Towery broke the story of Bascom Giles's involvement in bribery and financial abuse of state funds, in a two-story Victorian brick commercial building on East Main Street in Cuero, Texas. Photograph by the author, 2007.*

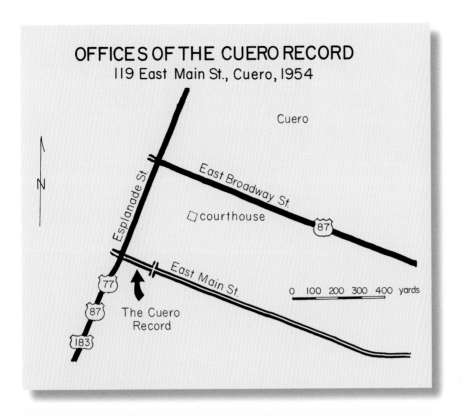

OFFICES OF THE CUERO RECORD
119 East Main St., Cuero, 1954

Cuero

East Broadway St.

Esplanade St.

☐ courthouse

87

East Main St.

0 100 200 300 400 yards

77
87 The Cuero Record

183

N

👉 **JUDGE THE EVIDENCE FOR YOURSELF**

Cox, Patrick L. "Land Commissioner Bascom Giles and the Texas Veterans' Land Board Scandals." M.A. thesis, Southwest Texas State University, 1988.

Cuero Record (Cuero, Tex.), November 14, 1954, pp. 1, 10; November 15, 1954, p. 1; November 16, 1954, p. 1; November 17, 1954, p. 1; November 18, 1954, p. 1; November 19, 1954, p. 1; November 21, 1954, p. 1; November 29, 1954, pp. 1, 6.

Dallas Morning News, November 18, 1954, part 1, p. 1; May 3, 1955, part 1, pp. 1, 7.

Houston Press, February 15, 1955, pp. 1, 5; February 16, 1955, pp. 1, 2; February 17, 1955, pp. 1, 2.

McSwain, Ross, and Harold Byler. *Texas Politics and Greed: A Historical Story of the Veterans' Land Scandal in the 1950's.* Bloomington, Ind.: Author House, 2005.

Towery, Ken. *As a POW & in Politics He Was Always the Chow Dipper: A Personal and Political Odyssey.* Austin: Eakin Press, 1994.

15 THE HOUSTON POLICE DOPE SCANDAL
SELLING HEROIN BACK TO THE DEALERS

Vivian Timms of Houston saw something most unusual taking place in her yard at 3306 Bacchus Street in a working-class African American neighborhood on the night of August 11, 1953. Two men carried a garbage can to a spot just outside her bathroom window, dug a hole, and buried it. After they departed, the young woman dug up the can and found inside two glass jars full of capsules and paper packets containing a whitish powder. She knew something about narcotics; her sister's boyfriend was Earl Voice, known as the "kingfish of the drug pushers" in Houston. Vivian called the police.

Three Houston police officers responded to the phone call and drove through the darkness to Bacchus Street, northwest of downtown. They were E. H. Bennett and J. T. Conley, both young lawmen, and Martin Albert Billnitzer, an old hand at narcotics investigation. The officers located the wood-frame house and the garbage can in question. Taking the two jars, they headed back to the nearly new Houston police headquarters across Buffalo Bayou from City Hall. What they learned from Vivian Timms is unknown.

The vice squad offices were upstairs in room 310A, where the three officers poured out the jars' contents on a table and began an inventory. The haul included hundreds of capsules, several paper packets about the size of a deck of cards, and about a dozen "bindles," or smaller packages wrapped in cellophane. Detective Bennett slit open several of the packets, withdrew samples for testing, and resealed the bindles with tape. The chemical reagent turned a deep purple color, indicating heroin. The men knew the street value for the narcotics was thousands of dollars.

As the inventory progressed, Captain Foy "Junior" Melton, head of the vice squad, wandered into the room. Detective Conley later remembered, "Melton came in and asked where we got the stuff." Then the captain left for a few minutes, informing them that he would secure the drugs and that only he and the three detectives knew about the haul. He wanted everything to stay hush-hush so as not to blow an important ongoing investigation. About half an hour later Melton reappeared, telling Conley that "he had put the stuff in the chief's safe."

J. T. Conley (left) and E. H. Bennett (right), the younger two members of the trio of Houston police officers who collected the two jars containing heroin that Vivian Timms dug up from her yard on Bacchus Street on August 11, 1953. Courtesy of Houston Metropolitan Research Center, Houston Public Library, image RG D5 folder 595A.

Houston Police detective Martin Albert Billnitzer posed holding dried marijuana confiscated in a narcotics raid. Courtesy of Houston Metropolitan Research Center, Houston Public Library, image RG D5 folder 6157.

Captain Foy "Junior" Melton, head of the Houston vice squad, who took charge of the containers of heroin that officers Conley, Bennett, and Billnitzer brought into police headquarters from Bacchus Street on the night of August 11, 1953. Courtesy of Houston Metropolitan Research Center, Houston Public Library, image RG D5 folder 4237.

(In reality the narcotics had gone into Melton's desk drawers.)

Within a week of the seizure, drug dealer Earl Voice received a personal visit from another Houston police detective, Sidney Smith. The two had had previous dealings, but this time the lawman carried some of the heroin seized on Bacchus Street. Voice later testified that he paid Smith $5,105 for the drugs, which he sold on the street through more than a dozen pushers for $7,200. He even remembered receiving packets that had been slit open and then resealed with tape. "Everything I got, I got from the Police Station," Voice declared. More installments of the Bacchus Street heroin kept coming.

In the meantime officers Billnitzer, Conley, and Bennett heard nothing of the purported hush-hush criminal investigation for which they were remaining silent. Two months passed and in fall 1953 they told fellow officer William C. Pool about the unusual proceedings, informing him that "something funny is going on." The officers feared being framed as "fall guys" in the disappearance of drugs. Then on April 29, 1954, federal drug agents arrested Earl Voice on a narcotics charge. Captain Joe Clark of the vice squad reported, "Shortly after his arrest, he asked personally for me. I don't know why he asked for me." In the surprise interview that followed, Voice told Clark that he had been selling drugs purchased from Detective Sidney Smith of the Houston force. Clark kept the story confidential, not knowing how involved other department members might be.

Detective Sidney L. Smith, who was accused of selling drug dealer Earl Voice his own heroin that had been impounded by lawmen on Bacchus Street. Courtesy of Houston Metropolitan Research Center, Houston Public Library, image RG D5 folder 469A.

Officer William C. Pool moved forward with his information on April 14, 1954. He told the Harris County district attorney and members of a local grand jury what he had learned from Bennett and Conley about the missing drugs. "They said it wasn't enough to go before the grand jury," he later told the press. According to Pool, Assistant District Attorney Ben Morris advised him to "forget about the whole thing," adding, "If you can't forget it, you'd better quit the police force." In what seemed like an unrelated event, Pool two weeks later interrogated a newly arrested Earl Voice. The drug dealer revealed his dealings with Detective Smith, and Pool combined this news with what he knew from Conley and Bennett about missing narcotics. "I had tried to get [our] local officers to act, and failed. So I decided to appeal for help from federal officers in Washington," he said. On May 21, 1954, a frustrated Pool

George White, the roving investigator from the U.S. Treasury Department who played a major role in exposing the resale to drug dealers of the heroin recovered by Houston police officers at the Bacchus Street residence. Courtesy of Houston Metropolitan Research Center, Houston Public Library, image RG D5 folder 6789 Dec. 3, 1958.

went to Al Scharff, a U.S. Customs agent in Houston, to report what he believed to be corruption in the Houston Police Department. The agent telephoned Fred J. Douglas, a Treasury Department enforcement agent in Washington, and the latter immediately made plans to travel to Texas. Three days later Pool was telling his story in person to Douglas at the Houston Federal Building. Realizing that "this thing is bigger than I thought," Douglas called for further assistance from roving supervisor George White and Kansas City division head Henry Giordano.

As soon as the three Treasury Department agents set up temporary headquarters in room 720 of the William Penn Hotel, Houston law officers and drug dealers heard of it. Houston police chief Lawrence Donald Morrison publicly announced full departmental support for the federal investigation, even though he knew there had been laxity in handling narcotics in his agency. It was common knowledge that certain detectives, as a matter of course, used "evidence" narcotics to buy intelligence and testimony from the criminal underworld.

As early as June 1 the three Treasury Department investigators met with head vice squad captain Foy Melton and detective E. H. Bennett about the missing heroin. That very day Melton asked Bennett to meet him privately in his home to find out what the younger detective had previously said. "Well, they're after one of the five of us," Melton declared, "Conley, Billnitzer, myself, Chief Morrison, or you." About the same time federal agents were interviewing J. T. Conley.

Chief L. D. Morrison had more to be concerned about than anyone expected. Since January 1952 he had suffered extreme neck pain from an automobile accident followed by a physical struggle with a prisoner. Twice he was treated at Hermann Hospital for a herniated or "slipped" disc in his neck. In early 1954, after two years of incessant pain, the chief started seeing Houston osteopath Julius McBride, who provided him with codeine. Morrison did not want Dr. McBride to keep written records of the prescriptions, stating, "I didn't want every Tom, Dick, and Harry to come in and examine the books." Consequently McBride recorded the codeine pills, a federal requirement for regulated drugs, as being dispensed to another patient, Billy Jackson. The chief usually visited the osteopath's office at 1710 Yale in the Heights neighborhood in the evenings about half past five every ten or twelve days, entering by a back door. He knew McBride was breaking federal law to protect him

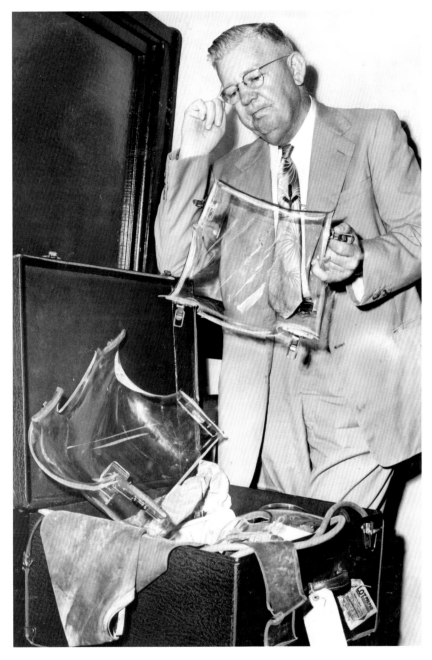

Houston police chief Lawrence Donald Morrison, whose personal use of codeine as a pain killer became public knowledge as a consequence of the federal investigation into his subordinates' handling of the Bacchus Street heroin cache. Courtesy of Houston Metropolitan Research Center, Houston Public Library, image RG D5 folder 4263.

from public exposure, so his greatest personal fear was that somehow the federal investigators would discover this secret.

On Wednesday, June 2, 1954, the three Treasury Department agents continued their probe by interviewing veteran narcotics detective Martin A. Billnitzer. Roving supervisor George White led the questioning, which focused on the missing heroin taken during the Bacchus Street seizure. Billnitzer stated that the haul was only a third or

HSP-89-10/19.Houston, Tex: Dr and Mrs Julius McBride. He was inficted on a narcotic charge and is being tried today at Corpus Christi. Man on extreme left is Ed Norton, Press Reporter.

Houston Press *reporter* Ed Norton (left) *with osteopath* Julius McBride (center) *and his wife, Evelyn Louise McBride* (right), *after the doctor was indicted on June 25, 1954, for improper handling of codeine. Courtesy of Houston Metropolitan Research Center, Houston Public Library, image RG D5 folder 6788.*

fourth the size that officers Bennett and Conley had described. Perhaps the detective, known as "Mr. Bill" in the underworld, feared the federal agents would discover his occasional practice of giving small amounts of confiscated narcotics to addicted stool pigeons in exchange for tips and testimony. Pondering the fact that his story had differed substantially from that of the other two officers, Billnitzer returned to room 720 of the William Penn Hotel about midnight on Thursday, June 3, to confer again with agents White, Douglas, and Giordano. This time he admitted that he had lied the day before about the volume of drugs recovered on Bacchus Street, and now his story matched that of the two younger men. That night he told his wife that he had "got a lot off his conscience" and that he "felt better than I have for a long time."

Lieutenant Billnitzer knew that he had to square up with Chief Morrison about what he had told the federal agents. During an interview on the morning of Friday, June 4, the detective admitted to the chief that he had given some small quantities of the Bacchus Street narcotics to criminal informers in exchange for information. This confession of a moral and legal breach clearly embarrassed Billnitzer.

At this point in the conversation, Will Sears, the city attorney, arrived for a scheduled appointment with the chief, so Billnitzer departed. He stepped across the hall to the vice squad offices, passed fellow officer George H. LaRue sitting at a desk, and entered room 310A, closing the door behind him. Detective LaRue described the next moments this way: "After about a minute, I heard a gunshot in that office and then I heard a . . . thud. I got up and rushed to the door and as I took hold of the door [k]nob, I heard another gunshot." Unable to open the portal, LaRue dashed into the chief's office to look for help. While the detective searched for a key, Olive Huston, secretary to the chief, entered the vice squad offices and pushed open the closed door, which was blocked by what she found: "I saw Detective M. A. Billnitzer lying on the floor with his head toward the door that I had opened," she told investigators, adding that "his shirt was covered with blood and he was gasping for breath." Within moments he expired, the victim of his own .38-caliber snub-nosed chrome-plated Smith & Wesson revolver. Although some people later claimed that it would be impossible for a man to shoot himself in the heart, fall to the floor, and then shoot himself in the heart a second time, Justice of the Peace Tom Maes declared the fatality a suicide.

Houston city attorney Will Sears, whose arrival for an appointment with Police Chief L. D. Morrison immediately preceded the mysterious death across the hallway of detective Martin Albert Billnitzer inside the Houston police headquarters on June 4, 1954. Courtesy of Houston Metropolitan Research Center, Houston Public Library, image RG D5 folder 2860A.

The death in police headquarters of a respected narcotics officer broke open the story of illegal drug handling in the department. The next day the local press carried the first of what became many stories about the missing heroin from Bacchus Street. The federal investigators, however, were following more criminal threads than one, and on June 5, the next day, they raided Dr. Julius McBride's clinic. "They tried to get me to sign a statement stating that the chief was a dope addict," McBride protested, "but I refused to do that." Agents White, Giordano, and Douglas did succeed in confiscating the osteopath's drug purchase and sales records. Sensing that the Treasury Department investigations were close to discovering all his personal and departmental secrets, Chief Morrison nominally announced full support for the federal investigators. At the same time he cautiously assigned officers to "trail" the agents and to report the names of any police officers who sought to meet with them. Within days a nervous Morrison loosed a verbal barrage in the press, describing the federal investigators as "visiting gestapo" who were "leaking stories which are more like those of a circus press agent than a law enforcement officer."

The Treasury Department investigators continued their work. They turned over their evidence to a federal grand jury, which began calling witnesses to the Houston Federal Building on Monday, June 21, 1954.

Among those who testified were Evelyn Louise McBride, wife of Dr. McBride; narcotics dealer Earl Voice, who purchased some of his own illegal heroin from a Houston officer; and Chief L. D. Morrison. Most people associated in any way with the Bacchus Street narcotics case were called in. Eventually the federal body concluded that three individuals should be indicted for crimes. These were Dr. Julius McBride, for dispensing controlled codeine to Chief L. D. Morrison under the name of another patient; Foy Melton, captain of the vice squad, for illegally concealing heroin from the Bacchus Street stash; and Detective Sidney L. Smith, for an unrelated minor narcotics charge.

The scandal grew, and by July 8 members of the Houston City Council were calling on Chief Morrison to resign. Constituents had contacted council members in the wake of daily headlines about the chief taking illegal codeine tablets; they condemned his behavior as unacceptable no matter how much his back hurt. By Monday, July 12, the chief had announced that he would step down as soon as a successor was chosen. Then his boss, Mayor Roy Hofheinz, met with the federal grand jury in an informational session. This was too much for him. On Friday, July 30, Chief L. D. Morrison submitted his resignation, which Hofheinz accepted.

On October 18, 1954, the first of a series of trials began. Dr. Julius McBride's trial was in Corpus Christi. All the principals in the case, including former chief Morrison, testified in the proceedings, but McBride himself was the star, entertaining the courtroom with homespun humor and jabbing wit. Even so, the jury on October 22 found him guilty of falsifying prescription drug records and dispensing narcotics "in bad faith and contrary to standard medical practice." A month later he received a thirty-month sentence in a federal corrections institution. Then came the first of two trials for Captain Foy Melton on illegal possession of large amounts of heroin from the Bacchus Street raid. The first trial, held in federal court in Brownsville in early November, ended in a hung jury, eight for acquittal and four for conviction. Another trial for Melton followed in Corpus Christi in February 1955, ending in acquittal. No one was ever convicted of any offenses associated with the illegal handling of the Bacchus Street heroin.

Former chief L. D. Morrison spent the remainder of his career in the Houston Police Department as a homicide investigator. Foy Melton also returned to law enforcement, but he, like Martin Billnitzer, died mysteriously. At age fifty-three on February 2, 1967, he was found shot to death in his car in the Houston courthouse parking lot, a .45-caliber pistol and a bottle of pain pills near his body. History repeated itself, with the medical examiner declaring Melton's death a suicide.

BACCHUS STREET NARCOTICS RAID,
3306 BACCHUS STREET, HOUSTON, AUGUST 11, 1953

The house where Vivian Timms lived at 3306 Bacchus Street and where she discovered the stash of heroin on the night of August 11, 1953, has been removed, but it is easy to find the long, narrow city lot in the Lincoln Heights neighborhood where it stood.

To reach the site, drive west 0.9 mile on North Loop 610 from Interstate 45 and take exit 16 marked for North Main and Yale streets. From Loop 610 turn north on North Main Street and drive two full blocks (0.1 mile) to its intersection with East Thirty-third Street. Turn east (right) on East Thirty-third Street and drive two blocks (0.1 mile) to Bacchus Street. Turn north (left) on Bacchus Street at the corner where the James D. Burrus Elementary School is located and drive one-fourth block north to the vacant lot on the east (right) side of the street between houses located at 3304 and 3308. This historic area retains much of its character as a twentieth-century African American community.

The now-vacant lot at 3306 Bacchus Street, where Vivian Timms discovered a cache of heroin outside her home on the night of August 11, 1953. Photograph by the author, 2010.

BACCHUS STREET NARCOTICS RAID
3306 Bacchus St., Houston, August 11, 1953

Bacchus St.

3306 Bacchus St.

East 33rd St.

North Main St.

N

45

610

45

To Downtown Houston

0   1/4   1/2   mile

1952 HOUSTON POLICE HEADQUARTERS, 61 RIESNER STREET, JUST OFF THE 1300 BLOCK OF LUBBOCK STREET, HOUSTON

Although many police department functions are today housed in other locations, the 1952 Houston Police Administration, Corporation Courts, and Jail building remains an active law enforcement facility. Its white limestone and pink Texas granite exterior, aluminum windows and doors, and polished granite and wood-paneled walls project the modern image that Houston sought to show the world during the early 1950s. Although the third floor, which once housed the offices of the vice squad and Chief L. D. Morrison, is not open to the general public, the lobby and information desk at the entry area has general access and conveys a feeling of what the building was like during decades past.

To reach the readily visible building, drive northwest from the central business district on Capitol Street and pass beneath the elevated Interstate 45 freeway (at the same time passing over Buffalo Bayou by bridge). Take the first right turn onto Lubbock Street and park in the for-fee public parking lot designated for the Municipal Courts Building. The multistory white limestone police headquarters stands just across Lubbock Street from the parking area.

The downtown Houston Police headquarters building, scene of multiple events, including the mysterious death of Lieutenant Martin A. Billnitzer during the 1954 Houston Police Drug Scandal. Photograph by the author, 2010.

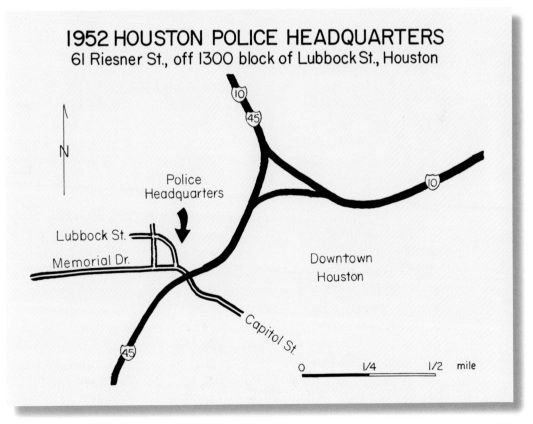

1952 HOUSTON POLICE HEADQUARTERS
61 Riesner St., off 1300 block of Lubbock St., Houston

Harris County, Tex. Justice of the Peace Court. Inquest into the Death of Martin Albert Billnitzer. Inquests and Views, V. 73, June 3, 1954, Justice of the Peace 1–2. Harris County Archives, Houston, Tex.

Houston Chronicle (Houston, Tex.), June 3, 1954, sec. A, p. 1; June 4, 1954, sec. A., pp. 1, 8, 9; June 5, 1954, sec. A, pp. 1, 5; June 6, 1954, sec. A, pp. 1, 21; June 7, 1954, sec. A, pp. 1, 8; June 9, 1954, sec. A, pp. 1, 7, 10; June 16, 1954, sec. A, pp. 1, 15; June 23, 1954, sec. A, pp. 1, 15; June 25, 1954, sec. A, pp. 1, 14; June 28, 1954, sec. A, pp. 1, 8; June 29, 1954, sec. A, p. 1; July 8, 1954, sec. A, pp. 1, 15; July 31, 1954, sec. A, pp. 1, 5; October 20, 1954, sec. A, pp. 1, 18; October 22, 1954, sec. A, pp. 1, 6; November 26, 1954, sec. A, p. 1; February 3, 1967, sec. 1, pp. 1, 6.

Houston Post (Houston, Tex.), June 3, 1954, sec. 1, pp. 1, 7; June 5, 1954, sec. 1, pp. 1, 14; June 6, 1954, sec. 1, pp. 1, 7; June 7, 1954, sec. 1, pp. 1, 8; June 8, 1954, sec. 1, pp. 1, 6; June 9, 1954, sec. 1, pp. 1, 6, 9; June 10, 1954, sec. 1, pp. 1, 12; June 23, 1954, sec. 1, pp. 1, 7; June 26, 1954, sec. 1, pp. 1, 12; July 8, 1954, sec. 1, pp. 1, 10; July 16, 1954, sec. 1, pp. 1, 6; October 19, 1954, sec. 1, pp. 1, 6; October 20, 1954, sec. 1, pp. 1, 3; October 22, 1954, sec. 1, pp. 1, 8; November 9, 1954, sec. 1, pp. 1, 6; November 16, 1954, sec. 1, pp. 1, 11; November 13, 1954, sec. 1, pp. 1, 7; November 27, 1954, sec. 1, pp. 1, 5; February 15, 1955, sec. 1, pp. 1, 6; February 19, 1955, sec. 1, pp. 1, 5.

Houston Press (Houston, Tex.), June 3, 1954, pp. 1, 13; June 4, 1954, pp. 1, 3; June 5, 1954, pp. 1, 2; June 7, 1954, pp. 1, 2; June 9, 1954, pp. 1, 12; June 10, 1954, pp. 1, 2; June 11, 1954, pp. 1, 11; June 15, 1954, pp. 1, 3; June 16, 1954, pp. 1, 24; June 21, 1954, p. 2; June 22, 1954, pp. 1, 18; June 23, 1954, pp. 1, 2; June 25, 1954, pp. 1, 2; June 29, 1954, p. 3; July 8, 1954, pp. 1, 5; July 9, 1954, pp. 1, 7; July 12, 1954, pp. 1, 5; July 13, 1954, pp. 1, 10; July 16, 1954, pp. 1, 2; July 31, 1954, pp. 1, 2, 11; October 18, 1954, pp. 1, 4; October 19, 1954, pp. 1, 2; October 20, 1954, pp. 1, 2; October 22, 1954, pp. 1, 11; October 26, 1954, p. 12; November 8, 1954, pp. 1, 16; November 9, 1954, pp. 1, 7; February 15, 1955, p. 4; February 19, 1955, p. 1.

Las Vegas Sun (Las Vegas, Nev.), September 1, 1955, pp. 1, 2; September 2, 1955, pp. 1, 15; September 3, 1955, pp. 1, 2; September 4, 1955, pp. 1, 4.

Phelan, James. "The Cops Who Sold Dope." *True, the Man's Magazine*, February 1960, 36–39, 96, 98, 115–16.

16 TWO BROTHERS AND GAMING OVER GULF WATERS
THE END OF THE GANGSTER ERA IN TEXAS

Today when one thinks of Galveston, images of family-style fun and sun at the beach come to mind, but the city over the years has meant other things to other people. Galveston Bay provided the only natural harbor for deep-water ships on the Texas Gulf coast, so it played an instrumental role in maritime history. The town became the largest city in Texas between 1830 and 1860. Shippers exported more cotton from its wharves than from any other American port. The seaside community also served as one of the precursors of modern-day casino gambling centers.

Certainly people wagered money at Galveston from its earliest days, but two Italian brothers brought big-time gaming to the port city. Rosario "Rose" Maceo and Salvatore "Sam" Maceo had immigrated to the United States from Sicily as boys at the turn of the twentieth century, settling first in Louisiana. As young men they relocated to Galveston in 1910, where they first worked as barbers. Sam, the more outgoing of the two, cut hair in the prestigious Galvez Hotel, while the quieter Rose followed his trade at the more plebeian Murdoch's Bath House. After prohibition ended legal production and sale of alcoholic beverages in Texas in 1918, the brothers entered bootlegging, eventually taking over the "beach gang," one of two groups of illicit rum runners on Galveston Island. They eventually pushed aside the "downtown gang" to gain near-complete control of the illegal alcohol trade in the city. Already by this time Galveston was attracting large numbers of tourists from the mainland, who came by train to enjoy its waterfront hotels and sandy beaches. The immigrant entrepreneurs had no shortage of customers.

The two Maceo brothers easily saw that the out-of-town visitors liked good food and entertainment with their booze, so in 1926 they built and opened the Hollywood Dinner Club. On what was the far southwest side of the city at Sixty-first Street and Avenue S, their impressive Spanish Renaissance revival–style night spot boasted dining rooms, a ballroom that could accommodate five hundred dancers, and less public areas where guests could wager at craps, blackjack, roulette, and other games. As the operations manager, "Big Sam" Maceo from the outset

Sam Maceo, as he appeared during the heyday of his family's gaming operations in Galveston. Courtesy of the Rosenberg Library, Galveston, Tex.

The Galvez Hotel just after its opening in 1911, about the time that Sam Maceo worked there as a barber. He later lived in the penthouse atop the luxurious hotel. Author's collection.

brought in well-known national orchestras and performers to entertain his guests. Always in the background, "Papa Rose" Maceo provided the brains and vision for the family enterprise.

The downtown area received the next infusion of the Maceo brothers' gambling profits. At 2216 Market Street they erected the three-story Turf Athletic Club. Guests entered through a ground-floor restaurant featuring steaks and seafood but took the elevator upstairs to the Western Bar and the Studio Lounge, actually the casino area, as well as to more private gaming chambers, not to mention athletic training rooms. A 1948 Turf Grill menu listed such delicacies as broiled red snapper steak browned in butter and half chickens served with spaghetti "à la Maceo." The dessert section included blue cheese with guava jelly.

Of all the Maceo enterprises, the beach-front Balinese Room, located on a pier over the waters of the Gulf of Mexico, conjured up the most exotic appearance. The prime location was diagonally opposite the seven-story Galvez Hotel. It began in the 1930s as the Grotto, then was expanded into the Sui Jen. The Maceos eventually further enlarged the structure and gave it a South Seas look in 1942 as the Balinese Room. The brothers' successful business strategy was to attract well-heeled gamblers from Houston and elsewhere with reasonably priced but elaborate meals combined with lavish floor shows featuring swing bands and motion picture stars. Among the nationally known performers who frequented its stage were singers Frank Sinatra, Peggy Lee,

and Sophie Tucker; comedians Jack Benny, Phil Silvers, Bob Hope, and Joe E. Lewis; and pianist Carmen Caballero. Bandleader and Balinese performer Phil Harris married actress Alice Faye in Sam Maceo's penthouse at the nearby Galvez Hotel. Arthur Murray and Fred Astaire, in addition to performing, were paid to teach the latest dance steps to the wives of high rollers. The whole purpose of bringing in such entertainers was to separate gamblers from their money, and the scheme worked. "The atmosphere was so friendly," reminisced one former customer, "that you almost enjoyed losing your money there."

Adolfo Zamora worked as a cook at the Balinese Room during the 1940s, and he described the casino from his perspective back in the kitchen: "At one time . . . we had 11 chefs. The old man couldn't stand a complaint." If law officers on a raid forced their way past the concierge at the seawall entry, the employee pushed a button for a buzzer at the casino over the water at the opposite end of the pier. According to Zamora, it took only thirty-two seconds for employees to clear all the dice tables: "As soon as that buzzer comes in, everybody, the cooks and everything, used to get the things [gambling paraphernalia] out." Officers would see only innocently legal pool tables and customers sipping soft drinks.

The Hollywood Dinner Club, the Turf Athletic Club, and the Balinese Room were only the most prominent of the Maceo brothers' many ventures. They also operated thousands of slot machines located in local stores and eating places. Mike Gaido of Gaido's seafood restaurant, a Galveston institution, once quipped, "The Maceos didn't ask you if you wanted their slots; they just asked how many." The brothers' operating company typically split the profits evenly with the business owners. Visitors to older Galveston commercial buildings even today can pick out the areas that decades ago were devoted to slot machines. The Maceos never entered prostitution, though the Post Office Street quarter constituted one of the largest red-light districts in the United States. The madams did not permit formal gambling, but they did install the Maceos' slot machines in their bordellos. Throughout the city were Maceo-run betting parlors where people wagered on horse races and baseball games. Even pinball machines offered cash payouts to skillful players. It has been estimated that 10 percent of the employed adults in Galveston during the late 1940s worked in one way or another for Maceo enterprises.

A female vocalist and her piano accompanist performing at the Balinese Room. Courtesy of the Rosenberg Library, Galveston, Tex.

Knowing that they needed the willing support of residents to succeed, the two brothers in many ways cultivated the people living in their seaside community. They generously supported local charities and even brought special events like the Miss Universe pageant to the city. Casino operators would allow locals to wager, but unless they were particularly wealthy, managers stopped them when their losses grew excessive. They knew that having lots of losers in town could hurt their generally favorable public relations. Although the two brothers were never convicted of bribery, they made generous campaign contributions to friends who were running for office. Galveston mayor Herbert Y. Cartwright declared of incumbents, "Once you were in, you were in." Lawmen turned "blind eyes" toward the illegal activity going on all around them. When Galveston County sheriff Frank Biaggne testified before a congressional commission in 1951, his widely publicized lame excuse for never raiding the Balinese Room was "because I was not a member." He elaborated, "I went to the door, but they wouldn't let me in."

From time to time locals and outsiders encouraged elected officials to "clean up" the town, but these efforts were sporadic at best. The attention led the Maceo brothers to hold things down for a while, but then the reform spirit passed and things returned to normal. One of

Sam Maceo (left); pianist Carmen Caballero, known as "the poet of the piano" (center); and Galveston mayor Herbert Y. Cartwright (right), all smiles at the Balinese Room during the early 1950s. Courtesy of the Rosenberg Library, Galveston, Tex.

these reform-minded periods came in June 1951, when Price Daniel, the Texas attorney general, used state court injunctions to end walk-in casino gambling at the port city. Slot machines disappeared from public places, while gaming houses like the Balinese Room became "private clubs." Dawson Duncan of the *Dallas Morning News* learned on a trip to the coast in August that "a mere push of a buzzer still opens doors to many bars that call themselves 'clubs.'" In October 1951 Thomas Mahr of the *Houston Post* visited the Turf Athletic Club, bypassed the ground-floor grill, and took the elevator to the lounge on the third story. "It breathes with splendor," he wrote, adding that he found a bar at one end of the room and at the other "a huge dice table and a roulette table."

Closure of the Galveston casinos came as the result of calculated efforts by local attorney Jim Simpson and newly elected Texas attorney general Will Wilson, both of whom opposed gaming on legal grounds. With hopes of election to other public offices, Wilson also sought the notoriety that closing the casinos of Galveston would bring him. In late

Lawmen using sledgehammers to break up confiscated illegal slot machines at Galveston in 1957. Courtesy of the Rosenberg Library, Galveston, Tex.

1956 the two men recruited undercover investigators James D. "Buddy" Givens and Carroll S. Yaws to visit dozens of Galveston gaming establishments in order to engage in gambling and then prepare detailed notes about their experiences. At the Balinese Room, for example, the men took their wives, drank scotch-and-soda cocktails, and saw two roulette wheels and three dice tables, and in a room behind the bar they observed slot machines and a "race horse machine." Givens placed bets at roulette and lost but broke even at throwing dice.

Under the Texas constitution, the attorney general cannot independently prosecute criminal cases but can use the power of civil injunctions to disrupt illegal activity. As Givens and Yaws undertook and recorded their visits to gaming establishments over a period of six months, Simpson prepared paperwork. On June 10, 1957, he delivered the first forty-seven of what would be many requests for injunctions for the gambling houses to cease their operations. A week later Texas Rangers began raiding gaming enterprises, removing illegal equipment and destroying it. They found almost four hundred slot machines in a storage building near Fort Travis and then an estimated two thousand more in the old Hollywood Dinner Club. This is not to mention roulette wheels, dice, chips, and gaming tables. Many Galvestonians opposed the actions, complaining, "It looks like Galveston is being made a whipping boy" and "Why do they have to close the Balinese?"

Even without the court injunctions and raids, the Gulf coast gaming operations faced doom. Promoters such as Texan Bennie Benion in the early 1950s introduced high-stakes gambling to Las Vegas, Nevada, where casinos were legal. The availability of air conditioning eliminated desert heat as an impediment to the setting, and airlines made it convenient for high rollers to travel quickly to the Strip from Los Angeles and other cities. Proximity to Hollywood made it easy for operators to attract prominent performers for nightclubs. Las Vegas thus superseded Galveston as America's "Sin City."

GALVEZ HOTEL, 2024 SEAWALL BOULEVARD, GALVESTON, BUILT IN 1911

Little remains to be seen from the Maceo brothers' gambling empire. The Hollywood Dining Club burned in 1959, and the Turf Athletic Club was razed in 1968 to make way for the construction of a downtown bank. The Balinese Room stood atop its pier over the surf along Seawall Boulevard until Hurricane Ike swept it away in September 2008. Surviving all of the casinos is the seven-story 1911 Galvez Hotel, also on Seawall Boulevard, which provided lodging for many thousands of the Maceo brothers' customers, not to mention the stage and screen personalities who entertained them. To this day it retains its historic character and continues to serve holiday makers as a favorite seaside resort.

GALVEZ HOTEL
2024 Seawall Blvd., Galveston, 1911– Present

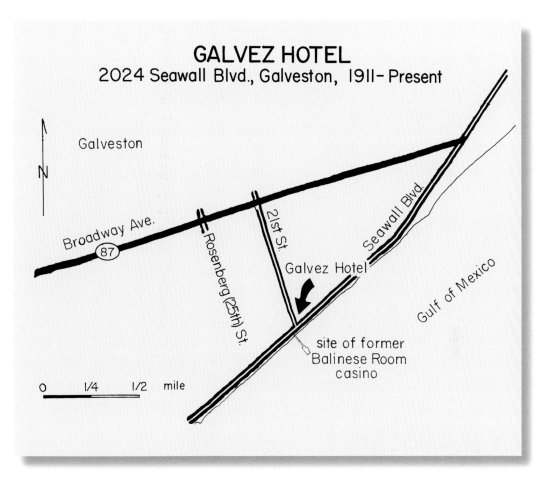

The Balinese Room as it appeared after the closure of its casino, when it was sometimes open as a restaurant and nightclub but frequently closed. Photograph by the author, 2005.

The 1911 Galvez Hotel, which provided lodging for many thousands of the Maceo brothers' gaming customers in Galveston, as well as many of the big-name entertainers who performed in the Maceo venues. Photograph by the author, 2005.

To reach the impressive, cream-colored hotel, drive southeast from Houston on Interstate 45 toward Galveston. When the freeway ends upon entering the built-up area of Galveston, it becomes Broadway Avenue. Proceed eastward on Broadway to its intersection with Twenty-first Street. Turn south (right) on Twenty-first and proceed twenty mostly short blocks a distance of 0.7 mile to its intersection and dead end on Seawall Boulevard. The hotel stands on the left side of this intersection, fronting on the wide street and the seawall. The Balinese Room stood above the Gulf on pilings diagonally opposite from the Galvez at the "T" intersection of Twenty-first Street at Seawall Boulevard.

JUDGE THE EVIDENCE FOR YOURSELF

Austin American-Statesman (Austin, Tex.), March 2, 1986, sec.
    D, pp. 65, 66.
Cartwright, Gary. "One Last Shot." *Texas Monthly* 21, no. 6
    (June 1983): 132–35, 182–83.
Dallas Morning News (Dallas, Tex.), August 9, 1951, sec. I,
    pp. 1, 4.
Galveston Daily News (Galveston, Tex.), October 17, 1948, p. 2;
    June 11, 1957, pp. 1, 2; September 25, 1957, p. 1; September
    27, 1957, pp. 1, 2; August 13, 1959, p. 1; December 4, 1965,
    sec. A, p. 1; May 22, 1966, sec. A, p. 1; sec. B, p. 1; April 10,
    1967, sec. D, pp. 1, 2; June 11, 1967, sec. A, pp. 1, 8; March
    15, 1968, sec. B, p. 1; June 3, 1968, sec. B, p. 1; August 3,
    1969, Tempo supplement, pp. 6–11; August 17, 1969, Tempo
    supplement, pp. 16–18, 20.
Henry, David. "A Time Past: Gambling in Galveston." *In
    Between* (Galveston, Tex.), no. 29 (August 1978): 23–25, 27,
    43–45.
Houston Chronicle (Houston, Tex.), June 30, 1963, magazine
    supplement, p. 22; January 15, 1984, sec. 3, pp. 1, 6; April
    27, 1990, sec. F, pp. 1, 4; July 25, 2002, sec. 10, p. 10.
Houston Post (Houston, Tex.), December 16, 1990, sec. M, pp.
    1, 2.
Houston Press (Houston, Tex.), November 1, 1951, pp. 1, 4.
Long, Steven. "Shutdown, June 10, 1957: The Day the Wheels
    Stopped Turning." *In Between*, no. 166 (December 1983):
    sec. 1, pp. 17–22, 29.
Waldman, Alan. "Isle of Illicit Pleasures: Big Sam & Papa
    Rose." *In Between*, no. 164 (November 1983): sec. 1, pp.
    9–12.
_____. "Isle of Illicit Pleasures: The Gamblers." *In Between*,
    no. 162 (October 1983): 23–25.
Williams, Janice. "The Galvez and the Gambling Years." *In
    Between*, no. 76 (June 1980): 15, 18–19, 20–21.

INDEX

Kallison Building, San Antonio, Tex., 175

Kansas: activities of John Romulus Brinkley in, 252-, 254–57; gubernatorial elections in, 256

Kassoff, Max, 210

Katy Limited (passenger train), 72, 85–88

Keene's drugstore, San Antonio, Tex., 166, 173–75

Kelley, Walter, 122, 124

Kelly, Machine Gun. *See* Barnes, George Kelly

Kelly, Kathryn, 180, 183, 184–89, 195, 197–200

Kemp, Tex., 7, 39–40

KFKB radio station, 254–56

kidnapping: of Charles F. Urschel, 180–204; of city marshal at Commerce, Okla., 22; during 1930s, 206; at Electra, Tex., 4–5, 8, 33–36; of Joe Johns, 9–10

Kilbourn, E. P. "Pack," 142

Kilday, Owen M., 168

Kirkpatrick, E.E., 180

Kirkpatrick, Mabel, 266

Kirk, Robert, 98

Kitchen, Lewis W., 241, 243–49

Kloepper, Kermit, 75

Kornegay, Chris, 67

LaGrange, Tex., 116–17

Laird, W.L., 98

Larson, Jimmy, 166–67

LaRue, George H., 303

Leavenworth federal penitentiary: Agapito Rueda inmate at, 97; William D. May inmate at, 208; George Kelly Barnes inmate at, 202; M.T. Howard inmate at, 221; Newton Boys inmates at, 76; O.D. Stevens inmate at, 206, 208, 221

Lennox, Thomas, 133, 135

Levein, E.H., 152

libel suit against Morris Fishbein, 262, 272

Liberty bonds, 66, 70, 74

Little, Elmer H., 140

Littleton, Vance, 134

Loe, C.M., 247

Long, E.C., 131

López, Anastacio, 98, 99, 100

Lowery, Dewey L., 245–47

lynching, 142–43, 156–59

Maccabee, Paul, xiii-xiv

Mace, Billie Jean, 16

Maceo, Rosario "Rose," 309, 311–13, 316, 318

Maceo, Salvatore "Sam," 309–14, 316, 318

Machine Gun Kelly. *See* Barnes, George Kelly

Maes, Tom, 303

Magness, Louise, 195

Magnolia Petroleum Company, 4, 33–35

Mahr, Thomas, 314

mail fraud, 262

marijuana, 298

Marshall, Beulah, 275

Martin, Joe L., 207–208, 210, 219

Mathis, Jim, 290

May, Mrs. William D., 212–13, 221

May, William D., 206–13, 216–18, 221, 224, 226–27

Memphis, Tex., 4

Marshall, Tex., 13, 50–51

Maxwell, C.G., 9

McBride, Evelyn Louise, 302, 304

McBride, Julius, 300, 302, 303, 304

McBride, Lillian, 11–12, 48–49

McCann, Ethel, 134

McCormick, A.F., 4–5, 33–35

McCormick, J.W., 277

McCullough, V.C., 244–47

McKamy-Campbell Funeral Home, Dallas, Tex., 25, 26, 61–62

McLarty, T.J., 290

McMillan, Robert J., 272

medical practice, 241, 243, 247, 252, 254–62, 265–67

Meers, Elizabeth, 101, 102, 105

Meers, Mrs. William H. "Bill," 100, 105

Meers, William H. "Bill," 98–100

Meers, William Jefferson "Jeff," 100, 101–102, 104–105, 107

Melton, Foy "Junior," 296, 298, 300, 304

Menn, Paul, 69–70

Methvin, Henry, 18, 21, 22, 56–57

Methvin, Iverson, 24

Mexicans: abused by Frank Nand Singh, 232; involvement in attempted robbery of Southern Pacific payroll, 97–102, 104–105, 109; murdered in frame-up, 122–29

Michelle, Eva, 245–46

Middleton, David, 77

Midland, Tex., 124, 125, 126

Milford, Kans., 252, 254, 257

Minjárez, Alejo, 97

Miss Universe pageant, 313

Mitchell Lake, San Antonio, Tex., 166–67, 175–77

Moates, Jack, 22

money laundering, 210

Moody, Dan, 3, 112

Moran, Tex., 132, 138

Schleyers, J.H., 117

Schmidt, Richard Allen "Smoot," 17–19, 24, 53, 189, 190

Sears, Will, 302–303

sex: exchanged for narcotics, 244; vitality restored, 252, 254–55, 260

Shafer, Jack, 101

Shannon, Armon, 188, 189–90

Shannon Farm, near Paradise, Tex., 182–86, 195–96, 202

Shannon, Oleta, 189

Shannon, Ora, 188–89, 192, 197

Shannon, Robert G. "Boss," 183, 187–90, 192, 194, 195, 202–204

Shannon's Funeral Chapel, Fort Worth, Tex., 143–44

Sheffield, B.R., 290

shooting. *See* gunfight and murder

shoot-out. *See* gunfight

Siebrecht, Carl, 10, 45–46

Sikes, Walter, 140

Simmons, Lee, 22

Simms Oil Refinery, Dallas, Tex., 4

Simpson, Jim, 314, 316

Singh, Asa, 229–33, 235–37

Singh, Bishan, 237

Singh, Concha, 233, 236

Singh, Delip, 233, 236

Singh, Frank Nand, 229, 231–33, 235–39

Singh, Guadalupe, 233, 235–36

Singh, Jagat, 237

Singh, Kishan, 237

Singh, Narain, 230, 231, 232–33, 245–37

Singh, Nidham, 232–34, 236–37

Singh, Trinidad, 232

Slick, Tom B., 180

slot machines, 313, 314, 315

Smith, Lee, 122–25, 127

Smith, Sidney L., 299, 304

smuggling: alcohol, 97, 309; immigrants, 229–40

Snyder, Mike, 100

Socorro, Tex., 231, 233

South Bend, Tex., 139, 148–52

Southern Ornamental Ironworks, Arlington, Tex., 277

Souther, William L., 3, 31–33

Southlake, Tex., 57–58

Spanish language: learned by William Jefferson "Jeff" Meers, 105; not spoken by William Guess, 102; spoken by Calvin Cidney Baze, 122, 126

Sparkman-Holtz-Brand Funeral Home, Dallas, Tex., 25, 58–60

Spears, Alex, 131, 133

stables, 276, 279, 280, 281, 283

Stafford, Spencer, 244–48, 249

Stanton, Tex., 122–29

Stanush, Claude, 77

Stephens, Altha, 166–67, 173, 175

Stephens, Lynn, 161–79

Stevens, Charlie, 161–78

Stevens, Olin DeWitt (alias R.H. Doyle, W.K. Krantz, and R.H. Strong), 206–13, 215–27

Stevens, Orley, 210–11, 219

Stinson, James P., 125

Stowe, Joe E., 99, 100

Stroebel, Freda, 134

Sturdivant, Ferman "Jack," 208–16, 217, 221, 223–24

Sturdivant, Melva, 211–12, 213

suicide: by Foy Melton, 304; by Martin Albert Billnitzer, 303, 304

Sui Jen (casino/restaurant), 311

Sulphur River, Tex., 73–74, 89

swimming pool, 276, 281

Taini, John, 266

Taylor, James T., 4–5, 33–35

Taylor, Koran, 270

tax evasion, 262

telephone lines, 66, 68, 74

Telico, Tex., 2

Temple, Tex., 10–11, 46–48

Texarkana, Tex./Ark., 73, 89, 111

Texas and Pacific Mail Robbery, 206–28

Texas Bankers Association: detective from, 69; magazine of, 71; reward from, for dead bank robbers, xiv, 123–24, 133

Texas Court of Criminal Appeals, 116–17, 125

Texas Department of Public Safety, 288

Texas General Land Office, 286–88, 290

Texas Prison Museum, Huntsville, Tex., 156

Texas Rangers: Charlie Stevens as, 161; escort José Carrasco, 102; pursue Barrow Gang, 22, 24; raids by, on Galveston casinos, 316; raids by, on Top O'Hill Terrace, 277–78, 280; in search for Cisco bank robbers, 139

Texas State Capitol, Austin, Tex., 286, 291–92

Texas State Historical Association, 112

Texas State Office Building (James E. Rudder Building), Austin, Tex., 286, 291–92